Scotland After the Virus is a gift of a bo⟨
with reflections and insights that give us
world can come from this wretched pand⟨
brate our priorities and recognise our com⟨
BARONESS HELENA KENNEDY

This book is a timely and welcome tonic for ⟨ne dark times we are living through. If we are to find any light through this, then it will emerge from the writers and thinkers who examine and articulate where we have been, where we are now and ideas and thoughts on where we are headed. The great collection of different voices in this book will help us navigate all of that as well as making us think and smile.
ELAINE C SMITH, actor and campaigner

What binds our nation is not birth but love. In *Scotland After the Virus* there are many voices which show many different interpretations of love of place, people and the connections which make us who we are.
IAN HAMILTON, QC and author

In the dark times, we need sparks of light like this to show the way forward to a brighter future.
VAL MCDERMID, author

Scotland After the Virus contains a powerful array of voices and stories in these unsettling times. They cover the full range of emotions, from love to loss and the search for meaning. It's a timely ray of hope for all of us.
STUART COSGROVE, writer and broadcaster

This impressive range of voices and genres indicates that coronavirus has affected us all in many different ways. The future for post-COVID Scotland will be a better one if we listen with open minds and speak to one another with compassion and care.
JAMES ROBERTSON, author

In this book the power of the written word gives us hope, inspiration and ambition at just the right time. So many at the start of COVID-19 dreamed of living a better life, of truly becoming a civilized and just society. This diverse range of voices beautifully show us that another world is possible, another Scotland is possible.
AAMER ANWAR, lawyer and former rector, University of Glasgow

THE IMAGE ON the cover was created by artist and weaver James Donald as a creative and charitable response to the lockdown associated with COVID-19 (Corona Virus Disease 2019).

James created 'mood boards' out of textures, patterns and shapes photographed during regular walks (ones which followed the guidance of the Scottish Government, naturally). Each walk adopted a colour theme. The colours were recorded on the artist's mobile phone and then curated in a grid of nine images which, combined in particular ways, seemed to illustrate the theme best.

Finished compositions were then posted out on James's PickOne web account (www.pickone.co.uk/nhs-fundraiser.html). The 16 most favoured pieces were turned into 14.8cm square postcards. These art cards come in a matt finish, and form a limited edition of 100 each. They are numbered, given a hand written title, and supplemented with additional information on the reverse.

Proceeds from the sale of these cards go to NHS Scotland. The aim is to support health and wellbeing, to show how the restrictions in our lives can generate creativity and to share the joy of art during a time of difficulty and pain for many. James's wee dog Domino also helped out during the walks that produced these images and ideas!

Further information on James Donald's work can be found here: www.pickone.co.uk

Scotland After the Virus

Edited by
GERRY HASSAN and SIMON BARROW

Luath Press Limited
EDINBURGH

www.luath.co.uk

In memory of Peter Macdonald (1958–2020), whose life was dedicated to working for justice, and Mercy Baguma (1986–2020) whose life was tragically cut short by injustice.

First published 2020

ISBN: 978-1-91002215-3

The paper used in this book is recyclable. It is made from low chlorine pulps produced in a low energy, low emission manner from renewable forests.

Printed and bound by
Bell & Bain Ltd, Glasgow

Typeset in 11 point Sabon LT Pro by
Carrie Hutchison

The authors' right to be identified as authors of this work under the Copyright, Designs and Patents Act 1988 has been asserted.

Contents

ACKNOWLEDGEMENTS   9

INTRODUCTION   A Nation and World Changed:
Imagining Scotland After the Virus   11
GERRY HASSAN AND SIMON BARROW

Section One – Stories of Our Times

CHAPTER 1   Droplets   28
KIRSTIN INNES

CHAPTER 2   Wynning   38
JULIE BERTAGNA

CHAPTER 3   Invisible Cities   44
THOMAS CLARK

CHAPTER 4   We Are the Lucky Ones   46
CATHERINE SIMPSON

CHAPTER 5   Blue Reflectin   50
ANNA STEWART

CHAPTER 6   Cardinal Dreams   58
LISA WILLIAMS

CHAPTER 7   Table Service Only   65
ALAN BISSETT

CHAPTER 8   Grief   71
MARJORIE LOTFI GILL

CHAPTER 9   Rewilding   75
SALLY GALES

Section Two – Politics and Money

CHAPTER 10   Sleeping Beauty Awaits the
Resurrected Streets   84
JANETTE AYACHI

CHAPTER 11   People and Politics:
Reshaping How We Debate,
Discuss and Listen   88
MICHAEL GRAY

CHAPTER 12   Leadership, Learning and Knowledge:
Lessons from COVID-19   95
JAMES MITCHELL

CHAPTER 13   How a Small Country Might Just
Be Able to Lead a Big Change   101
KATHERINE TREBECK

CHAPTER 14   Breaking with Growth:
Creating an Economy of Life   108
BRONAGH GALLAGHER AND MIKE SMALL

Section Three – Public Spaces

CHAPTER 15   Hairdresser   118
CHERYL FOLLON

CHAPTER 16   Futures in Common:
Democratic Life Beyond the Crisis   119
OLIVER ESCOBAR

CHAPTER 17   Lessons in Civics:
What Do We Do About the Rise and
Fall of Civil Society in Scotland?   127
GERRY HASSAN

CHAPTER 18   How Parks Got Our Attention   135
WILLIE SULLIVAN

Section Four – Relational Scotland: Care, Life and Wellbeing

CHAPTER 19   The New Old Age   142
HUGH MCMILLAN

CHAPTER 20   Towards a Caring Economy   144
ANGELA O'HAGAN

CHAPTER 21   Death in the Time of COVID-19   154
DANI GARAVELLI

CONTENTS

CHAPTER 22   A Fable for Today   161
KAPKA KASSABOVA

CHAPTER 23   Casting Long Shadows:
Children and Young People and the Importance of Trust in a COVID-19 World   167
SUZANNE ZEEDYK

CHAPTER 24   Mental Health, Wellbeing and the
Psychological Challenge of COVID-19   176
CATHERINE SHEA

Section Five – Justice, Equality and Belief

CHAPTER 25   New Abnormal   186
STEPHEN WATT

CHAPTER 26   Changing Scottish Justice Will Take
Courage and Cooperation   188
HANNAH GRAHAM

CHAPTER 27   There is No Race Problem:
Theorising the Absence of Racial and
Ethnic Disparity Data in Scotland After
COVID-19   195
TOMMY J CURRY

CHAPTER 28   Spirituality:
Nurturing Life Before, Within and
Beyond COVID-19   203
ALISON PHIPPS, ALASTAIR MCINTOSH AND
SIMON BARROW

Section Six – Art, Culture, Sport and Media

CHAPTER 29   Sìth Sealach   214
ANNE C FRATER/ ANNA C FRATER

CHAPTER 30   Changing Landscape for Arts and
the Media   216
CLAIRE SAWERS

CHAPTER 31   COVID-19: Accelerating the (Un)Social
Media Landscape   221
JENNIFER JONES

CHAPTER 32   'Abandon All Hope, Ye Who Enter Here':
From Hell to Creative Scotland Form Filling
A Short Journey   227
FLAVIA D'AVILA

CHAPTER 33   Scottish Football in the Wake of the
Pandemic: Do or Die?   232
PAUL GOODWIN AND SIMON BARROW

Section Seven – Ideas Scotland: The Power of the Past and the Future

CHAPTER 34   Zero Traces of Cringe 2.0   238
CHRISTIE WILLIAMSON

CHAPTER 35   Scotland as Ark, Scotland as Lab   239
PAT KANE

CHAPTER 36   High Noon for an Imperfect Union:
The Search for a 'Settled Will'   246
HENRY MCLEISH

CHAPTER 37   Sure Foundations:
The Constitutional Basis of
Scottish Statehood   254
W. ELLIOT BULMER

CHAPTER 38   The Changing Risks of Independence   261
MARCO G BIAGI

CHAPTER 39   Scotland, Brexit and Europe:
Challenges Ahead   268
KIRSTY HUGHES

CHAPTER 40   From Downton Abbey to the Blitz Spirit:
Living with the Ghosting of Britain   275
GERRY HASSAN AND PATRICK WRIGHT

AFTERWORD   What Could It Mean to Flourish
'After the Virus'?   283
SIMON BARROW AND GERRY HASSAN

CONTRIBUTORS   296

Acknowledgements

THIS BOOK AIMS to understand the Scotland of recent times, the world of disruption under COVID-19 and the related crises created and magnified by it; and to map our future choices and directions when we eventually emerge from the pandemic.

This project is deliberately different from others that we have undertaken. It combines a breadth of perspectives in a range of formats to address a wide tapestry and palette of human emotions, intelligence and imagination in relation to the unprecedented times we have seen unfold in 2020 that may be with us for some time.

A book like this is a collective effort. First and foremost, we would like to thank the stellar range of contributors who gave their time, insights and expertise. We often asked the impossible in terms of briefs, and in each and every case were met with encouragement, positivity and engagement. The wider context of this book – the COVID-19 crisis – has magnified this experience and made it even more stimulating and supportive where we have as editors and contributors become a living community trying to make sense of the times we are in the midst of.

Many others aided the creation of this book with numerous assists, advice and recommendations. These include James Robertson on the opening section of short stories, alongside Zoe Strachan and Colin Herd of Glasgow University Creative Writing. Also generous in time and recommendations was Asif Khan of the Scottish Poetry Library in suggestions for poetry contributions. In related commissions, Malcolm Dickson of Street Level Photoworks, Richard Walker of the *Sunday National* and Joyce McMillan were enormously supportive of the entire project.

A whole range of other people gave of their time and insights to aid this book come to fruition. These include Danny Dorling, Peter Taylor-Gooby, Jim McCormick, Cathy McCulloch, Willie Storrar, Ian Fraser, Angela Haggerty, Douglas Fraser, Isabel Fraser, Alex Bell, Verene Nicolas, Ben Jackson, Lesley Orr, Jordan Tchilingirian, Shona Tchilingirian, Doug Hynd, Devi Sridhar (for her important public health analyses), Lisa Clark, Ian Dommett, Paul Martin and Lindsay

Paterson. We would also like to take this opportunity to thank the patience, fortitude and acute observations of our partners Rosie Ilett and Carla J Roth.

A major debt of gratitude is owed to Gerry's partner, Rosie, who – as with all of his publications and writings – read and proofed the entire text up to near-final sign-off. The book and its contents are sharper, more focused and better argued for having the benefit of Rosie's professional editing skills and overall insights. A particular note should be made of the conversation with Patrick Wright which benefited from her informed and subtle editing.

The very existence of this book with so many creative voices, talents and perspectives in this book has also been aided by the encouragement and support of Creative Scotland and in particular we would like to acknowledge the advice of Alan Bett – as well as other members of staff and advisers.

Many thanks to James Donald for the cover image which continues our tradition of striking, original covers. Finally and critically, we would like to thank the magnificent people who make up Luath Press – Gavin MacDougall, Carrie Hutchison, Lauren Grieve, Daniel Miele and Jennie Renton. They are passionate about books, ideas and writers, and it has been a pleasure and privilege to work with them. We want to record our gratitude for their support, and pay tribute to the wider contribution that Gavin and the Luath team have made to the public life of Scotland in recent years. Our country would be a less vibrant, dynamic and interesting place without their efforts – and this should be widely acknowledged and honoured.

Gerry Hassan   *Simon Barrow*
gerry@gerryhassan.com   simonbarrowuk@gmail.com

A Nation and World Changed: Imagining Scotland After the Virus

Gerry Hassan and Simon Barrow

THE WORLD IN 2020 was once the subject of far-reaching predictions: an imagined future typically filled with progress, possibilities and the contribution of new technologies that would transform what it was to be human.

The world that arrived in 2020 has proved to be very different and not one many would have predicted. It is a place where COVID-19 has caused global death and illness and dramatic changes to our lives. Alongside this massive disruption to how societies are run, there's economic dislocation, cultural dislocation, psychological uncertainty and massive social readjustment too.

All of this is true of Scotland and the UK. The former is the subject of this book, examining how Scotland has been affected and changed by the pandemic and how we might come out of this experience changed as individuals, and as part of the wider communities to which we belong or affiliate. It looks in different ways at how we each see the world, organise ourselves and think about our future. This introduction looks at the broader picture of how Scotland has changed, the nature of the UK, the future post-COVID-19 and the personal experiences of those who have contributed to this book.

As co-editors, we are conscious of our own different experiences of a tumultuous year with the pandemic. This has been, on a very human level, one with a range of heightened emotions, hopes, fears and anxieties. We experienced all of this living in Scotland – and this book is one small contribution to trying to make some sense of what we have lived through, as well as offering some glimmer of hope, reprieve and relief. To this end, we have commissioned an array of talented writers, many well-known and well-regarded, others emerging and newer, to share their insights in a variety of forms: fiction, poetry, non-fiction and a cover which emerged particularly out of living with lockdown.

Scotland, the UK and the Global Context

These have been difficult and stressful times – with doubts about the nature of the economy, jobs, prosperity and how people will manage post-furlough, particularly as the UK Government winds down the support schemes it unveiled at the beginning of the pandemic. The scale of economic and social disruption we have witnessed raises huge questions about the character of our society and its long-term direction.

One huge question concerns the role of government and public intervention. All across the world, governments have at least temporarily reversed the fiscal belt-tightening adopted recently, and have created economic support packages unprecedented in peacetime. Ones which, in many ways, fly in the face of free market capitalism. All of this comes barely a decade after the global banking crash.

The UK Government appears to have done something of an about-turn in reversing – to a degree – the previous ten years of austerity. As a result of cutbacks, public services (not least the NHS, education, social care, public health and local government) were not in a healthy or well-resourced place as they faced the unexpected and unprecedented challenge of COVID-19. Of the four countries of the UK, this was more so for England, but it has also been true for Scotland, Wales and Northern Ireland, where Westminster-led cuts have had a significant impact.

That said, Scotland, despite largely being required to follow the UK lead, has been able to chart a slightly different path on COVID-19. Nicola Sturgeon has shown more conscientious leadership than her UK counterpart, grasping the detail and putting science, evidence and independent expertise at the heart of government advice. The actual scale of divergence between Scotland and England in terms of deaths per head from the virus has been small. Up to the end of September 2020, England had the highest excess deaths per head in Europe during the pandemic and Scotland the third highest – a bleak reality. The UK has once again become known as 'the sick man of Europe'.

Yet Scotland has increasingly felt like a different place in terms of response to COVID-19, and this feeling builds on an already gathering sense of revulsion at the direction of UK politics and actions of UK Governments in recent years. This does give the impression of being a significant and potentially long-lasting change in how Scots see themselves and their future, but only time will tell.

One critical area central to the post-COVID-19 future is the nature of the economy – in Scotland, the UK and internationally. The nature and viability of work, employment and countless businesses (many once hugely successful), along with high streets and physical retail, is now a major concern. It raises questions both about the future of city and town centres, and also the adequacy of planning, taxation and regulation, particularly in relation to online shopping and corporate behemoths such as Amazon. The connection (or lack of it) between urban and rural local economies is also in the spotlight again.

One consequence of the pandemic crisis is that the public discourse which has framed the past 40 years (economic, social, cultural and political) is now even more open to challenge and reformation. The economic model of recent decades – free market capitalism, corporate power, anti-social individualism, validation of grotesque levels of wealth and inequality alongside parsimonious state attitudes to welfare and public spending – has become even more discredited.

This has huge implications for the planet and future of humanity. It also has major consequences for the UK and Scotland, with the UK over those decades being one of the leading advocates for a deregulated, unconstrained corporate capitalism – both domestically, in international forums and globally. Brexit is both an expression of, and catalyst for, pushing further in this direction.

The contest over the future state of the economy and society involves proponents and defenders of a view of the planet which is unsustainable economically, socially and environmentally. Such people will not simply concede that they are wrong and give up power. The capitalist leviathan built in recent times will not budge unless forced to do so by alternative forces. In the UK we can already see that the UK Government, while prepared to consider a bigger, more proactive state for survival purposes, is already pushing to further weaken regulations and planning in favour of big business, and to ride roughshod over local government in England. The 'small state' conservative will see this as a setback. What they are pushing for instead is a 'client state' – one that offers support for corporate interests, and sufficient (but increasingly conditional) social protection to retain electoral support.

Scotland has the potential for a different path here – something which is explored in this book. It is a path which includes but goes way beyond politics. It includes how we see ourselves, how we under-stand our mutual responsibilities to each other and how we express our connectedness and shared values. This, after all, is a core part of what is to be human. But in recent times these have sometimes seemed like revolutionary principles in the age of crony corporate capitalism where McKinsey can charge the UK Government £19,000 per day for management consultancy to advise civil servants.

The coming storm after COVID-19 will have unimaginable ramifi-cations. It will accelerate pressures on public services, such as the NHS and education. It will raise questions about affordability and sustain-ability in right-wing think tank circles – and in the Dominic Cummings-shaped 'Vote Leave' faction influencing Number 10 Downing Street. In England, the cover of the crisis will be used to remove the indepen-dence of public health experts and to bring them under the control of a centralised model to avoid talking about realities like health and social inequalities. Already we have seen health and education bodies punished for mistakes in handling the pandemic which were clearly the fault of the UK Government.

This will have a human cost across the UK and knock-on effects in Scotland, especially affecting those most vulnerable and disadvan-taged, not least disabled people. Think of the loss of life in care homes from COVID-19 and the stress, worry and anxieties thousands have been put through – whether residents, their families or staff. It raises so many questions. How do we, in an ageing society, nake available appropriate support to those elderly citizens who have to go into care? Who should run and own care homes, and are private equity firms really suited to the task? How do we economically support the legion of unpaid carers, recognising their vital role? Moreover, how do we strengthen the inter-generational social compact meant to connect the young to the old – and which has been left to wither in the UK?

What Does This Crisis Say About the Nature of the UK?

Central to these discussions is the nature of the UK and Scotland's place in it. This book is being published months before the May 2021 Scottish Parliament elections – one which will mark 22 years of devo-lution for Scotland, alongside Wales. In this time the dominant UK po-litical class has often considered devolution as a box ticked 'done', or has just forgotten about it. To Westminster and Whitehall, devolution has always been about pesky, complaining far-flung places, and never about the political centre and its problematic take of the entire UK.

This points to more serious and degenerative views of the UK and the nature of the power that lies at its heart. First, we have the view that devolution is not 'big boy' politics, and that the Scottish Parliament's wishes can be over-ridden, all connected to an absolutist sovereignty. This has been expressed by broadcaster and commentator Andrew Neil talking about Holyrood: 'It can be easily over-ruled by Westminster. Westminster is sovereign. Holyrood is devolved. Power devolved is power that can be superseded' (Neil, 2020).

Second, such absolutist sovereignty has a long lineage in the English political tradition. It is what Bernard Crick called 'the English ideology', which lost the UK the American colonies in 1775–76 and Ireland in 1921 through its refusal to compromise (Crick, 2008). Long thought dead, this absolutism resurrected itself under Thatcherism, and has reached an unapologetic full throttle in right-wing support for Brexit, and in *The Daily Telegraph* and *The Spectator's* worldviews. It is the grotesque thinking behind the UK Internal Market Bill which proposes to drive a horse and cart through the UK Government's Brexit Withdrawal Agreement, undermine the Good Friday Agreement and break international law. Crick believed that the whole UK edifice was held together by smoke and mirrors, and thought that 'Our rulers have ended up believing their own rhetoric, and therein often lies ruin and disaster' (Crick, 1990).

Third, and more seriously, it needs to be recognised that none of this is some arcane debate about abstract principles. Rather such a narrow, doctrinaire version of sovereignty has become directly linked to the imposition of a nakedly right-wing agenda, celebrating so-called 'winners, success and talent'. Related to this, it views those who struggle or need compassion and support as 'losers' and less than fully human. In many respects, this is a British version of what Naomi Klein has called 'disaster capitalism' – which has been practised much more brutally in Chile and Argentina in the 1970s (Klein, 2007). But that understates the uniquely British-English homegrown nature of this revolution – which has then been, in typical 'British exceptionalist' style, trumpeted around the world as the future.

This brings us to how Scotland sits in the strange hybrid that is the current UK. Scotland post-1707 has more or less enjoyed a privileged status in the union. As a nation it was never conquered or assimilated in the way that Wales was, and that was attempted in Ireland. Twenty plus years of the Scottish Parliament have built on this, showing capacity and resourcefulness, plus the need for further work and some honest conversations about where we fall short.

A major factor in the continuing journey of Scottish self-government is the relationship between the Scottish economy and UK economy – the latter fixated on the growth powerhouse of London and the south-east, and interests of the City and finance capitalism. Whatever Scotland's constitutional status, the dynamics of the rest of the UK economy and economic policy will be a major factor in the decisions we make here; London operating as virtually a city state in economic terms is a significant part of that.

Take the nature of the UK economy. The World Inequality Database has calculated that the ratio of wealth in relation to income in the UK is 605 per cent in the direction of wealth to income. That is the highest it has been since 1913 – having nearly doubled in the last 40 years, rising from 337 per cent in 1977 (World Inequality Database, 2020). This reflects the scale of investment in the UK in terms of assets, shares, property, offshore holdings and the 'hidden economy' – something increasingly disconnected from the real economy most people work in. It is difficult to be able fully to measure the figures for Scotland, but one estimate of the Scottish income to wealth ratio is, in the words of Professor Danny Dorling of Oxford University, that 'the Scottish figure is likely to be similar to the UK figure, possibly slightly lower' (Dorling, 2020a).

Secondly, a large portion of the independence debate has become fixated on the degree of fiscal transfer from the UK. This leads to heated debates about Barnett (the formula which works out the Westminster annual block to Scotland, Wales and Northern Ireland) and the reliability or otherwise of Government Expenditure and Revenue Scotland (GERS) figures, particularly for the purposes of making estimates about an independent Scotland – for which GERS seems ill-suited by design. Germane to this debate is the economically unbalanced nature of the UK. It is the most unequal country in Western Europe. Similarly, when fiscal transfers to Scotland from the centre are discussed, every part of the UK is a beneficiary of transfers from the political centre apart from London, the south-east and east of England. The reason for this is the greater degree to which the greater south-east concentrates wealth and power and crowds out the potential for other areas to blossom – notably, many English regions.

Much attention is paid to the fiscal transfer per year from Westminster to Scotland, which is estimated at £1,941 per head (see Scottish Government, 2020). This is offered as proof of the 'union dividend', and is held by some to demonstrate that any independent Scotland would have to make savage cuts to its budget to 'balance the books'. What this perspective wilfully misses is the difficulties of disaggregating large parts of UK public spending and locating them at the level of devolved nations and regions. It also underlines that the union has never been a static entity, but always changing. Relevant here are ten years of Tory austerity and cuts, beginning with George Osborne's aim to reduce the state and public spending back to 1930s levels. This has resulted in savage cuts across the UK – from 44.5 per cent of GDP in 2010 to 38.3 per cent in 2020 pre-COVID-19 – the difference between the two – 6.2 per cent of GDP. This has had a commensurate effect on public spending in Scotland which has not risen to the degree it could have (Dorling, 2020b).

Any 'union cutback' does not mean that Scotland, along with Wales and Northern Ireland, do not gain from Barnett consequences. But the important point here is that they have also been affected by UK-wide decisions and cuts, which has impacted on public spending in Scotland, due to the choices of Westminster. What the above underlines is that financial decisions and flows cannot be seen in isolation, or assessed in one direction, but have to be seen in the round. This indicates that while Scotland gains from Westminster, it is also affected by Westminster decisions and priorities being made for us. Ones over which we have very little say, given that MPs elected from Scotland are hugely outnumbered.

Future Scotland and Lessons From 'Past Futures'

The scale of crisis and the degree of upheaval that COVID-19 has produced calls for the most fundamental rethink of everything we know about public life, politics and society. If we go back to the harsh economic climate of the 1930s, and the domestic 'people's war' of Britain in the Second World War, there was an array of ambitious, far-reaching plans in Scotland for reconstruction and recovery, which played a major role in the foundations of post-war society.

The scale of ambition these embodied, building popular support and achieving change, offers some pointers for negotiating the crises of the present. Hence such publications as *Plan for Scotland* (Burns,

1937), *Scotland 1938* (Allan, 1938) and *The Future of Scotland* (Bowie, 1939); then, during the war, *The Real Rulers of Scotland* (Burns, 1940), *The New Scotland* (Maclean, 1942) and numerous publications from the Scottish Convention of the 1940s – such as *The Culture of the Scot* (Power, 1943). These were informed by concepts of modernity, progress and belief in the power of the state – alongside a determination not to repeat the past failures which had led to economic depression and war.

Several of these publications demonstrate impressive quality and content, still evident decades later. *The Real Rulers of Scotland* itemises who has economic power. *The Culture of the Scot* calls for a new age of Enlightenment, and a Scottish Broadcasting Corporation capable of nurturing culture and talent (see Finlay, 2004). The most comprehensive plan is *The New Scotland*, from 1942, with its 17 chapters offering a kind of Scottish mini-Beveridge, but actually going much further – with proposals for economic planning, cooperation, democratising banking, worker and trade union rights and more.

There are similarities between then and now, and also obvious differences. Scotland after the virus needs a similar ambition, analysis and determination. We have to be clear that there can be no return to the old ways, to the society pre-COVID-19 which gave sustenance to a rotten economic and social order – one that reduces workers and successful businesses to being pawns of finance capital and which seems incapable of thinking long-term.

The New Scotland made the case for economic planning, a crusade to end privilege and vested interests, and the extension of democracy – including a Parliament. But it also goes further, arguing that:

> The mere setting up of a bourgeois Parliament at Edinburgh without sturdy local self-government to control it will simply make new jobs for Edinburgh lawyers and Glasgow business men – and the real people of Scotland will have as little liberty and self-government as at present (Burns, 1942).

This vision of Scotland was one of greater democracy and self-government, not just a Parliament. It had roots in the early days of Labour, Keir Hardie and the Independent Labour Party. It drew from anti-state traditions, but was conceived at a critical junction where it would soon be subsumed in statism. This was an approach which was to dominate Labour and Scottish politics well into the 1970s. With it came a transformative agenda which remade Scotland – lifting working-class people out of poverty, using education as a liberator, improving health and life expectancy, clearing away the old slums and introducing hydro-electric power to the Highlands. This Labour Scotland of progress and modernity lasted from 1945 to 1974 – and a lynchpin of it was that the Labour Party had emphatically turned its back on its earlier traditions of supporting a Parliament, anti-statism and community organisation. Eventually this shift from redistributing power to using it for (rather than with) the people came back to undermine Labour and some of the achievements of this era. These became perceived as paternalist and bureaucratic, opening the way for the Thatcherite critique of 'dependency Scotland'.

Scotland's Parliament was re-established under the conditions of devolution in 1999. It was in part a product of Scottish autonomy and distinctiveness, and in part a reaction to the onslaught of Thatcherism. It has since become a central pillar of political life, reflecting our priorities and values, yet it is still unclear whether it is an end in itself or a means to a greater end. Is it about power accruing in this institution, or does it mean using its prestige to aid the further dispersal of power to communities and regions?

These questions pose a larger one about the unfulfilled promise and possibility of the earlier tradition of self-government, expressed in *The New Scotland* of 1942. It is this which politics turned its back on after 1945. This earlier vision was one of dispersed popular power, aiming to avoid politicians becoming 'a privileged ruling class', and instead having a Parliament which

> would act not so much as the sovereign assembly dictating its will to the people (for this is English Constitutional Law, and the immemorial Scottish one which recognises the People, and not the King in Parliament, as Sovereign)

but rather 'as a central co-ordinating bond linking the Sovereign self-governing People' (Burns, 1942).

Post-COVID-19, this terrain will surely become a major issue again. Where do we want power to sit? What should be the role of Parliament and national politicians? How do we aid greater autonomy and decentralisation throughout society? How can we nurture a different vision of the economy to that of the prevailing (and failed) orthodoxy of recent times? There is already one possible future on the table – the direction taken by the UK Government of further diluting regulations and planning in England, contributing to the creation of what John Harris has called 'unplaces' which offer the prospect of being a 'hyper-individualised future... with no sense of place, no dependable local news, no spaces to gather' and no 'kind of collective self-help' (Harris, 2020).

Here is the future we need to avoid. But while England offers a desolate landscape, lacking popular agency, we should not be blind to our shortcomings here. Scotland's traditions and practices of local government and decentralism have been atrophying for decades, and the arrival of the Scottish Parliament and Government has further accelerated the tendency toward centralisation. Post-COVID-19, one possible future for Scotland and elsewhere, driven by pressures on public spending, would be further to concentrate political power, and to say that these crises forced us to erode local democracy even more, along with the powers of public agencies. In some respects, this could even be seen as re-treading the road from 1945, when we should rather have had the confidence to embrace the missionary zeal with which people went about improving society, instead of embracing the same old top-down approach.

The COVID-19 Life Stories in This Book

This book contains fiction, poetry and non-fiction. It is not just about politics, but about many areas of human life. It concerns the powers of the human imagination and the human spirit. It is also about the people in these pages who gave their time and energies in the midst of lockdown and a pandemic. All of the 40 plus contributors were invited – after they had completed their contributions – to reflect on how COVID-19 had affected them, their families and friends, and to consider what wider impact the pandemic and lockdown was having. We asked for such accounts anonymously, in order to paint a snapshot that showed the general picture. None of our contributors had been diagnosed with the virus, although many fell ill and had worries and anxieties that it might be COVID-19.

These contributions offered a picture which combines bleakness, adaptability and finding new experiences in something none of us expected. At first, the pandemic and lockdown seemingly changed everything and challenged what most of us thought about ourselves and the world. One contributor said: 'The pandemic felt like the earth cracking open at my feet. Normality disappeared one week [in] March.'

An obvious strand was the hit that many people took in income, with work opportunities and monies drying up – particularly for younger freelancers. One writer stated: 'I lost a fair amount of work throughout the pandemic, but I found the social isolation by far the hardest aspect.' A related theme was the changing world of work, retreat from the office and home as a place of work. This challenged the identities of many people – one person wrote of the artists and musicians they know: 'Their wee light and identity [is] rubbing away. People used to [the] limelight and being loved – [their] identity created by what we do.'

Another put it: 'The biggest challenges were psychological and relational: dealing with lockdown, juggling home-working with home-schooling, trying to manage everyday tasks while keeping safe.' Connected to this has been families living more closely together than in past years, with resultant pressures. This was something in which some found an upside:

> We found lockdown a very intense bonding experience. My three boys have become much closer and we did more as a family than we had done for years.

But there was a downside for others: 'When a neighbour turned threatening and violent, it became unsafe even to venture into the garden. Social breakdown was on our doorstep.'

This has divided families, with people not being able to see family members they love dearly. That can be acute, with one person worrying about his '91-year-old mother in hospital, and severe visiting limitations'. There were the shared experiences of missing friends, including what happens when a friend dies. One contributor recalled hearing of a suicide:

> During lockdown restrictions, hearing the news of the death of someone my age having taken their own life meant people couldn't go to his funeral. Though living in the same city, a group of us shared memories, photos, stories, played songs and sang over a Zoom call.

They signed off their thoughts by saying: 'Watching people in need of a hug and not being able to give it' is one of the hardest things imaginable.'

There was the wider sense of feeling cut off, isolated and an absence during lockdown of shared communal moments. There was sadness about this, but also some sense that it allowed for other ways of looking at life. It forced change in long-established behaviours too:

> The lockdown, if not the virus, has significantly impacted my reading life. Two or three text streams disappeared overnight – borrowing libraries (and The Mitchell Library).

The opportunity to halt or move away from the incessant rush that was life pre-COVID-19 was for some a sort of liberation:

> COVID completely changed my view of normal. Pre-lockdown I was constantly chasing new experiences and checking off boxes on my to-do list. I didn't stop to appreciate the experiences and moments I was having.

Connected to this, there was a changing relationship with the environment – from feeling the lack of rush and noise right through to the cleaner air and the slower, more deliberate pace of activities, such as walking and going to public parks. One person talked powerfully of 'a kind of cycling between rest and reprieve – the freshness of the unpolluted air, time to sit in the garden, time to explore new skills.'

Big political decisions impacted people, including the insensitive, inhumane policies of the UK Government on asylum seekers which has been felt acutely, especially in Glasgow. Someone involved in trying to mitigate and challenge this stated:

> The Home Office decanted asylum seekers in the city into hotel accommodation at 30 minutes notice... and I ended up deeply engaged in the co-ordination and advocacy around what was an unfolding humanitarian disaster.

Another view from someone who has chosen to come to the UK for work was: 'As a migrant, there were days when I felt the weight of closed borders on my shoulders.'

The long-term impact of COVID-19 will be felt for years, and one writer thought about this internationally:

> I keep thinking about people in other countries too, in years to come, what will be the knock-on effect of coronavirus? This situation reminds me of the 2008 financial crash, in the way that a big world event affected people so personally, and how people were confused by it and encouraged to feel like it was their own fault.

Finally, in the immediate future, the UK and global economy will inevitably see an upsurge in unemployment, business closures and greater inequality and hardship. One voice referenced on this the words of the Bard stating: 'Robert Burns captured fear of the future in his poem, "To a Mouse".' They cited the following (emphasis added):

> Still thou are blest, compared wi' me!
> The *present* only toucheth thee:
> But Och! I *backward* cast my e'e,
> On prospects drear!
> An' *forward*, tho' I canna *see*,
> I *guess* an' *fear*!

Across the range of these observations forged in the midst of a pandemic, there were similarities as well as some noticeable differences. In a book with a majority of women contributors, women writers were markedly more fulsome in their reflections. Men, in general, were more focused on the practicalities of what was happening in work and home. There was also a definite difference in response by age. Older writers – and those with homes and assets – felt that they could fall back on these, with many stating how 'lucky' they were in that respect. But some of the perspectives offered by people in their 20s and 30s unsurprisingly showed more worry and anxiety.

The House of Scotland

This is a very human book, borne out of experiences up and down our land, and across the world. None of us know in detail what the near-future will hold – whether a vaccine will be found, and whether national and local lockdowns will be unique to the spring and summer of 2020, or will instead become a recurring feature that permanently alters how we live. But we have already been changed in ways we do not yet fully comprehend, and as one of the voices above suggested, the long-term effects will take years to pan out and understand.

We cannot go back to the old 'normal', people feel. But, on the other hand, the 'new normal' is an oxymoron which makes little sense right now. And isn't it a bit rich that many of those who glibly parrot these phrases, and especially those want to put the economy ahead of health, are the same ones who have continually told us that the status quo is not an option and that we have to embrace change? The conservatism of recent times, which has turned the lives of millions upside down, ripped up the social contract in the UK and elsewhere, and celebrated irresponsible capitalism, has shown itself to be particularly lacking when times get hard – such as the 2008 crash or 2020 COVID-19 crash. These ideologies do not have the capacity to address fundamental and permanent change. Instead they end up resting on old orthodoxies concerned much more with preserving power, order and privilege for the governing and owning classes.

All of this will be felt at a very human level over the coming years. It would be beneficial if the handling of public affairs and matters of state could show the degree of humanity, empathy and insight evident in the contributors to this volume. We need to be able to have public conversations and debates worthy of the tasks we have to face. There will always be noise and point-scoring in our politics, but more than ever there has to be substance and generosity behind such characteristics – something we explore further in the afterword.

There can be no standing still. But we should see part of this task as one of remaking Scotland as a home that aspires to look after all of its citizens. As Green MSP Andy Wightman said of modern Scotland a couple of years back:

> We are like a house that hasn't been lived in for a long time. You go in, and you can see familiar things, but nothing really works, and you know the water needs [to be] sorted out and switched on again, and there is a lot of dust around (Hassan, 2016).

Scotland's journey in the near future needs to be one of continual learning, maturity and self-discovery – what Irish writer Fintan O'Toole called 'the art of growing up'. This will involve confronting some unpalatable truths about our society and acting upon them (Hassan, 2014). That will be up to us. We will have to learn and relearn every day how we do this, and recognise that we do indeed – if we work together and overcome some of our divisions – have the power to make Scotland post-COVID-19 a place we are proud to call our collective home.

References

Allan, JR, 1938, *Scotland 1938: Twenty-Five Impressions,* Edinburgh, Oliver and Boyd.

Bowie, JA, 1939, *The Future of Scotland: A Survey of the Present Position with some Proposals for Future Policy,* Edinburgh, W & R Chambers.

Burns, T, 1937, *Plan for Scotland,* Glasgow, A MacLaren & Sons and London Scots Self-Government Committee.

Burns, T, 1940, *The Real Rulers of Scotland,* Glasgow, Civic Press and London Scots Self-Government Committee.

Crick, B, 1990, 'On Devolution, Decentralism and the Constitution, reprinted in Crick, B, *Political Thoughts and Polemics,* Edinburgh, Edinburgh University Press, 104–25.

Crick, B, 2008, 'In conversation', *Changin' Scotland weekend,* The Ceilidh Place, Ullapool, 15 March.

Dorling, D, 2020a, 'Personal communication to authors', 19 August.

Dorling, D, 2020b, 'Personal communication to authors', 31 August.

Finlay, R, 2004, *Modern Scotland 1914–2000,* London, Profile Books.

Harris, J, 2020, 'No news, no shared space, no voice – the Tories are creating a cookie-cutter Britain', *The Guardian,* 16 August, accessed at: www.theguardian.com/commentisfree/2020/aug/16/ news-britain-covid-local-communities-tories

Hassan, G, 2014, *Caledonian Dreaming: The Quest for a Different Scotland,* Edinburgh, Luath Press.

Hassan, G, 2016, *Scotland the Bold: How Our Nation Has Changed and Why There is No Going Back,* Glasgow, Freight Books.

Klein, N, 2007, *The Shock Doctrine: The Rise of Disaster Capitalism,* London, Allen Lane.

Maclean, N (ed.), 1942, *The New Scotland: 17 Chapters on Reconstruction,* Glasgow, Civic Press and London Scots Self-Government Committee.

Neil, A, 20 August 2020, accessed at: www.twitter.com/afneil/
   status/1296513956954152962
Power, W, 1943, *The Culture of the Scot: Its Past and Future*,
   Glasgow, Scottish Convention.
Scottish Government (2020), *Government
   Expenditure and Revenue Scotland (GERS) 2019–
   2020*, accessed at: www.gov.scot/publications/
   government-expenditure-revenue-scotland-gers-2019-20/
World Inequality Database, 2020, 'United Kingdom', accessed at:
   www.wid.world/country/united-kingdom/

Section One – Stories of Our Times

CHAPTER I

Droplets

Kirstin Innes

THERE IS NOTHING
no that's not it. There are too too many too many things

tiny things, many of them
little
bits
of
lists
that nip away at the bits of her brain that
she'd intended to use for better
Back when all – this – had begun, it had seemed like the best way to
survive it was to imagine the experience as a crucible, a forge maybe,
where all the bits that were wrong, cruel, broken could be burned
away. There were hopes, those hopes were announced and agreed
with, all over the internet. When all this was over* society was going
to emerge

(*a thing everyone all said a lot at first, *when this
is all over*; talking with the same mouth about how
everything and nothing would change.)

emerge from this leaner, bruised but resilient, a white-hot new thing
that gleamed and was fit for purpose

was that the baby

and it – oh, everybody meant
well. There were great intentions. Within three days they had a set up

a local volunteer network, had posted info in the windows of the shops on the High Street – if you need us, we're here. She felt herself made new with the work. Weird, isn't it, she'd said to Debbie, who coordinated the volunteers in what they'd decided was Zone 4, it took being stuck in the house most of the time to really make me feel connected to the community again. One of the terrifyingly organised mums on the primary school council had sourced compost in bulk, distributed it throughout the village. Doorstep drop-offs. Tap-door-run. The dirt stuck under her children's fingernails as they pushed tiny sprouting tatties, khaki balls, into the depths of the bags she'd lined up along the one sunny wall of their wee bit of garden. The baby had been fascinated by the feel of it, rubbed it into his hair; she'd gone to scold him and ended up laughing instead because what did it matter? Who would see? Maybe they would grow up green-fingered, her children, freed by a change in circumstances from plastic-wrapped supermarket potatoes. When the first bits of green began to sprout her daughter had thought it was a miracle, named each tiny plant after a different favourite cartoon character, made a video to send to the friends she couldn't play with.

All these beginnings. All these ideas. It was terrifying but the possibility of it; well, *fundamentally changing society should be terrifying. That's the point we're trying to make – hang on; I'll elaborate later –*

– arms outstretched at the top of the stairs to her and a wordless keening

back to bed. Back to bed sweetheart. Sssh-sssh. Mummy cuddle. Sssh. There. She drew leisurely hearts on his back with a finger, readying herself for the long wait until his slightly curdled milk-breath slowed. The arm sandwiched between his heavy head and the flat little pillow began to tingle. It's not working this, still stuffing him with bottles throughout the night, just to stop him from screaming and waking his sister, he's getting too old really

and the relief as she took out her phone and her thumb pulled the screen down and down and in it came because she needed to check, keep checking, because the world changed every time she hit refresh now, got worse and worse and she needed to know, STAY ALERT to it.

over two-thirds of people who have recovered from the virus report heart conditions, study says

the spike of outrage and anger, a mashing of buttons that weren't even there, just points under sensitive glass, pull down again and on to the next one. Angry people jumping on fragments without context, spinning them into a mob, a resignation, a lack of resignation and a shrug, a scroll, a pull-down-and-refresh-and-on-to-the-next

emoji flags
like pitchforks–

– face buried in the crook of her elbow he shuddered out a sigh, raised his bum in the air and farted happily in his sleep; she had to drop the phone to muffle the laugh

in the desert, wind blowing his hair, the President of the United States thumped a bible from the kids' bedroom rug

she might as well just sleep here again

Hope you don't mind me getting in touch like this! I work for an organisation trying to connect community organisers, to help put the scaffolding down for a new and positive future. You've been recommended to us – by several sources actually! – as exactly the sort of person who we need to help us rebuild our post-virus society–

– no, no, it's your sister's turn. Okay. Okay petal, how about we choose something you can both watch together. Hey Duggee. It's not really for babies, though, is it? This one? No petal, please. Just pick one. Okay. Let's just let Mummy oh are you alright darling, did you have a wee fall, oh, bumped your head. You're fine. You're fine. Okay, Mummy's just going to drink her coffee now –

– doorbell (hooking the elastic round her ears): a woman from up the road, dropping off stuff for the foodbank. Ach, I just thought I'd drop them in. I just thought there's someone who'd get the use out of them and that lassie who's doing the foodbank will know better than me. More pasta, tins of tomatoes and peaches, teabags, a sliced loaf.

Experience of working with community groups and social enterprises. Background in care. Furlough pay so didn't need, couldn't be paid – could she help them and she'd said yes, of course; ended up taking charge while everyone else in the meeting in their sealed boxes had looked away from their webcams, tried to deflect.

> *Just had a loaf dropped off. Out of date tomorrow – anyone know a service user who*

– please baby I just need to do this one wee thing could you WATCH THAT CUP! I've got hot coffee here look, could you both just sit down. On your bottoms. Please just watch the programme. Watch the fu

let's just watch the programme okay? Mummy's just going to get more coffee now.

fingernail marks in the flesh of her palm–
> *might want it today?*

Kitchen. When had she stopped cooking? When was it. Dinners of beans and chips. Fishfingers every third day for variety. Somewhere around the second month? The third?

> STAY ALERT the smoothed-out Health Minister, all his parts ironed by his mammy, opened his mouth as her thumb brushed his face and said that controlling the virus was responsibility of the individual

screams of laughter funnelled through the open window OHMIGOD I HATE YOU GET OFF ME YA TOTAL MINGER from the empty carpark across the street where a snakepit of teenage bodies smoked weed all day and probably fucked while their parents stayed locked at home. They'd started early this morning, maybe hadn't gone to bed yet.
AAAA
AAAA
YOU'VE GOT THE RONA NOW

AAAA
GET OFF ME STOP TOUCHING ME FUCK YOUSE IM
GOING HOME –
– and there it was again. The bone-deep ache. Her joints too heavy to
let her think. She put jammy toast crusts in her mouth, washed them
down with cold, cold coffee how long had she been in here

> *Hi Frances,*
> *Thanks so much for thinking of me.*
> *I'd love to be involved and find out*
> *more – shall we get a chat at some*
> *point this week? When sui*

– DID YOU JUST HIT HIM? WELL, WHY'S HE CRYING? DID
YOU BITE HER?
> 28 new cases from one pub

they were out of toilet roll and running low on binbags, she needed to
remember that.

> 9am. New notification from the school app.
> ▮▮▮▮▮*Good Morning!! It's time to start*
> *another day!!!*

– oh jesus fucking god, handwriting again. Her daughter making fists
around the pencil, unable to get the grip, throwing it away in frustration, both of them screaming at each other. A wee high electrical
pitch, ticking through her brain. The baby, plonked down in front of
Teletubbies, had removed his nappy and pissed a drippy trail across
the carpet.

> Donna was the first to reply: *Use bicarb*
> *of soda. It works on the mattresses when*
> *they wet those too. Gets the smell out like*
> *nothing else.*
> hair care advert (how did they know she had curly hair,
> those worms inside her phone?)
> that guy who used to be on the telly taking selfies
> of his angry face, a grim maskless etching shot from
> the chin up, in the aisles of Asda, Tesco, Aldi. Just to
> prove he could–

– why does the baby's pee smell like that, anyway? She hadn't been getting him drinking enough water, maybe. She filled a bottle from the tap, Elsa's doll-perfect face scratched and peeling off it, took it through to him. He threw it onto the carpet by the pee stain and laughed.

he was thirteen. Thirteen, and he died alone, without his mother, surrounded by strangers in plastic alien face screens. He'd had asthma

no

someone had started a fan account for the gold chain round the thick neck of the actor playing an Irish teenager in that new sexy programme

Everyone had put rainbows in their windows at the start, a tiny gesture of support for each other, their felt pen stripes fading in the sunlight as the weeks ticked on. When was it decided that they should take them down? About the same time as they stopped clapping for the keyworkers? She'd found the ones her kids had done under the sofa, dust, hair and nail clippings stuck to the old Sellotape around the edges.

ts you? Evenings are usually better for me, after the kids are down, but could try and do Zoom over a naptime? I'll stick the big one in front of Fro

oh just FUCKING STOP IT STOP IT LEAVE EACH OTHER ALONE

the Chancellor has announced that there will be no extension to the furlough scheme
that pretty boy who did the exercises on YouTube, his big blank living room, how sweaty it must smell crowded English beaches, people squeezing up their pink flesh against each other.
saltire-draped blockades across the motorway, three old men trying to close a border

the chaotic weightiness of this big unwieldy world squeezing her; she imagined it cracking rib, flattening organ, gasped for breath. She reached behind herself. Fuck, still no bog roll. Thump, thump, thump as one of the children demanded entry, demanded her. WHY DID YOU LOCK THE DOOOOOOR? MUMMMMEEEEE! I NEED TO TELL YOU SOMETHING URGENTLY

Right, so. It's about – what it's about is putting a structure in place now. Setting down markers, a scaffolding for a new society that we can build on when all this is over. The trouble is that this new society, it requires a – just a minute love – it requires us, those of us who care, to do that work on behalf of ourselves and of the people who haven't – please, Mummy's working – sorry, I've got a thirsty five year old here; I'm just going to get her a drink then I'll be right back – I'll just put myself on mute, you all carry on.

protests on the news, people scorched with righteous anger and nothing left to lose seizing their moment to burn it all down and she shrank away, scrolled on where she once would have rejoiced only a shiver at how close they stood

Their potato plants grew too high, struggling up the pebbledash to reach the sunshine, the stalks browning, falling over, breaking one after another and she didn't do anything to help them.

left the shopping at your door doll receipts in the bag no rush lol xxx

the yoghurts and pre-packaged toddler snacks she couldn't get to the supermarket to buy, not on the bus with a toddler and an asthmatic child, the driver's hacking cough; the only things the baby would eat some days. Good neighbours. Good neighbours. Another shopping bag tucked behind the door, she'd only just noticed. That foodbank drop off from last week. Tins. Pasta. The loaf of bread turned blue, wasted and eating itself inside the plastic bag. Her phone. The message to the volunteer group still hovering there in drafts. She sank onto the doormat, bristles through her leggings, wet face wet hands as the waste of it overwhelmed her; the person

who could have eaten it and went hungry; her own stupid fucking
uselessness.

SUBJECT: Post-furlough redundancies
a statue of a murderer toppled into a harbour
due to unavoidable circumstances
a white man made a cast iron statue of a
beyond our control
black woman with her fist raised
please contact HR to discuss packages
but he was problematic, had a history of profiting from
deeply saddened

*Swing park open again! Bring your
two down. Come on. We all need this.*
xxx

She stuck an ankle out of her front door and it felt like dangerous waters, but her daughter jumped, feet first. Come ooooon Mum!
Bundling the buggy, no don't touch the door handle darling don't
touch don't touch other people's cars
swagger
    swagger
      swagger
they were coming closer and closer and it didn't look like they
were going to step off the pavement. The bigger one's eyes glazed, his
face swollen with it. Their shoulders bumped off each other, cunts and
fucks fired messily from limp machine gun mouths. Cans of energy
drink in their fists. She tried to manoeuvre the buggy behind one of
the parked cars, realised too late her daughter was frozen in their
path. Eyes huge, fresh, young, asthma-hooked lungs ready to receive
any droplets they spat her way. The smaller one's head swivelled like
something out of a horror movie, swerved and bent down at her tiny
tiny girl, opening his mouth into the cruellest smile. She jumped,
moved her whole body into his way, hauled the nappy bag over a
shoulder at him and felt something crunch as the baby's full bottle in
the side pocket met his ear.

Get away from her.
You get away from her.
Get the fuck away from her.
GET THE FUCK AWAY FROM HER.

It had been a long, long time since she'd touched another adult. Since touch had been a gift, for her not from her, loving not needing. Who had it been? That brief, slack, photocopy of a hug from Claire after an awkward coffee in February? If she'd known that would be the last one she'd have gone in for a snog or something, rubbed her skin on that over-blushered cheek, wrapped a hand round the bare skin of her neck. Made it count.

But here was the woman who worked in the chemist, mask still round her chin, hand brushing her back, gently pushing her back along the pavement to her house. Come on love. Come on. It's okay. It's okay now. All the ill people who must walk into the chemist. The germs on that mask.

In the distance, through a Vaseline lens, the bigger of the two boys made fists at her from behind the small crowd who had gathered around his friend.

Build Back Better. Her handwriting, on an envelope tucked behind the toaster. Underlined. Red biro. She had no memory of writing it. On the sofa, her children's legs tangled up as they lay back together on a cushion and let Elsa lull them off – a slow sweet song to a drowned child

> most people I know have loved lockdown, said the woman whose husband had singlehandedly shattered it, writing from beneath her aristocratic caricature on a newspaper website, and hardly anyone was as angry as they should have been, would have been weeks ago
> 49 new cases.
> 104 new cases.
> he'd taken a selfie, his wide-eyed slab of a face doing cartoon outrage, pointing out to sea at an orange smudge battered by waves. Look over there.

CHAPTER 1: DROPLETS

Hi Frances, I'm so sorry I haven't replied

Delete draft?
Delete.

There was nothing she could do to stop any of this.
There was nothing she could do to change any of this.
There was nothing she could do.
There was nothing
There was n

        o bog roll. Again. She dropped the phone down
the toilet. Water splashed up, dripped down her thighs,
and she flushed.

CHAPTER 2

Wynning

Julie Bertagna

THE CITIES WERE scattering us in a great tide of coughs and sneezes, all across the land.

Waves of lockdown had wrecked our roaming years, our little eras of exploration when we'd widen our horizons, pick up some bar work or teaching, be bold and free. Before settling down to work till we're 75 or so.

That was then.

Now the next tide was coming in, the really big one, and Wynners had to be ready. I was sick of my shadow half-life, waiting, worrying, wondering. The New Enlightenment was rising. I'd steer my own fate.

'You can't just sail out into the world, Siddie,' my mother kept saying. 'Not this world.'

'Come with me then.'

I knew there was little chance of that.

'But all our *things*.' She'd open her arms, encapsulating a lifetime of accumulated stuff.

My mind raced through the rooms of our house, past sofas and chairs and cushions, tables and lamps, pictures, curtains, books, mirrors, beds, rugs, potted plants, TVs, toaster, fridge freezer, microwave, washing machine, dishwasher, cooker, juicer, blender, coffeemaker – I stopped, mind spinning. If I thought of it all, I'd never be able to go. How could I exist without so much stuff?

Existing was all I was doing. Home was my prison. At the start of the pandemic I'd bolted back here to be with my parents, glad to be safe. Now I was stuck. No job, no money of my own, minimal outside contact. We'd lost Dad, early on. Overweight, taxi driver, diabetes type 2. The perfect COVID combo.

'Start again,' I said to my mother. 'Take what we can pack in the car. It's just stuff.'

For three seconds, the possibility trembled in her.

'Ach, I'm too old to just jump up and go. And you're too young, Siddie, with everything that's going on.'

'What's the perfect age,' I wondered, 'to save your life?'

The way she looked at me, I felt my eyes well up.

'Listen, after the Great Wars people rebuilt the world, yeah? The Roaring Twenties, the NHS. Even after the Black Death. That's what we're trying to do.'

'Why run off into the blue to do it? Here, you've got food deliveries, you've got...' She tried to think.

'People are moving out of the cities, Mum. It's the Clearances in reverse. You get drone deliveries anywhere. What's a city *for* now, if you've a 5G phone with RuralBoost, SmartMed and PanDr, the Internet of Things, a Starswarm satellite connection, AgriSmart and WaterTech...'

In the Remote Revolution, everything from eye tests to dental checks could be done via phone. Digitised systems and voice-tech reduced human contact everywhere. If you were young, the choice was: live apart from vulnerable family members or live with them in a remote world where you rarely see anyone else.

Entire ecosystems of small business were gone. Once the offices emptied, the cafes and sandwich bars, gyms and shops, restaurants and pubs and suppliers collapsed. As everything went online, tech and entertainment, supermarkets and home deliveries boomed and all the wealth lost by small business was concentrated in the coffers of the biggest. But big government and companies had mostly proved vast enough and fast enough to cope with a complex global crisis. Were they agile enough for the really big one? It seemed as if COVID had been a dry-run for the Climate test. Tech had stepped up to that challenge. Could it make the giant leap humankind needed now?

That was up to us.

'Once I'm settled, Oto could bring you to visit.'

'We'll see.' Mum sighed. 'If you're set on going, you'd better take him.'

'Oto? Really?'

Oto would make everything a lot easier.

But I couldn't. He was needed here.

'Your Aunt Cathy's bagged your room,' my mother pressed on. 'She's on her own too, so we'll muddle along together. We'll have her car. Everything's delivered anyway. I'll be happier if you've at least got, well, *somebody*. And your Dad would want you to have Oto. He'd want you to live your life.'

So she was all organised. I was free.

The lights blinked. It was one of those dim Glasgow days that could be any month of the year, when the sky was so low you needed the lamps on, though not jumpers any more. It was muggy, even in March.

'You go on ahead,' said Mum, over the ominous roll of thunder, the batter of hailstones outside. 'We'll maybe catch you up.'

As if I were eight years old, racing along Troon beach where the tide was so far out it was just a silver line at the bottom of the sky and the wet sands were shining after an ordinary rainstorm and our lives lay calm and all before us.

*****

'What about the Black Death?' Mum asked, as Oto opened the car boot and I heaved my backpack in.

Had she been thinking about that all night? I wanted to leave her with hope.

'After, the survivors remade the world. A golden age of new tech. The rich grew richer but land was up for grabs so the serfs broke free.' I hesitated. 'I've found an old lodge on a loch in the heart of Scotland. Absentee owner. Very absent now. Dead. He lived in the Netherlands so it's... up for grabs.'

'Be careful, Sidera.' My full name. This was the big goodbye then. 'My girl of the stars.'

'Don't get soppy. I'll call when I'm there.'

'Ready?' Oto locked the seat belt.

We eased down the driveway and I didn't look back.

'Do you want to drive?' purred Oto.

Mum kept him on Sean Connery voice setting. She liked a virtual James Bond at the wheel. (Was there a Janey Godley or Val McDermid setting? Check later, Sid.) The car sensors had tracked my concentrated stare through the windscreen, but I was just trying not to cry. The steering wheel hatch slid open in front of me.

'No, thanks. Stuff to do.'

I really didn't need to thank or explain to a self-driving car, like my mother did. He'd been Dad's last instruction. Use the life insurance to get one of those new electric self-drives, they'll do everything, even self-charge, you won't need to go out. Cost a small fortune, but Oto was proving his worth right now as I merged my phone and tablet with his systems.

The car breezed a burst of clean air through the vents and dimmed the windows as we drove through the worst of the streets. I made myself look at the boarded-up wreckage of a once-teeming city. Yet there were signs of life in the empty shops and buildings, in the art gallery and museum. The dispossessed were reclaiming the cityscape. I hoped they were Wynning.

Wynning. Old Scots word. The action or state of occupying a place.

Wynning meant building arks of all kinds, however, wherever we could. It meant future-proofing the planet, creating new codes for change that could help us all surf the storms of the coming climate chaos.

Generation iGen, the most tech-savvy in history. We turned our energies inwards, locked down in a world changing at exponential speed and bloomed into Generation GeniUs, interconnected seed-bedders, growing a new world in the cracks and broken places of the old one. There was a lot to fix.

Our tech toys became survival tools, doorways to each other, work channels, innovation hubs, shopping malls for food, clothes, meds, masks. And memory lanes to our past selves Before COVID, our stories entombed on Netflix and Amazon Prime, all our Photoshoppery and Insta-existences suspended forever in the clouds. Though our realest selves were inside books – the whole beautiful, sprawling human mess of us.

Our Ecoversities were digging up the old universities made for a world of endless growth, mulching ideas anew. In virtual cafes, like the coffee houses of the 17th century Enlightenment, we were re-thinking our dynamic with the world, retuning all our senses, remaking who we were, how we might live and love and be human.

We've learned we're not gods in charge of the Earth or our even our own destinies. We're part of a vast complex ecosystem in a vast complex universe. The COVID-Climate intersection is teaching us, as we fast-forward into a new era, that real time is not measured by us.

After the Black Death we invented clocks, thinking the Earth could be tamed by harvests and machines and human time. Now the planet has reclaimed time and we must re-set our imaginations to the deep time the Earth works by, to the many layers of time, all working at once, with tipping points and chaos we can't control, only adapt to.

The choice? Extinction or change.

* * *

This first evening of my new life I'm face to face with my aloneness as the sun drops behind the mountains in the empty heart of Scotland. The lodge on the loch looks like it's been derelict a hundred years. Tomorrow I'll unshutter the windows, clear some dust before the others arrive. Tonight I'll sleep in the car by the loch, where the moon is laying a silver pathway, my invitation into the unknown.

I sit on a rock by the water and raise my face to the night. I am Sidera, a girl made of stars (as we all are). Jupiter, brightest star of all, is rising above the loch. Its three hundred year old storm, three times the size of Earth, feeds on the storms in its path. Ours is a storm in a teacup compared to its raging Red Spot.

Something swoops overhead. What's that? Sparrowhawk, evening hunt, says Oto. So many things I've not seen or heard before. That hoot? Tawny owl. Silvery trees? Ancient birch. The loch gives a great sigh and turns glassy, the waves smooth and calm. Do lochs have tides, like the sea?

'Hey, Oto. Show me the others?'

The dread of loneliness lifts as my phone screen lights up with a star-scatter of settlements and innovation hubs around and beyond the loch, all across once-empty lands.

A sound ripples across the moon path on the loch. A song, plaintive and strong. If the moon had a voice, this would be it. Others join in, distant and near. Voices adrift in the night, connecting across empty space, a song new to me that feels ancient. I know it in my bones.

Wynning means reclaiming what was lost, before we lose everything.

* * *

The politician stands on a podium. (Though not too often, these days.) A hot March wind ruffles the flags at his back. Sunlight is bright on tousled, unmoving hair. And you don't know what's real, do you? The wind or the sun, his will or his words. This is where we are, he says. All in hand. He squints and points towards something indeterminate only he can see. Let's go!

Where are we going?

Waken up.

Our GeniUs is to know that we don't yet know where we are. At the end of the old world? The beginning of the new? Some murky transition in between? We're harvesting our lockdown years, drawing new kinds of maps for where we're going. The old ones don't even show where we are.

Senses set to emergency, set to survive, we're alert and agile, young and brave. Careless and caring, smart and selfish, we're all of that too. But not weakened by prosperity, ageing immune systems or a lifetime of habit. Our biggest blessing? Having nothing. None of your old certainties. That means we have nothing to lose. So we connect all across our land, all across our world. We gather, sometimes we party, virtually and for real, stay up all night, sleep late. But we do not slumber, like you.

The world you once held in your hands is slipping through your fingers. (Don't you feel it?) Feeling our way, we don't yet have the words to tell you what the new world might be. We're only at the beginning of our Wynning.

What we do know is that the future will not be whatever you expect it to be.

CHAPTER 3

Invisible Cities
Thomas Clark

IT IS ANELY efter a journey o some months that ye come at last tae the waws o Cadzow, thon sunless city, whaur the skrunkelt trees stent up in spires o smuir an the dairkness is – at aw times – absolute. In Cadzow, there are nae greys, faur less shades o white – insteid, frae the nearmaist ben, the hale toon lies afore ye as a range o owerlappin dairknesses, naethin visible but the lines delineatin wan thing frae anither, or at ony rate the livin frae the deid, the city itsel frae the presumed horizon it goves upon.

As ye shuffle doon its blind wynds an cleekit closes, ye dae sae wi baith hauns held oot in somethin kin tae supplication; no that ye micht save yersel frae the wind-bitten corners o the toon haw, the slammin shut o an auld kirk door, but tae haud aff aw the ithers, unseein an unseeable, as they pass by in gropin pilgrimage. Some hae contrived ingenious schemes tae steer awa frae the uncomfortable proximity o anither's elbae, their unusual breith, an as yer hauns find their weys alang the still-wet waws, ye micht hear noo an then the alarum o anither body shauchlin by – the chink o square-end bottles banged thegither, a dull-tongued bell, a low an steady pant. Ahint the mask o black which aw noo weir, each stauchers hame busket up in their ain, inviolable bubble o the nicht, the shortest gate frae hither tae thither a lang, stumblin zig-zag atween sirens an shipwracks.

This aw came tae pass in the usual wey, although naebody noo can mind jist whit that means. A disaster, mebbes, a flood, a plague; the rake o some lang-suspectit croupier ruggin aff the thin skeins that held the toon thegither an replacin them wi shaddaes. But wha kens. Science, like history, has itsel become a kind o superstition. No lang syne, the city-faithers feared the sky micht cowp upon their heids – but tae them that bide in Cadzow noo, it is as if the heivens abuin

44

hae been reived awa awthegither, like the lid o a midden, a circus tent snecked up bi the wind.

This much alane is kent – that at the cusp o the disaster, while the guid-fowk chittert in their sindry hames, the nicht sky tremmled wi a delicate licht. First there wis yin glent – then, anither – each wan follaein the last like the minims o some patient symphony, until as they luiked up through dicht-hole windaes in their stour-shelled hames, the fowk o Cadzow could read these wirds athwart the sky: 'BE SAFE'.

An sleep came easier thon nicht, an for mony nichts there-efter, as wan bi wan the citizens o Cadzow turnt their dwaumie beacons on the retina o the sky, an flashed in spreckelt sparks the things they wished they'd said. Ilka morn, sic wee bit morn there wis, the burghers o the toon breenged tae their windaes tae see whit news wis written up alaft.

'STEY HAME, AWBODY.'

'TAK TENT O YERSELS.'

'AW LIVES MAITTER.'

'OPEN FOR DELIVERIES.'

In time, the messages in the sky became a kind o digital geography, a portrait in binary o the toon that lay ablo, the guidin stars bi which fowk, forgettin ony ither custom, wirked their weys frae wan place tae the next. In the reflectit city that pulsed abuin their heids, the fowk o Cadzow saw their gates mapped oot, a fankelt wab o possibilities that circled an coagulated aroond each ither. Aw at wance, their choices had become baith myriad an dimly reckonable.

The cataclysm, if it ever it wis, is ower – but still the fowk o Cadzow keep cooncil anely wi theirsels, bide in their hooses, share nocht wi their neeburs but the sky an the waws. The ceaseless screen that lours owerheid has nae mair room for them, their missives absorbed in an instant bi the neon leam o the restless bombardiers o heiven, a bricht guddle o injunction sae tichtly weaved bi noo as tae resemble naethin sae much as a skinklin void, a blindin snawdrift in which neither ben nor haugh nor omen can be descried.

Leave Cadzow, noo – drift frae aneath its mirrored loans, cast aff yer maps, walk yer weys unaided bi the fause freends o precedent an example. Forget these transparent heivens, an whitever paths lie ayont, abuin. Airt wi yer een; find wi yer feet; send scuttlin stanes. There are skies elsewhaur.

CHAPTER 4

We Are the Lucky Ones
Catherine Simpson

SUMMER, 2019: I am in an out-of-town hotel – brown decor, piped muzak, spluttering coffee urns – attending a meeting of 'cancer survivors' where I am part of a semi-circle of shell-shocked women still reeling and disbelieving from our encounters with breast cancer.

We have all gone through – and are still enduring the side-effects of – a smorgasbord of treatments from lumpectomies or mastectomies to chemotherapy, radiotherapy and ongoing hormone therapy. We are guests of a cancer charity, who tell us that these support meetings are 'the other half' of our treatment – not so much caring for our bodies (although there is some of that) but for our minds.

And I need care for my mind. Mentally, the cancer diagnosis has hit me like a train. I used to take comfort from the phrase 'This too shall pass' and toyed with getting it tattooed on my forearm. Now I am glad I did not as I do not like to imagine the mortician's raised eyebrow, seeing me on the slab with that inked on my skin; because yes, all things pass, but some things kill us in the passing.

A breast care nurse from the Western General Hospital in Edinburgh is leading this session. She is a young woman bursting with energy who probably dashes everywhere in her blue NHS uniform, ponytail bobbing. She looks no-nonsense, efficient, and effective, and not cancerous. Definitely not cancerous.

I assume I am not the only person in the room who, post-cancer, is jealous of those who radiate energy and glowing good health and the confidence that comes with it. Pre-cancer I had taken so many things for granted – health and energy and confidence among them. I assume I am not the only one who admires this woman's professional presence and remembers longingly when they had that too. I know I will not be the only one sad about who I used to be and what I have lost.

'You probably want your old life back,' the nurse says, 'your old selves,' and I am all ears, pen poised, notebook at the ready, yes, indeed I do want those things back. It has been terrifying watching my old life and my old self disappearing, becoming ever smaller, vanishing into the past in life's rear-view mirror. I want this robust, determined nurse to tell me how to turn back time to when 'cancer' was an unpleasant word not a terrifying diagnosis.

'You probably want your "old normal" back,' she goes on, then shakes her head, 'but you can't have it because it's gone. Your life has changed for good. The old normal will not come back and you need to work on creating a "new normal".'

The group lets out a collective breath. It is rare to encounter such honesty, and both devastating and strangely comforting when you do because at least she is giving it to us straight. There is no flannel here.

We silently absorb her message: we must create a 'new normal'. It is the first time I have heard this phrase. Now, more than a year and a pandemic later, it is commonplace, with everyone, everywhere, urging us to create our new normal. But what does it mean?

In early spring 2020 when we were put into lockdown to control the spread of coronavirus I watched as the entire country appeared to experience its own cancer diagnosis.

As with my cancer diagnosis there was the shock and disbelief that we could be facing a deadly pandemic at all, but especially that it could *happen to us*. This kind of catastrophe was something we saw on the news, in stories and films, not in our own real lives. How could this disaster be invading our well-ordered world? Surely some mistake?

We cast about in a panic: there must be a quick solution! Scientists, politicians, medics, someone, anyone, must be able to sort this thing out and get us back to normal straight away. But no.

As with the cancer diagnosis, normal life vanished overnight. Simple pleasures were suddenly out of reach. Straightforward tasks became difficult. Just dealing with the nuts and bolts of the day – buying basic groceries, getting fresh air and any exercise at all – seemed to take forever.

As with the cancer (at least for those of us in lockdown as opposed to key workers facing the dangers of the virus everyday) there was a sense of unreality, an otherworldliness. The outside world became distant, and close family all-important. We were in our own bubbles, gazing out. Listening to the birds. Even in the city centre it was possible to listen to the birds without the usual backdrop of sirens, traffic and revellers. Weeds sprouted between parked cars in front of shuttered shops and began to create a post-apocalyptic vibe.

As with the cancer, there was much killing time. With cancer it is waiting for results, waiting for treatments to start, treatments to end, appointments to arrive, side-effects to subside. You do your best to be constructive, take your mind off it, make the best of things. Likewise, in COVID lockdown we passed the time cleaning, baking, crafting, keeping busy, filling the days, Zooming, TikTok-ing, Skyping. Trying to do something useful with these nebulous, floating hours – what day was it? What week? What month?

As with the cancer, hair became an issue – but this time not whether I would lose it all, but whether I could face going grey.

As with the cancer, we tried to keep our weight down and our fitness levels up despite the odds being against us

As with the cancer, there was a surreal sense of time standing still, of anxious breath-bated waiting. And a fury that it had happened at all. 'I'm sick of it! I wish it would all just go away!' I heard someone say. Well, yes. Fury is a part of grief and grief does not only manifest after a death.

As with the cancer, fear of an unknown future hovered. The unfortunate became ill, some chronically so. The most unfortunate died or were bereaved. Life pre-coronavirus suddenly seemed long ago. Beyond our reach. Vanished.

As with the cancer, when the catastrophe appeared to be receding a little and lockdown began to ease, the fear of its return was real, a lurking worry. Would COVID always hover in the back of our minds from now on? Would we ever regain that carefree ability to jump on a plane without considering how far away the doctors would be? Or would we adapt and learn to live with its presence among us?

As with the cancer, there was a deep unease that life had changed forever. We had to acknowledge that a world we had once taken for granted could change overnight and become unknown, and if it had done it once it could do it again.

But as with the cancer, there was also a sense that perhaps not all the changes were for the worse. The unreality created by COVID also created freedom from the tyranny of the usual 'shoulds' and 'musts' and 'oughts'. *I must go to… I should visit… I really ought to…*

No, suddenly the old rules did not apply. I am an introvert, and often find socialising more problematic than being alone. Both cancer and COVID gave me an excuse to stay quiet at home. An excuse to be semi-detached from the demands of 'out there'. Why is that so hard to achieve? Why does it take a cancer diagnosis or a pandemic to let us off the hook, to be able to hunker down with our own thoughts, alone, guilt-free?

Being in my own bubble, gazing out at empty, silent streets, made me realise how enmeshed I usually am in the chaos of social media. What a noise it made. What a constant, unbearable racket. Certain aspects of social media continued to give me pleasure and connection but feeling a separation from the world allowed me to let go of some of the more toxic competitive elements. Competitive social media was not what mattered. Silence, space, the chance to think, to create were what mattered.

Post-traumatic growth was another phrase I had never heard until I got cancer. Post-traumatic growth is the positive change brought about by living through trauma and includes a greater appreciation for life, a changed sense of what is important, a recognition of our own resilience and the opportunity to rethink the path we are on.

We are all COVID survivors, not something we ever thought we would be, but a title we are lucky enough to have attained. Like in the storybook bear hunt, we couldn't go under it, we couldn't go over it, we had to go through it. We are the ones who got through. We are the ones who survived. We are the ones fortunate enough to have another go at life, putting into practice the lessons a pandemic taught us. We are the ones with the opportunity to be flexible, adaptable, to wear the world differently and not only to survive but to thrive, to create a new normal, a different normal, a better normal. We have the time to work out what we want and need, not what we should... must... ought to want and need. We are the ones who can still listen to the birds.

We are the lucky ones.

CHAPTER 5

Blue Reflectin

Anna Stewart

I'M IN MA flat smokin a rollie. It glows a wee light when I inhale. A piece o paper covers the side o the wa, I speak tae it and ma voice sounds loud, and I remember I've been alane.

Now yir lookin tae me like yi could be a forest, minding me o that time wi the deer when its shape flashed up in the headlights and ma dad put the brakes on. The car slowed, but we still clipped it. Dad said efter we go intae toon we'll come back and check the wood at the side o the road, and if we foond the deer wis deid we'd tak its meat so's it wouldnae be a waste. We'd use his knife and he'd show me how tae 'gralloch' it. Gralloch wis the wird he used, even though I didnae ken then whit it meant. But by the time we got back someone had beat us to it, and there wis nothin left o the animal worth takkin, just its heid aw perfect and still, and it's skin; a rag o blood and fur in the snaw. Now, tae mak a thing like that, that would be half decent.

Ma doorbell rings, I dinnae answer, instead I sit on the settee, smokin. Aroond uz, I can see ma front door, the wooden meter cupboard, the windee wi closed curtains, the coffee table, ma single bed, and the piece o paper on the wa. I can see ma kitchenette wi linoleum flair, and the clock ower the sink: it's ten past three. I've nae time fir whaever it wis at the door anyhow, I've got tae git this finished. I'm no really sure whit I'm daein wi it yet. I need time tae think. It's no good light in here. I switch on the lamp. Nut, these friggin energy savin affairs, nae use tae man nor beast. I stand on the settee, I tak the lampshade aff leavin the bulb bare. I look at the piece o paper. That's no makkin a blind bit o difference. I go tae the windee and pull the curtains back, behind them are the pink nets that were here when I moved in. I wouldnae mind gettin rid o these like, so's I could see better. I dinnae want any Joe Bloggs seein in though, that's the problem. I look through the nets at the piece o paper. See if yi could get the light goin on it like that, in these wee lines like, that would be better, that would be half decent. Shards, that's the wird, shards. I better write that doon. I write on the back o an envelope. It looks different now fae here. Aye that mighto helped a bit right enough, takkin this daft lampshade aff. I stub ma cigarette oot and roll the lampshade atween ma haunds. Wha wants aw this finery anyhow? Tassels. Who'd have thunk it, me wi a lampshade like this in ma hoose, nae danger. I put the lampshade on ma heid, maybe I'll mak somethin aboot the economic climate? Aye somethin political, I roll a cigarette, lick the rizla, I spit in ma haund and wipe it on ma jeans... Arab spring? I light the cigarette and inhale. Or internet? Exhale. It's aw there, Charlie, it's aw there. The lampshade slides aff ma heid and ontae the flair. Maybe its somethin else, some other state o affairs. A corner o the paper curls doon and aff the wa and I see the lump o blue tack, hingin on. Wis that meant tae happen? Did yi mean tae dae that? Tae leave it there, or no tae leave it there? But that blue tack's no very bonnie... but whit is *bonnie,* whit does it even matter? Maybe it's the fates, the fates moved it, makkin yi question things again, there's nae point staundin still and acceptin things as fact, the way they are. It's happened afore and it'll happen again. It's aw connected, it's a connection wi the wurld. Write that doon, yi better write that last thing yi said doon coz yi'll want tae re-member that. I write on an envelope, I inhale ma fag. Blue tack – who wouldo thought such a simple thing as that. And how come it's *blue*? Oot o aw the colours o the wurld, how come that ane? The colour o the sea and the air above oor heids, except that's kindo clear and all, and just reflectin is it no? Reflection... now there's a wird. I write it doon. Blue reflectin, whit's that aw aboot eh? *Blue reflectin.* Aye yir speakin tae me noo. I drink fae a mug on the coffee table. Ach. I spit in the cup: dowpies! I pull a soakin cigarette fae ma mooth. Didnae see that comin did I? It's ane unexpected occurrence efter the ither. Put the kettle on. Fresh cup. I lean on the bunker waitin fir the kettle tae boil, I look at the paper on the wa. Fae here it's like a kindo kite, that triangle bit, I jump ower the back o the settee and write on the envelope. Get back ower here though, there's mair tae see. Maybe no. Maybe that wis it fir this end o the room, just 'kite'. The kettle clicks aff and I pour the water. Ah ya! I drop the kettle on the bunker. Need a new kettle, Charlie, need a new kettle. Every *time* that happens, I need tae get some organisation aboot this place. I go tae sit doon but trip ower a curl in the carpet and splash tea aw ower the flair, the wa, and the piece o paper. Aw fir fucksakes! I kick the carpet. It's nae good this, nae fuckin good! I slam the tea doon. Need tae get this shite sorted fir a start. I go tae the cupboard aneath the sink and haul oot the cardboard box, I rake through it. Yi'v got aw the brigalia in the wurld in here, Charlie, but can yi ever find whit it is yir lookin fir? I chuck awthin fae the box on the flair. Ah ha! I find a blue roll o leccie tape, I pick at the end o it. It's no easy this. It's the stickiness that does it, it's damn sticky. I unravel a length and haud it up tae the light: blue... aye. I stick the tape on the carpet and look at the paper, I see whaur the tea has made a mark and it minds me o antlers. I get in bed and look at them, until I faw asleep.

When I wauken I cough, so I light a fag. I reach aneath the bed and get ma tape deck and press play, Bowie blares oot like fae a tin can. I cough, tak a deep breath. There's snot jammin ma nostrils. I feel aneath ma pillow and find a tissue then spit it aw oot, some o it lands on ma haunds and I wipe it on the blanket. I look at the piece o paper – it's no cheenged, except fir the tea stain, that's still there.

It's been weeks like this, started aff just a wee sniffle, whit I'd like tae ken is wha I got it fae, it's no as if I've been oot and aboot, its like, how do these things mutate? How do they get yi? Couldo been fae the postie, couldo been on any o them letters, friggin junk mail, how are they sendin me aw that? Sendin me diseases through the fuckin post. Keepin the masses doon, that's whit they're daein, so's we'll buy aw their drugs. Well no me, I tell yi, no me. I'll fight this bastard on ma ane. Plenty o fluids, that's aw I need. And exercise, I'll do a bit o that later on, get the legs wirkin, flush the bastard oot. Time tae get oot the auld pit I suppose. And you dinnae help. I'm fed up wi it aw... this is nae life. Fuckin piece o paper starin at uz day in, day oot, no a line on it, feel like settin the fucker on fire, naw but yi cannae dae that... how no? How could yi no dae it? Set the hale lot on fire, get rid o it, stop the mind games, aw the controllin looks it's gein yi, aye do this, do that, mak somethin, mak somethin happen, Eh'll mak it happen awright, Eh'll mak it fuckin happen. Smoke inhalation though, got tae bear that in mind, got tae think o the consequences o yir actions, yi cannae just go roond tearin shit up coz yi dinnae like it, yi'v got tae use yir noggin son... wha's that? At the door, wha's that? The letterbox opens, twa eyes, starin at uz: wantin in:

'Gonnae let uz in Charlie? Charlie gonnae let uz in, em no jokin it's Baltic oot here. Aw ma legs, I'm pure near greetin oot here. I've got this awfy pain in ma legs I need tae speak tae yi aboot. Charlie, Charlie are yi there?'

'I'm no lettin yi in Elaine.'

'How no Charlie?'

'Dinnae, *how no Charlie* me. Yi ken fine well how no.'

'But I dinnae Charlie, honest I dinnae ken, how no?'

'Yi ken whit I'm daein in here Elaine! Yi ken whit I'm daein!' She starts the greetin, 'Aw dinnae greet.'

The letterbox closes fir a minute then opens again.

'... I'll awa up the road then.'

'This is how I dinnae let yi in Elaine.'

'Eh?'

'The greetin and aw that. Yi distract uz.'

'Sorry Charlie.'

'Yir ay sorry aboot it, but yi ay dae it. See that pain in yir legs, that fuckin naggin, that's whit it's like inside ma heid aw the time. I dinnae need these distractions.'

'Aye, I ken Charlie, it's no easy wi that heid o yours.'

'Whit's that supposed tae mean?'

'I wis just meanin, yir heid, ken, yi think too much aboot stuff eh?'

I hear her blaw her nose: just blaw yir nose and dinnae think how yiv cut me tae the core, blaw awa hen!

'Charlie?'

'I better get on now Elaine.'

'Yir no offended are yi?'

'How would I be offended?'

'Coz o me sayin that heid thing.'

See, she does ken. She kens whit she's sayin. How could anybody no be offended at that? This is the problem, I've naebody aroond that unnerstaunds. Yi try tae talk tae fowk. Christ, there's times I'll talk tae anybody: the wifey at the shop, the fuckin lollipop man, ma brother, fucksakes, ma brother – he fir ane doesnae unnerstaund. And now her, whit the fuck does she want fae me? I cannae speak tae her, she doesnae hae a clue whit I'm tryin tae dae here. How did I end up here, wi these fowk, these numpties? Aw she does aw day is zoom aroond in that electric chair chattin wi any idiot that's daft enough tae engage wi her. How come I attract this kindo shite in ma life? These belters. But she's had her share o shite, whit kindo a man thinks they things?

'I'm tired Elaine, I need tae get on, ma nose is aw bunged up, I need tae get mysel sorted oot.'

'Yiv got the cald Charlie?'

'I've the bloody flu!'

'How's yir paintin goin?' she says, breezy as anythin, like it's just a wee daft hobby.

'Dinnae ask that Elaine, dinnae ask uz.'

Sorry, she says, sorry sorry sorry. She wis just wonderin.

'It's no goin Elaine, it's no fuckin goin.'

Then she starts on again how it's a shame she cannae see me, see how like I am? And how she's tried ma door loads, she thought I wis oot, have I been busy? Aye I'm busy, I'm busy. She says yir lucky yiv an occupation Charlie, somethin yi can just dae yirsel, and how she's ay needed someone tae tell her whit tae dae. Or just chattin, she's just happy chattin. Fucksakes, I ken that. Aye, well there wi go eh, wi cannae aw be the same, I say. She's ay been stuck in the chair she says, she's got tae thinkin whit's the point? Whit's the point even tryin kindo thing. Bring oot the violins! Some mornings, it taks her aw her energy just tae get oot o bed. She'd like tae be like me, wi some kindo ambition.

'That's whit you've got Charlie, that's how I admire yi fir that, wantin tae be an artist.'

'I cannae let yi in Elaine.'

'I ken, I ken. But whit aboot if I just stayed here fir a bit, at this side o the door? If I just   stayed here, and I let yi get on, and I didnae say anythin.'

'I need tae get on, Elaine.'

'I ken, I ken. Just you get on then, I'll be here: quiet.'

I'm resigned tae her noo. I go tae the kitchenette, switch the kettle on, then she's askin, 'S'that you puttin the kettle on Charlie?'

I'm no makkin yi anythin Elaine. I ken, she says, I'm just bein here – quiet. She's just bein here *quiet* ma arse. I cannae fit a cup through the letterbox anyhow. Nah, dinnae worry aboot me she says, Eh'm no in the mood fir tea. If I'd a wee-er cup, ane that would fit through, I'd gie her ane. I'm no bein stingy or anythin, it's just the situation wi the door, ken? Then I spot the bowl on the drainer, I could maybe get a bowl through... I tak the bowl ower tae the letterbox tae check if it fits. Honest Eh'm no bothered, she's sayin. I try tae shove the bowl through but I cannae, nah, its too big. She says she'd hae trouble drinkin fae it anyhow. But I think, maybe a wee-er ane. I go and look in the cupboard, she's shoutin through,

'Eh'm no bothered Charlie honest.'

I find a slimmer bowl, ah ha! Just the ticket, put a teabag, pour the water. 'Are yi still cuttin oot the sugar?'

'Nah, I gave up on that diet.'

No good fir yi though is it? Afore sugar yi shouldo seen fowks skulls; perfect teeth, no a rotten ane in the mooth. Shame that eh, coz it tastes so good. I lift the bowl tae the letterbox.

'Yi ready?'

'Wait a minute.'

I hear her shift, a thud, then her floppy-like fingers poke through the letterbox: that's fae her arthrogryposis. She minds me o a cloth dolly wi those haunds, they look as though they shouldnae be able tae move, but they do.

'Ready... I'm ready Charlie.'

I gie her the bowl o tea, careful, 'Now watch... Waaatch! Dinnae spill it, it's boilin.'

Her fingers grasp fir the bowl and it disappears through the letterbox,

'Yiv got it okay?'

'I've got it.'

I hear her sippin, 'It's awfy sweet Charlie.'

'Ach!'

'But I like it like that, I like it.'

I lean against the door,

'Aw that effort and I still dae it wrang.'

'Naw Charlie it's good, on a second sip... aye, its awfy good, I've been needin that, it's daein uz the wurld o good, coz it's cald oot.'

I kent she'd be needin somethin sittin oot there. But then she maks a gripe aboot it no bein real milk. There's ay somethin wi her, there's ay somethin. I suppose it's good tae hae a wee break, awbody's enti-tled a break, part o the wirkin day. I look at that piece o paper, that tea stain... could be antlers. I tell her, 'It's hard tae ken when a deer's deid coz o the eyes, they've that much life in them.'

Then she says, 'Mind wi were drunk when yi telt uz aboot yir dad knockin doon the deer, mind yi took a haud o ma haund? That wis funny eh... how come yi did that Charlie?'

I cannae stand it, her bringin stuff like that intae it. It's nothin aboot that, it's nothin aboot her.

'I need tae get on Elaine,' I say. She bangs the door, I get intae bed and put the cover ower ma heid. I can still hear her though,

'I'll no say anythin else, just gonnae let uz see yi? Let uz see yir awright? Charlie!'

I press play on the tape deck and haud it tae ma ear.

* * *

She's no come back like, Elaine. It's no like her. It's been days and no a peep. It's no as if I can go roond, no in the state I'm in. I've got this paintin tae contend wi. But there's her legs. Whit kindo pain is that, in her legs that can hardly move? Must be *some* pain. A walk would do me good, a walk roond tae hers, if I could gear mysel up tae it, bring mysel roond. Just hae a dander ower and see she's awright. I cannae rely on any other bastard coz I'm the ane that kens her. But she's the mair ootdoors ane, she doesnae mind poppin oot and seein uz. How come she's no bothered then? These past few days? How come? Suppose I could head oot fir a bit o fresh air, I need some milk, aye real milk fir a cheenge, that would be good. But then yi promised yirsel Charlie, yi made yirsel a promise. Yi better stick tae it coz yi ay gie up, never see anything through. Its hailin hailstanes. If I wis in a different mood I'd write that doon. But I'm no in the mood. It's a cald air afore it hits. But yi cannae build a man or go sledgin, so naebody likes it. It's the noise o it, that batterin sound; a violent element, maks yi ill at ease. I roll a cigarette. That's some racket right enough. It'll soon stop and then it'll be too quiet. I light the fag: inhale. At least this damn flu seems tae have shifted. I can smoke in peace now. I'll be oot o baccie soon and then I'll really hae tae go oot. But whaur is she? She'd have brought uz baccie. She wis good like that. If I could only kick the habit, coz that's aw it is wi me, a bad habit. I'm no addicted, I'm no addicted tae anything, its just no in ma nature coz I'm a changeable bastard. I've ay been that way, could never stick at anything. Except the fags, fir some reason I've managed tae stick tae the fags, suppose that's some achievement: an auld friend now, are yi no?

Fuck wis that! Somethin banged ma windee. There's a noise o scrapin, a kindo flappin, I open the windee and look oot – a bird, fuckin gull oot there! Did yi see that? Whit a shock! Near gave uz a heart attack, Jesus Christ! Aye, its flappin aboot oot there, musto done some damage, fuck sakes, maybe its wing... or its leg... or even its *neck,* fuck, maybe the poor bastard's fucked its neck. There's nae hope then is there? I'm inclined tae help it, this is a predicament. I pace the room and hear the hailstanes and the bird flappin. I look oot the windee again. It's still stugglin, it's still fuckin strugglin. Whit a shame, whit a fuckin shame. It's hard tae witness. Musto been the hail, distracted it, went blind wi it, poor bastard. I see someone oot the windee, passin,

'Hey! Hey mate! Aye, you. Look… can yi see, there's a bird here. It's knocked intae ma windee, gonnae dae uz a favour and see it's awright? It'll only tak twa minutes, gonnae just check its awright? Mate? Mate!'

That's ignorance right there. Fuckin disaster. I pull the nets back and open the windee right up, I speak tae the bird, try tae reassure it, tell it tae calm doon – calm the fuck doon. But it's no listenin, it keeps flappin. So I hae tae climb oot the fuckin windee and pick it up and bring it in. I look through the yella pages fir the RSPB or whitever it is, begins wi R. The pages are awfy thin and keep stickin tae my fingers coz o the tremmlin. The bird scrapes and flaps on ma flair. The hail goes quiet and sun glares in ma room, I watch the bird, how it slows then stops. I put the phone doon. I sit oan the settee. The sun goes and there's darkness fir a while till the glimmer o street lights. Then, there's a noise ootside the windee and I hear her voice:

'Are yi wantin baccie Charlie? Eh'm awa tae the shops. Yi ken yir windee's wide open?'

I tak money fae the tin, reach intae the open air and put a note in her upturned haund.

CHAPTER 6

Cardinal Dreams
Lisa Williams

Monday – PRIDE

Every statue in Edinburgh has crumbled into a fine dust that's hundreds of years old. Our masks have done nothing to stop us from gagging. There are crowds of people with white skin and black masks. Everyone is sneezing into the crease of their elbow. The names of freedom fighters stud the length of the Royal Mile, like the stars along Hollywood Boulevard. Yet there is a lone man, red faced and sputtering with laughter, who is rhythmically trampling on them with sturdy ghillie brogues. Perhaps he is a descendant of one of the Edinburgh men who, two hundred years ago, placed the severed heads of resistance leaders on spikes across the island of Dominica. Or one of those who decimated the Garifuna people of St Vincent by isolating thousands of them on a barren rock to starve. The prideful faces of these kinds of men stare down at us from the walls of the National Gallery, but the walls behind the portraits are dripping with centuries of blood, creating pools on the floor. The bodies of the people they've killed are all over the cold marble, and I step between them like Scarlett O'Hara at the end of *Gone with the Wind*.

I've kicked off the duvet in the night and my feet are cold. I blink hard and rub my eyelids. A Nigerian friend calls and breaks my reverie to ask for the name of a good lawyer. Her son has ended up on the hard surface of a littered Edinburgh street. Due to vigorous self-defence from an attack by two white guys, he's going to trial for attempted murder. Five years on, Scotland is still waiting for Sheku Bayoh's death at the hands of police to be fully investigated. Neither of these situations are part of the dream. I wish my friend a happy Eid nonetheless.

Tuesday – GREED

I'm riding through beautiful stretches of Scottish countryside, the train hurtling along on tracks originally laid down with slave compensation money. The names of the stations and stately homes flood me with ugly facts and figures I wish I didn't know, because I am trying to enjoy the scenery. During the Second World War, the Duke of Buccleuch complained about having Black men on his land, the same men who had left their tropical homes to help defeat the Nazis. The bitter face of our old neighbour, now in prison for several years, looms through the train window and sucks me into an airless tunnel.

I wake to a chorus of clanking metal and breaking glass; my son is washing a saucepan in the overflowing sink. With my eyes still closed, I remember giving an impassioned interview to Scottish television about the white supremacist neighbour who had been making bombs in his council flat. They cut out the part where I suggested the government didn't take white terrorism seriously enough. I decide to concentrate on the passengers who patted my son enthusiastically on a real train home from Glasgow when he hesitatingly tried to explain where he was from. 'It disnae matter where you were born. You're one of us, son! You're a Scot now!' He's partial to Irn-Bru and can certainly strip the willow if needed, having learned the steps wearing a full head of Rasta locks and a tartan cummerbund.

I forget that many non-Muslims are frightened of Muslims. PROVOCATIVE HEADLINES wipe out the fact that Britain makes a fortune from arming Saudi Arabia while demonising the Muslim people in our own communities. My daughter's boyfriend would prefer to stack supermarket shelves with his double engineering degree than accept a job in the lucrative arms trade. Serco has just evicted traumatised and vulnerable refugees in Glasgow in the middle of a pandemic. Not just managing detention centres but dozens of defence contracts, they effectively create their own customer base. Raytheon helps to keep the people of Glenrothes out of the foodbank queues by employing locals to make the 'smart' part of their bombs; the same bombs that litter the countries from which refugees trickle to Scotland. The Army advertise at my son's career fairs, and the scandalous marking down of grades of pupils in struggling schools, if allowed, will be a blessing for the army recruiters. Bearing in mind the close ties SQA has with the Saudi regime, will Scottish pupils ever face an exam question about their Saudi peers receiving the death penalty up to 2019?

Wednesday – WRATH

I wake from a dream where the angry face emoticons on Facebook have become flying demons. They pulsate and burn my hands when I try to swat them away. I wonder who created their algorithms. Would Muhammad ibn Musa al-Khwarizmi have approved of the use of his invention? Does anyone learn his name or where he was from as they struggle with algebra? I peer through the blinds to see if it's worth getting up. A Black man walks away from the football field opposite the house. The boys who've climbed onto the roof of the community centre are shouting 'Black Lives Matter!' in his direction. I hope that it's heartfelt, but something about the tone of it makes me wonder if it isn't a version of 'Special Needs!' hurled by neurotypical children at an anxious loner in the playground.

A young friend suffers a Twitter pile-on after venturing a sarcastic comment, and she tearfully DMs me from Glasgow after they have targeted her workplace. 'You should be skinned alive, you black c**t!' says one tweet. I armour myself for a potentially rancorous Zoom call with editors who are anxious for new spreads on Black Scottish history, to explain why I'd like them to capitalise the b in black, and now I wonder how important it really is. I want to support friends' efforts on Twitter pointing out how our racist past still affects us, but I'm wary of their engagements with accounts with British flags, aggressive fonts and zero followers.

Against my better judgement, I dive into the comment sections that viciously trail friends' articles in the press. Perhaps I could rearrange words like 'ridiculous' and 'snowflake' and make poetry out of their sentences. My daughter suggests I have too much idle imagination. I never like to waste anything. 'Inherited immigrant syndrome', my daughter laughingly calls it, despairing of finding yet another cupboard overflowing with empty yoghurt pots that 'might come in useful'. Toxicity on Twitter is a given now, even though many of the far right have moved over to another platform. Even friends who pride themselves on fighting 'the good fight' have been sending me alt-right memes during the lockdown, suggesting the virus is a sinister lie and likening masks to slaves' bridles. Will I grieve for these friendships as well? Well-funded and organised online cults have sucked them in with clever psychology. Would I walk away so easily if they had joined a cult somewhere in the countryside and needed to be rescued?

Thursday – ENVY

The loud voices that boom outside my window from the shared garden interrupt a dream I no longer recall. I've been shrinking away from them for weeks, but I decide today is the day I speak to humans face to face. One neighbour has a voice that echoes around the walls of our building, and I can identify her purely from her volume. The curtains of her flat are permanently shut, but whenever we meet, she beams at me without fail. I stumble outside to the garden and she, still wearing her nightdress, indicates the window of a man who illuminates his flat at three o'clock in the morning in order to peer directly towards hers. I don't know whether to worry about him, or for him, like the elderly disabled man I've only just discovered lives alone at the top of our building. Part of me wants to climb the stairs to sit and chat with him too, but the lingering thought of passing on a killer virus stops me.

Wherever we've lived, our Scottish neighbours have gone all out to make us feel welcome. This vociferous neighbour regularly dispatches one of her twins to our door, bearing plates piled high with full dinners and creamy slices of cake. I weigh up whether I still need to disinfect the foil wrappers away from the kitchen area. I hope that people will no longer scoff at me when I ask them to wash their hands when they enter the house, something I've had drilled into me by a Caribbean mother. The day before, I tiptoed through spattered globs of phlegm on the ground outside the local pub, so the odds are not high.

However, I'm enjoying the novelty of witnessing other humans in their post-lockdown 3D splendour, even at two metres away. They may have grown up using imperial measurements, like me, and they may think two feet does them just fine. I've asked them to stand back, with a smile, and they've apologised. Their vegetables are flourishing, and I'm envious of their shiny green leaves, as my excited efforts have withered and died. Even the pots have been savaged by feral, rag-gedy foxes, creatures that through a rainy window during lockdown seemed magnificent and free. It strikes me that it's my punishment for ordering from Amazon. My daughter reminds me of the workers who pee their own pants because they aren't allowed breaks. I think about the children who refused to eat sugar produced by slaves and how we admire their caring hearts today. My friend from Trinidad has been texting me throughout lockdown, updating me on the hole he is digging in his garden. In the absence of live theatre, I find the progress fascinating, as do his neighbours. They linger by the fence and comment approvingly on his stamina. I ask him whether it's the husband or the wife who comments. Both, he says. I suggest he sells them some *bwa banday*, that the old men in Trinidad consume with an everlasting hope for the pleasures of life.

Friday – LUST

I'm hugging strangers through the new plastic body sheeting that hangs from the lurid anti-terror barriers on the Royal Mile, and it's strangely satisfying. I remember the people I have hugged without permission before the virus, and before accepting that Scottish people don't touch each other in the way Caribbean people do. Asking people if they 'hug' feels awkward though, so I have simply learned to no longer initiate. Now I can wave at people instead, and it's easier all round. I remember the many men who have touched me without permission in the past; stroking my hair in amazement while I'm ordering a drink or taking the chance to rub their hands all over me as make my way across a crowded dance floor.

My phone surprises me with consistent buzzing, and I scroll through a series of WhatsApp messages from old flames I'd forgotten that I'd messaged out of boredom. I hear that men are being forced these days to make an effort beyond 'hey' and 'wyd' in this extended period of waiting expectantly for that first meeting. I've read that STDs have been almost extinguished across Scotland, because the only things exchanged in the past few months have been words and pictures. I'm relieved for the young. I've gladly let my hair turn silver and spend my evenings scouring through photos of rescue dogs, favouring the sweet natured and the well trained.

This morning I walk to town to test my legs. Along the way, I glimpse the 'national barrier assets' I've been dreaming of, installed in the centre of town and paid for by the Home Office. It almost surprises me that the protective sheeting is absent from the yellow metal arcs that tempt fate like upside down horseshoes. I walk past the string of beauty shops that formerly had gaunt beauticians smoking in the doorways, watched carefully by pock-marked, broad shouldered receptionists in jeans. Their doors are padlocked. I wonder whether the staff have gone back to their original homes. While waiting for Universal Credit, some women have turned to selling sex to pay their bills. Not a pretty situation, but perhaps sex work will finally be de-criminalised in Scotland, to usher in an era where sex workers are respected and can access full protection from unions and the police. Two hundred years ago, the Beggar's Benison was flourishing in Edinburgh. George IV gifted them his snuff box of women's pubic hair on his visit to Scotland and Governor Melville exported the 'Tropical Chapter' of this sex club to the colonies. We might even pay attention to the fate of young girls currently being trafficked by gangs across this country of ours.

Saturday – GLUTTONY

Customers, as a matter of practice, leave beautifully wrapped gifts as tips for the staff in the local Chinese take away. They learn the courtesy phrases of Cantonese and Mandarin that they might need to place their orders with grace. Cantonese might not make their children economically competitive when they leave school in the way that Mandarin will, but they are proud to learn it anyway; just to be friendly and appreciative. They hold cooking classes every week when the whole community brings one ingredient and learns to cook up a feast together. The fortune cookies encourage everyone to smile and share wisdom for coping with difficult life situations.

A lightning bolt of a toothache wakes me from my slumber this morning. I tip the takeaway boxes into the bin. I call the dentist with trepidation, imagining the virus lacing the surfaces of the surgery. Laughter ricochets around the walls of the office when I tell them that I think I've cracked my tooth biting down on a Dorito. It must be my comic delivery, I tell myself. I didn't bang a pot for the NHS on any of the Thursday evenings, so at least I can give them some light relief. Truth is, my whole being has been breaking a little. How have we been able to live with thousands of deaths by baking banana bread and laughing at viral memes? Perhaps these have been our only cushioning against an all-encompassing grief.

I recall a shaman I met once, from Burkina Faso, who drew a triangle between three points of compulsive eating, inadequate community support and a lack of grieving rituals. Doritos, these alluring triangles of salt, sugar and fat, have been carefully designed to hit the 'Bliss Point'. I stream Radio 4 just to hear a human voice, as my son is temporarily reluctant to engage in conversation. The experts are 'tackling obesity' with the same old worn out formulas for success. What's even more convenient than convenience food itself is their omissions of unequal access to land and property, social isolation, childhood abuse and the resulting addictions in all their forms. No wonder we need cushioning.

Sunday – SLOTH

Nursery children, with fat cheeks and innocent eyes, have a place where friendly animals come to visit. They enjoy cataloguing the display of seed packets by colour, and they each have their own wee pot with their name painted on it. On entering primary school, they'll each be allocated a patch of earth to plant during lunchtimes. Half of their lessons take place in the forest or in a park, where they're allowed to splash in muddy puddles and throw autumn leaves in giddy, good natured play fights. They can sing the name of every plant and animal they come across, first in English, then in Gaelic. They video link with children across the world every Friday and learn to pronounce their pretty-sounding names just like they do with the friends they see every day.

I wake, naturally and well rested, to a silent house. I've turned off my phone. I hope my son is soundly sleeping rather than staring at the wall wondering what to do with himself. He and his friends have been listless recently, even though their grades have been good enough to carry them through to the next stage of life. Sadness and sloth were merged into a cardinal sin hundreds of years ago by Pope Gregory, but it's time for us to unpick this hasty bundling of experiences. I'm startled to see how pale my chatty neighbour's son has become as I meet him out by the row of bins for our flats. He's also been lying on the sofa for months with a remote in his hand, but his face brightens at having a conversation. I place my bare feet on the shared, freshly mown lawn. I look up at the sky. I breathe deeply and stretch gently. My son will wake soon. Perhaps he'll join me. Maybe the neighbours will too.

CHAPTER 7

Table Service Only

Alan Bissett

THEY SHIFTED AND peered through the frosted glass of the Joiners' Arms, like parched cave dwellers who'd shambled into the light, waiting to greet the pink shape looming towards the door. 11.01. The sun blinked through the clouds, teasing the possibility of a beer garden. There was perfunctory, amiable village-chat among what resembled a queue – two old guys with broken-veined noses, a smattering of furloughed office workers, a foursome of tanned, rotund retirees – all gingerly stepping while they calculated the space between them. 'How's yer lockdown been?' 'Honest, if I have to do another bloody Zoom call.' 'Left the weans with him, I've done ma shift.' 'Had to be there for the grand re-opening, show support, know?' Sage nodding all round. They knew.

July. Four months. Mouths moved, feet twitched, as the key turned in the door and Gary appeared as though from a parallel dimension, face creased with either a smile or a frown, they couldn't tell yet. The gathering on the pavement cheered, applauded: a not-quite-key-worker-but-still.

'Ho,' Gary said, raising hands, 'Whoah. Listen. Canny huv that in here. Nae cheerin, nae singin, nae raised voices. Guidelines.'

'Can we still swear?' chuckled one of the retirees, as Gary hooked the door open.

His eyes narrowed as he glanced down the street, at the village ambling to and fro: parents on their hundred and twentieth day of weans; teenagers searching for *anything* to do; the old dears, ecstatic in lavender at the thought of shops open again. 'Swearin's fine, long as it's no oot loud.'

A smattering of laughter then they were inching forwards – slow but inevitable, jovial zombies – and Gary was backing up and reaching for the temperature gun and wrists were suddenly in front of him and Janice had bustled to his side, the opening doors seeming a surprise to her, even though she'd been in since half eight that morning wiping everything down, and she was taking phone numbers and doling out banter and then, numb with wonder, they'd filed past him one by one into the pub, looking round at tables spread out as though refusing to talk to each, the Perspex covering the bar, the serving-girls with their robotic face-shields, a sci-fi layer draped over the *ancien regime* of the dartboard, the whisky barrels and framed, sepia photographs of the village past, their hatted gentlemen and barefoot kids peering into this odd future. It was an eerie dream to Gary and to stay alert he built mental furniture: assigned punters seats, took drinks orders, while the vision of this he'd been playing in his mind for four months unspooled uselessly around him. He touched his forehead. Sweating already. As he took the order from two of his regulars, Frank and Jack, reunited in denim and babbling, he wondered if that meant if that meant if the sweat meant if his fingertips

TABLE SERVICE ONLY
PLEASE STAY SEATED UNLESS GOING TO THE TOILET OR
OUT TO SMOKE
CONTACT POINTS IN THESE TOILETS WILL BE SANITISED
EVERY FIFTEEN MINUTES ONE PERSON IN THE TOILET
PER TIME PLEASE BE UNDERSTANDING DURING THIS

Spraying down tables, so the punters could see him doing it, then standing with the cloth still in his hand and saying to Josie, Helen and Yvonne, the Ladies Who Lunch/Lunched/Who'd Hopefully Still Lunch, 'I just huv tay get the weekend under ma belt. Psychologically. Mair drunk folk, happy to see each other, spillin aboot the place. I mean, maist understand like, but ye've always got that natural rule-breaker.' Gary's gaze lifted into Saturday, the bustle beyond the table, The Natural Rulebreaker swaying in front of him, eyes rheumy. *Sayin I cannay even talk tay ma mate ower there? Montay fuck, Gary, no seen the cunt since March.*

A shift in the air then a blaze of light from the door and he glanced round to see Senga ambling her fuzzy bulk into the room, wearing the same Iron Maiden t-shirt he'd last seen her in, mid-March. Senga leaned on her walking stick and took in the pub, big shoulders slumped, as though discovering a childhood field that was now all houses. Gary nodded at Janice, who went to her.

He saw Senga blink at Janice, who was smiling with the cocked temperature gun, before Senga proffered a pale, tattooed wrist, muttering 'government' and 'microchip'. Then Janice was leading Senga to a table before flitting back to the door, where two of the local Young Team had turned up, wafting a weed smell before them like dry ice announcing the arrival of a rock band.

Gary went to Senga, wriggling her big arse in the confines of the chair, coughing freely. Some of the punters glanced over. He raised an eyebrow at her. 'Sorry, Gary,' she grumbled, dabbed her mouth belatedly with the back of her hand. 'It's just a tickly throat, no the virus.'

'How dae ye know?' he said, fishing the pad and pen from his back pocket.

'Eh cos it doesnay exist?' she laughed throatily and peered through grey hair at him, eyes twinkling with mischief.

He tutted. 'Well for the purposes of being here, just pretend it does.'

'Will it mean me gettin a pint?'

'Hunner per cent.'

'Then I'll pretend.'

'Good. What can I get ye?'

'Strongbow.'

'Strongbow.' He wrote it on the pad, a whiff of something gamey from her reaching his nostrils. 'Anythin else?'

'Aye,' she said, 'Gonnay tell me how we're supposed tay live like this?'

He stuck the pad in his back pocket and glanced round to see the first drinks arrive at the first tables, like gifts being borne from The New World, met by chortles and hands already-cupped, and then satisfied supping. *Ahhhh.* 'Dunno, Senga, I dunno. Just gottay get on wi it. Aw in it the gither.'

'Aye, I've heard that wan afore. "Aw in it the gither".' She chuckled and cracked a knuckle. 'But are we? I mean, dae ye *know* anybody wha's had this virus?'

Gary shrugged. 'Heard aboot this guy fae Kilbirnie.'

'But dae ye *know* anybody? Personally?'

He shook his head. 'But that's cos folk are takin precautions.'

She wiggled her ringed fingers and made a ghostie noise. 'Whooh.

Fear! Got us whaur they want us noo eh?'

Gary took a deep breath and let it go. 'Onywey, Senga, Strongbow comin right up.'

She snorted, as though the idea of being brought the drink she'd ordered was now offensive. 'Afore ye go, goat a newspaper?'

He reached for the paper-rack mounted on the wall, took the solitary *Herald* out and placed it on her table. As she picked it up, he wondered about his fingertips again, *her* fingertips, about how you disinfect paper, about about about about.

'Ho,' she said, staring at the headline, 'Whit the fuck's this?'

'Ih?' he said, noticing the Young Team had already disappeared towards the smoking area. He'd better check what they were rolling out there. She held up the newspaper in front of Gary. It read: Last Orders as Pubs, Clubs and Restaurants Forced To Close.

Cold surged through him. They hadn't been open fifteen minutes! He'd been prepping this for four months, had gone through numerous incredibly-tense staff training-sessions during which he'd had to answer the question But Why? repeated endlessly, as though from the lips of children, had invested in the Perspex, in the PPE, in the pain of it all, and now they were being told –

'All pubs, bars, restaurants and cafes have been ordered to close throughout the UK,' said Senga, reading aloud, almost proudly, 'as efforts to halt the spread of coronavirus were ramped up after new advice from scientists.'

Gary looked to Janice, who was briskly carrying drinks to a table. The force of his shock made her frown, stare back at him worriedly as she placed each down in front of punters. She hurried over, tray under her elbow, brows furrowed. 'Whit? Whit's the matter, Gary? Whit's wrong?' Her tone was clipped, short, all the uncertainty of the past few months trapped and fluttering in her throat.

'Show her,' Gary said to Senga, and Senga held up the newspaper, eyebrows raised above it like a cartoon peering over a wall.

Janice looked at Gary, faintly amused. Gary opened his hands. 'Whit's funny?' Janice took the newspaper and waved it in front of Gary, tapping the date.

'Saturday March 21st 2020. Kept the paper from the day afore lockdown. For a laugh, like.'

In the time it took for Gary to process this, Senga was indeed laughing, the catarrh giving it a rough, mocking underlay. Gary rubbed his forehead as Janice returned to the bar and Senga flicked through the paper, squinting from inside her grey fronds of hair. 'Opinion: The Mortal Threat From Coronavirus Could Change Us All For The Better.' She cackled again, mouth fully open now, head thrown back, and Gary was reminded of a shark breaking the water. He strode towards the fire exit, feeling his veins twitch with adrenaline, hearing Senga's fanged voice trill across the pub:

'Telt ye, Gary, we canny live like this!'

He paused, turned, held up a hand as though to oncoming traffic. 'Senga. Please. Nae raised voices.'

'Sorry,' she said, 'Forgot we were in a library. Shh!' She did exaggerated shushing and the other punters giggled nervously along.

Outside, the two lads were sparking up, standing either side of a barrel, the lighter paused as Gary was spotted. He approached, peering. 'Sorry, Gaz, just a wee blunt,' said the tall one in the bomber jacket. 'Tay celebrate you bein back, like.'

'We can take it aff the premises,' the smaller one almost squeaked, 'If ye want?' The sun had gone again and the sky above them was as pale and lifeless as their skin: a lockdown spent with the blinds drawn, the telly on and a bong.

Gary held out his hand, thumb and forefinger touching. The taller one swallowed and passed Gary the blunt. Gary put it to his lips and sucked, before holding his breath and blowing out a cloud of dull, scented smoke. Then he passed it back to the taller one, who took it as though it were an alien object, touched by alien saliva.

'Needed that,' Gary said, feeling the smoke stroke his lungs with grey fingers, 'Whit's yer names, boays?'

'Mikey,' said the taller one, nipping the blunt then wiping his fingers.

'Kev,' said the smaller one, seeing this, disappointed.

'Yese believe the virus is real?' said Gary, and they glanced at each other, as though presented with a difficult question on Dragon's Den. Mikey scratched the back of his neck.

'Well, likes, aye sortay.'

'Sortay?'

He made a face. 'Ma papa says it's the Illuminati. Says Bill Gates has goat the only vaccine. They're tryin tay stoap us meetin up in real life so we canny, like, overthrow them.'

Gary looked at Kev, who had his hands in his pockets, slumped away from the question. 'Whit aboot you, wee man?'

Kev's eyes checked in with Mikey before he spoke. 'Eh, I heard it was the Chinese done it. Like a biological weapon sortay hing? Release it oan the West an watch it cause havoc.'

'Well,' said Gary, taking a tube of sanitiser from his pocket and squeezing some over his hands. 'It's workin then, int it?'

As the sharp alcohol smell met him he offered it to Kev and Mikey. They held out their hands and he gave a generous slug each, which they quickly rubbed into their skin. The sun breached the clouds once more and the boys' faces turned upwards, like flowers in the underbrush edging towards the light.

'Whit yese drinkin, lads?'

'Kopperberg,' said Mikey.

'Kopperberg,' said Kev.

'We've only goat Summer Fruits, that alright?'

'Aye,' they both said, and Gary left them and pushed open the heavy fire exit door, hearing shouts and laughter from inside, and Iron Maiden being belted out across the pub with a rough voice.

CHAPTER 8

Grief

Marjorie Lotfi Gill

'AGAIN?'

She's already been to California twice in the past six months, once more than she's visited in the past three years.

The morning after she'd dreamt Baba was sitting cross legged on the only Persian carpet they got out of Iran (Tabriz, of course), holding his chai glass along the rim with his fingers, tilting his head to the side and entreating '*beshini, beshini, dokhtaar e man*' (sit, sit, my daughter) – she'd bought a flight home.

She went on her own for that first visit, choosing Thanksgiving so they wouldn't be alone. Baba wasn't well enough to travel to her brother's and Mom's voice had cracked when she described their quiet plans.

'We'll be fine, honey. We'll go out to eat. The restaurants here do a lovely spread.'

She thought back to year on year of dozens of family around Mom's table for the holiday. Her own children complained when they realised when she was going away.

'What about our turkey and fixin's?' (She was secretly proud of their use of this slang.) 'What about the mini pies for school?'

Since nursery, she'd been visiting their classes on Thanksgiving, making handprint turkeys and telling the story of the first pilgrim feast in America. She'd produce mini pumpkin pies for all the children, replete with a squirt of whipped cream, before conjuring up the full meal at home later that evening: turkey, stuffing, corn goo, sweet potatoes, mashed potatoes with gravy, cranberry sauce, green Jell-O salad, green beans, homemade rolls and pumpkin pie. It was the only day of the year she cooked sweet potato, let alone the version with marshmallows and maple syrup.

'It's not really a holiday here, you guys. I'll make it up to you.'

That first visit wasn't a long one – it'd felt like she was in the air longer than she was on the ground. The sixth time she'd had to slam on the brakes barely missing hitting the car ahead on the drive down, she booked into a nameless hotel and slept off the flight. When she arrived early the next morning, she took them both to the beach, saying she needed someone to watch this middle-aged woman getting into a winter Pacific without a wetsuit. But really, she wanted them to have the confidence to go out into the world again, drink strong coffee amidst strangers, walk along a boardwalk warming in the sun. They stood on the sidewalk with their lattes and said to the early morning dog walkers

'She's not trying to kill herself, honest. She lives in Scotland and thinks the weather is WARM!'

They did ordinary things on that visit: shopping, watching TV, playing cards. Baba kept saying, 'I've had a good life', as if he were trying to convince himself.

On her last night, she took Mom out for a margarita at the local Mexican, and heard the full story of her worry, peppered with questions.

'I can't put my finger on it, but something's changed beyond the health problems. You're the only other one that really knows him, that can really tell. Does he seem any different to you?'

She hadn't known how to answer after only three days.

And then as she was packing to go, he'd said – 'Here, let me show you where I keep all the paperwork, just in case your mother forgets.'

She went back a second time for February half-term, this time with the two youngest children, those that couldn't be left in the flat alone and didn't have summer exams to work towards. Even a longer visit – this time almost a week – didn't seem long enough. He was more himself, but she wasn't sure if it was an act put on for the children. Persians were good at smiling, at pretending. 'I'm fine', he kept repeating when asked, 'I'm absolutely fine.'

Every morning, he rose jet-lag early to accompany her to Peet's coffee, where they waited for the guy wearing a BOB nametag to open the door in the 5am darkness. He looked more like a Behrooz than a Bob. If she ever had to wear a nametag at work, she decided, she'd choose something simple, too. Baba had done the same; she was still startled when people called him by his American name.

On the second visit, Baba wanted her to come with him to doctor's appointments. At one, he asked to be able to drive again, which she took as a good sign. The doctor looked at his latest results on his computer – *who even used paper anymore*, she wondered – and granted his wish. She flew home telling herself that all was on the mend.

They got ill on arriving back – temperature, coughs. The GP was sure it wasn't coronavirus because they hadn't travelled through an affected country. Her younger daughter stopped eating because she said everything tasted *really weird*. She made their favourite Persian stew in the slow cooker, chicken with pomegranates and ground walnuts. The others spent the afternoon asking when they could eat already, claimed she was torturing them with the smell.

So when her daughter asked, 'What's for dinner?' they all laughed, thinking she was joking.

'You can't smell that?'

'What?'

'It's been driving us all mad all day – the stew. It's Khorest e Fesenjan!'

'I can't smell a thing', she'd said, lifting the lid to the pot to peer inside.

They woke to the headlines that one of the clearest signs of the virus was a lack of smell. She left the newspaper on the table so her daughter could read it for herself.

Three days later she received the text message saying that Baba had just come out of surgery. 'He's fine, and recovering well in post-op, it said. It all happened so fast that we didn't have time to call you.' She'd known this was a lie, that her mother would have waited alone during the surgery with a phone in her hand; she chose not to ring.

Baba called when he was able, unusually upbeat, and she knew he was trying to set her at ease. She made a mental note that parents never stop being parents, and that someday her own children would want the actual truth from her. *Truth's relative when you're a parent,* she thought, *especially a Persian parent.*

Now she wants to go to California again.

'Again?'

Mom gets the virus, struggles to breathe at night, and Baba seems to be holding, despite the recent surgery. But she's not sure he would say if it were otherwise. He's busy nursing Mom.

Public Health Scotland pleads with her to stay put.

'You'll undo everyone's good work if you travel abroad unnecessarily right now.'

'What's the definition of "necessary"?' she asks herself.

A week later she runs into an old American friend, Jane, in the Sainsbury's queue. Jane's parents are also in California, and they ask after one another's family. She tells Jane that her father is back in hospital, struggling this time.

'So when are you going home? Have you got a ticket?'

'Public Health Scotland have asked me not to go'. It sounds like a lame excuse when she says it aloud. But what else can she do? How can she put others at risk?

'You have to go,' Jane insists. 'You'll never regret going, but you'll regret not going, especially if something happens once the airports are shut.'

They decide this exile from home is a form of grief in its own right. A Sainsbury's employee asks them to move along, conduct their conversation outside.

'I never realised how my willingness to live here was conditional on my ability to go back when I choose,' Jane says on their way out.

That night, neither of her parents answer their mobile phones. She tries to tell herself they've run out of battery, forgotten the chargers at home, but when she drifts off to sleep she can hear Baba calling her, using his old pet name – 'zeebah dookhtar, kodjah ee?' (beautiful daughter, where are you?).

Early the next morning she books herself a one-way ticket for later in the week. At a decent hour, she rings Jane to tell her.

'No one could ever blame you, Jane says, and adds I'd call this necessary, anyone would. And anyway, what's the worst that can happen?'

She's still sipping her coffee and thinking through how she'll tell them that she's going home again, debating the exact words she'll use, when the phone rings.

CHAPTER 9

Rewilding

Sally Gales

AMELIA SLIPPED OUT of bed as soon as Ewan's breathing slowed and small puffs of sleep punctuated the air. Haggis raised his head from the foot of their bed and watched her through slitted eyes. She reached out and scratched between his mismatched ears and whispered. 'Stay.'

Of course, the cat did exactly the opposite. Lifting his tail high in the air, he stretched out his front paws and yawned, oblivious of the man still asleep in the bed. Amelia smiled. Grabbing a hoodie from the floor, she snuck out of their room, with Haggis sauntering behind her.

* * *

'... everything is fine here, Mom. Things are opening back up but we're staying local. Ewan is training and I've just started–'

'He's praying? Oh my God! What happened?'

Ewan smiled. He was on the other side of the garden finishing up his pistol squats when Mia's mom had video called. It was the same routine every Sunday. They'd survived lockdown, restrictions were being lifted and still she panicked.

'No, Mom, no.' Amelia sighed. 'He isn't praying. He's train-ing.'

'Oh, training. What is he training for? He's not planning on going to any races, is he?'

Amelia threw back her head and groaned. Her mother knew exactly how to drive her insane and still, Amelia was disappointed she wouldn't be able to fly back home that year.

'Mia? Why aren't you answering me? Is this a bad connection? Can you hear me?'

Ewan wiped the sweat from his face and came to his fiancée's rescue. 'Hi, Barbara. Don't worry. We're both staying put. I'm just training for...'

While Ewan explained himself to Mia's mom, a kitten stumbled out of the bushes that delineated their garden. Tufts of long brown hair stuck out in every direction camouflaging him in the shadows, with the exception of one white ear. The creature sat, legs splayed inelegantly beneath him, and watched Ewan rest his hand on Amelia's shoulder.

The kitten chirruped. No one paid him any attention. Yawning, he begrudgingly lifted himself from his spot and trotted towards a leaf being batted about by the wind.

'Oh my God!'

Ewan's head snapped up.

From the dropped phone on the floor, Amelia's mom screeched, 'What's wrong? What's wrong? Someone talk to me!'

The kitten didn't notice the fuss. Scrambling to grab her phone, Amelia held out her other hand to Ewan. 'Shh, shh. Mom, stop screaming.' All eyes stared at her. 'Look.' She pointed.

At this point the nameless kitten had cornered its prey and pounced on the unsuspecting leaf.

'Mom, I have to call you back.'

'Mia, don't–'

Amelia hung up. Slinking down to the floor, she crawled closer to the kitten who was now watching her with wary eyes. 'Hey, buddy.' She stopped a few feet away and held out her hand. 'Oh, sweet baby. Pspsps. Come here.'

Ewan stepped around her and the kitten arched its back.

'Get back,' Amelia whispered. 'You're scaring him.'

Ewan watched Amelia grovel with the kitten for over thirty minutes. He'd never had a cat before but it seemed to him that the wee creature knew exactly what it was doing as it coaxed more promises from her lips. At last, it tottered over with a final, 'Mew.'

Amelia scooped the kitten up into her arms and made noises Ewan had never heard before.

'He looks just like those Haggis toys.' She wiggled her fingers and squeed when the kitten batted at them. 'Oh my God! We should name him, Haggis!'

Ewan corralled his fiancée and their new pet towards the house. 'Aye, maybe? Why don't we get him inside and see if he's hungry?

Then we can brainstorm a few more ideas and see which suit him best.' He refused to own a pet with such a cliché name.

* * *

Haggis strode past Amelia and straight through the kitchen to the backdoor.

Amelia took her time. It was an old house; the floors creaked. She walked down the hall and through the living room, grabbing her wellies from the closet. She took out a flashlight – torch, Ewan always did like to tease her for her American words – from the kitchen drawer and glanced back, down the hall.

She wasn't nervous. She'd been sneaking out for over a fortnight now and he was none the wiser. No, it wasn't nerves that made her pause, it was guilt. She'd promised him she would stop.

Amelia shook her head. She just needed one more night. Opening the door, she followed Haggis out into the garden.

* * *

Amelia had been searching for a cat tree when she accidentally clicked on the ad: 'REWILDING: DID LOCKDOWN BRING BACK THE FAIRIES.'

She scrolled through the article. A fluff piece, it'd used stock images of blurred out white horses with sun flare and shadows in water to imply the return of unicorns and Nessie.

'I wasn't aware Nessie ever left,' she muttered under her breath.

Over the rest of the week, more articles and ads about 'Scotland's Rewilding' peppered Amelia's social media accounts:

WOMAN IN STORNOWAY SAW BLUE TINGED MEN DIVE IN THE MINGE

RETURN OF THE BROWNIES: 86-YEAR-OLD MAN CLAIMS HOUSEHOLD SPIRITS ARE HIS FRIENDS

A BIRD STOLE MY BULL: RANCHER IN DUIRINISH BLAMES GIANT BIRD FOR DISAPPEARANCE OF PRIZE HIGHLAND COW

THE STONES HAVE EYES: VILLAGERS IN SHETLAND ARE BAFFLED BY MYSTERIOUS APPEARANCE OF STONES IN THEIR FIELDS

The last one peaked her interest. Ewan and Amelia had planned on getting married in the Shetland islands – it was where they'd first declared their love for each other – and she liked to imagine them living there one day. She read through the article.

At least a dozen witnesses all collaborated the same story. Stones kept showing up out of nowhere. The height of young children, it wasn't their size, or even their strange materialisation, that caught the attention of the town. No, every single person agreed. If you looked at the stones from the right angle and the sun hit them a certain way, a face was visible in the grey rock. The last line was a quote from the oldest woman in town. 'My great-grannie used to tell us tales. I know what they are. The trows are back.'

Amelia reread the line. Trows? She'd never heard of such a thing. She opened a new tab on Google.

One tab led to twenty and before she knew it, Ewan was behind her telling her dinner was ready. She blinked. She'd read every single article and searched the internet for more. There were tales of Blue Men, Brownies, Boobries, Kelpies and Cu Sith. All over Scotland, people were spotting things that belonged in myths and stories.

'And there is this one couple, close by actually, in Kingussie, that's claiming their baby is a Changeling.' Amelia slurped up the last of her curry.

Ewan chuckled. 'What a bunch of muppets.' He grabbed Amelia's plate and headed for the kitchen.

'I know but it's been fascinating learning so much about Scotland's beasties.' Ewan laughed from the kitchen.

Sitting back into the sofa, Amelia turned on the BBC Evening News. Ewan sat down beside her and extended a tray of tea cakes. She smiled as she grabbed one and nestled against him.

'… and later tonight we will speak with a university professor who claims he's seen the Stoor Worm…'

Haggis scaled the side of the couch at the sound of foil being unwrapped and stared at Amelia, waiting for her to throw it.

* * *

The stars still captivated Amelia. Growing up in cities, she'd never really seen the night sky until she moved to Scotland. Ewan had surprised her on their trip to Shetland with a midnight picnic on top of a hill. Wrapped up together in a blanket, they'd had Hot Toddy's and tea cakes. They'd watched the sun come up.

She wasn't always 100 per cent sure she'd made the right choice moving out to the Cairngorms with him but at night, staring at the stars, her doubts disappeared.

'Mew.'

'Right, tonight's the night Haggis.' Amelia tore her gaze away.

Haggis cleaned a spot on his paw, beside the bushes where he'd first appeared.

Amelia crouched onto her knees beside him and wedged half her body into the shrubbery.

***

It started off as a shared interest. Amelia ordered books and Ewan recalled childhood stories. Everyday during lunch, they sorted through the flood of new sightings posted online. They went on excursions.

'Have you ever heard of the Monster of Loch Garten?'

'Garten? No. Is it like Nessie?'

'Nah, this wee beastie is more akin to a Kelpie. Half bull, half stallion, it supposedly stole lambs and children in the dead o' night.'

Amelia shivered. The pair went hiking and biking, reintegrating their old habits back into their lives, but now they stayed alert for a glimpse of the impossible.

Time passed and Haggis grew as kittens do, quickly and without warning. Ewan forgot about the promise of adventures but Amelia still checked the blogs and reddit posts for daily updates.

'What's Haggis doing?'

They were having breakfast out in their garden. Ewan grunted into his cup of tea, 'Probably just got sight of a mouse.'

From their small table, Haggis' hindquarters and tail were prominently displayed sticking out of the bush where he'd first appeared. He lifted his left leg and then his right. His tail swished side to side.

'I think he's stuck.' Amelia pushed her chair back.

'He's fine, Mia.'

Haggis' tail fluffed to three times its size. Amelia went to his rescue.

'What you got there, big guy?' She approached slowly and made sure to talk calmly so as not to startle the cat. 'Are you stuck?' She placed her hands around his waist, intending to pull him free, when he popped out and sat back with a thud.

Haggis looked up at Amelia, not sure what she was doing there, before getting to his feet and strolling away.

'See.' Ewan watched from across the garden. 'Told you he was fine.'

'Yeah, yeah.' Amelia brushed her hands on her jeans when something within the bush glittered. She bent closer. 'Ewan.'

Before he could respond, she stuck her head and shoulders into the bushes, and he laughed at the sight.

'Ewan!' She called out in a higher pitch. 'Ewan, come over. You have to see this.'

* * *

Even in the middle of the night, the stone was clearer than it'd been that day. Of course, in the two months since she'd discovered it, it had grown nearly ten times its original size. The grey rock was now more akin to a small boulder. And at its centre the faint outline of a single arch door had turned into an elaborate etching, clear even in the moonlight.

The overall outline of the door was the clearest but across its surface the faint filligrees and imagery was becoming clearer. Ivy grew and flowered along the bottom edges, amidst the thistle, foxglove and heather. At the centre, a mountainscape loomed in the distance. Deer grazed in fields. A rabbit leapt out of the gorse. And a golden eagle, soared up into the clouds puttering across the top.

Haggis chirruped and rubbed his side against Amelia's arm.

The rabbit fled.

'Wha–'

Amelia leaned in closer.

* * *

'Mia, you have to stop.'

'How can you say that?' She threw her hands up in the air and started pacing. 'You've seen it. It's growing.'

'You think it's growing. It could just be a trick of the light. Or maybe Haggis or another animal is digging around it exposing more of its surface. But you want it to be more...'

'Are you calling me crazy?'

'No. Obsessed.' Ewan pulled his fingers through his hair and sighed. 'Mia.'

She stepped back.

'Mia, I'm worried about you. About us.' He stared at her. 'You haven't painted in almost two months. You don't hike, bike, read. The only thing you do is stare at that rock or talk about it on your forums.'

Amelia breathed.

'Mia, I don't care if that rock is a trow or a gateway to Fairy. I only care about us. I miss you.'

'Ewan.' She reached out and touched his arm. She couldn't deny the distance that had been growing between them. She shook her head. 'I'm sorry.'

He took her hand in his. Kissed it. 'You have nothing to apologise for.'

She smiled and put her head against his shoulder. His heart beat against hers – solid, real. It wouldn't be easy but she could do it. For him. 'I'll stop.'

Ewan lifted her off her feet and squeezed. 'Thank you,' he whispered, his lips brushing against her ear.

That night they started planning their wedding. They made dinner together. They reconnected. One week later, Amelia snuck out of bed and followed Haggis out into the garden.

* * *

'Purrr-rup.' Haggis trilled. He leapt up and butted his head against Amelia's chin.

'Ow, Haggis. What are you–'

His front paws landed beside the deer and they scattered. They ran towards the mountains and out of sight. Amelia blinked. The deer were gone.

She looked at the door and back at Haggis. His eyes glowed, unblinking.

Amelia reached out and traced the eagle etched into the sky. It didn't move.

Haggis pounced on her fingers, inches from the eagle. It came to life. Diving down, it plucked a hare from the grouse before wheeling around in the sky and flying towards the mountains.

'Haggis are you–' Amelia stopped, feeling self conscious.

The cat purred.

'What are you?'

As if in response, he purred louder and got to his feet. Tiptoeing across the door, his paws rustled the heather, scared a family of voles and made a flower bloom. At last he finished his circuticous route and stopped at the door's header.

Amelia sat frozen in shock.

'Mew.'

A knob appeared beside her hand. Golden, it shimmered despite the dim light.

Haggis waited to see what she might do.

Amelia glanced back at the house and back down at the door knob. She looked to her cat but he refused to give her any answers.

Taking a deep breath, she grabbed the door knob – warm in her palm – and opened the door.

Section Two – Politics and Money

CHAPTER 10

Sleeping Beauty Awaits the Resurrected Streets
Janette Ayachi

'I breathed in air the dead breathed out' Dannie Abse, 1948.

Beyond the overgrown briar rose
I slept with all the books that I have harvested
I listened to the conversations from my garden;
women talk about how their husbands'
fixed their drinks as they watched the heavy rain
humidity still glazed across their cheeks
I hear of sons who forget their fathers' birthday
cloned lovers who argue in Spanish
young girls talking about young boys
neighbours learning the names of plants
'we are making plans for every eventuality'
is the general school of thought
but I can't quite imagine it
I can't tune my clairaudio to the outside world.
What does a country represent
when it has succeeded its stabbing;
every district did it differently
up and down like the notes on a flute various prints pressed,
timescales and a cruel crescendo of corpses
bones dug up in the too far away future
when they call us Medieval
and have evolved to something more technological.

So much of it is about belonging.
Lockdown loosens, near yelps to stay apart
coughs that echo down empty roads

graffiti over MDF boards on the shops
statues defaced and signs pulled down
the homeless pegged-up in train stations
gangs hide from running in circles
strays under strobe street lamps
so lonely now they reach delusional
taunt the jumped-up activists into rogues.
I watch the sky like a cinema screen drinking projections,
tiny cranium pavement cracks and
clouds showing slow-motion re-enactions
of cave paintings,
karma sutra lit couples argue over answering the door
to parcels they never ordered
as dismal as a candle flame in direct sunlight.
I hear an opera voice from an open window
the sound that breaks your heart strings
after you have not listened long enough
to the harmony in your own arteries.

Virus diminishing,
you saved yourself from the thorns;
but what about when lockdown lifts
and you have no one to run to
except the alluvial depths of the ocean
beckoning you closer with a pinch
a solar eclipse on the summer solstice
an improper and crude jacked-up new moon.
The world has changed in a myriad of ways
but consumers are comforted too quickly
streets are resurrected too soon
a second coming; what are the dead singing
when to dress up, when to unveil
so much of it is about unbelonging.
Sleeping fists opened, lockjaw unclipped
bring us back home they cry in soft whisps
as ships of people return from frontline battle
back to littering the beaches
so much of it is still to be healed.
In the liminal luminary world of lockdown

anything was possible
but only the probable has happened.
I used to love walking into the noise
now I long to move closer to the sea
lodge myself under a dervish whirl
of waves that cascade over a Scottish bay
I am not sure if I can ever be more distant
because the epidermis of the computer screen
has responded to my touch
and the steady meditation of field animals
is the nearest to normality I know;
to graze the earth all day with fat tongues
for sustenance and sky bathe under an arcadian clock
with no concern concocted other than to feed
the slow conveyance of bright mornings.

Beyond that, catacombed parks before and after dark
an impressive periscope
of exotic full-throttle birds. Oh, unsullied sun
I have not wasted an hour indoors
every day writing – I feel more than reborn
transformations from all the upgrades, universal downloads;
speak up, act out, change, redefine our past to empower our future
as phantom-fevered brains are unblocked
the world's despair gnawing, terror growing
but shutters pop, curtains open
people remember the taste of coffee
baptised by a brothel of baristas
relish in catching glimpse of strangers
as the moon's bleached skeleton
takes to her throne every night
upright enamel in our shared patch of ether.

Bars and museums unmuzzled
look what we have been gifted
an amphora of sun-consoled seafarers walking the land again
to anchor themselves into the arms of their long-limbed beloveds.
Under the circus stances
of all that has been impoverished

still an uncanny circumference of longing
with no one to run to in your city
after your country lifts its restrictions
and everyone you are yet to love
is still so, so far away.
I save-up my coins for a fortune teller
with hands made of sun beams
and a hot-ride in an air balloon
to balance across unpolluted skies;
a landscape of human contact

yet to be mapped.

CHAPTER 11

People and Politics:
Reshaping How We Debate, Discuss and Listen

Michael Gray

IN TIMES OF CRISIS all kinds of change seems possible – even to democracy itself. COVID-19's wartime spirit paused party-political hostilities. A laser-focus on health solutions and the public good emerged. Experts and science were elevated. Were these the early days of a better democracy?

The seriousness of the crisis emphasised the crucial tools of liberal democracy: how we discuss, debate and listen. The life or death consequences of government decision making dominated politics.

Despite this unifying storyline, the COVID-19 crisis was not without conflict. No appraisal of democracy in post-COVID-19 Scotland can be conflict free either. While liberal democratic tools are essential for a better world, they are not enough. When lauding democratic consensus and stability, we can too easily drown out inequalities of power. Who can't buy a seat at democracy's table?

For Scotland to have a more democratic future we must go beyond the dominant conception of democracy that excludes questions of economic control and collective organisation. How we constitute democracy is the foundation for how we deal with various imminent challenges – not least the constitutional questions that will continue to dominate political debate.

A New Approach to Constitutional Debate

How we debate and discuss Scotland's constitutional status will be a defining democratic challenge in the decade ahead. Since 2011 the questions of independence and then Brexit overturned many old features of political life. This trajectory looks set to intensify.

While analyses of this change differ, there is broad agreement that constitutional debate has taken on an added potency compared to parliamentary politics. The consequences of independence or Brexit are considered to be deeper and longer lasting than normal electoral cycles. This, I believe, means we should expect a higher quality of deliberation on those changes.

Fortunately Scotland has plenty of examples to learn from. Scotland's referendum of 1997 was a 'confirmatory vote'. The 74 per cent vote for a Scottish Parliament confirmed a national consensus. The referendums of 1979 (devolution), 2014 (independence) and 2016 (Brexit) were tightly contested. None of these processes led to a settled 'national will'.

The crucial lesson from contested constitutional events is that they fail to achieve their purpose – determining agreed rules for the national community. The legitimacy of Scotland-UK and UK-EU relations have become the subject of far greater polarisation since their respective referendums. The urgent challenge, as we look to the future, is what alternative approach exists for people in Scotland?

My answer is a call for realism and gradualism. Supporters of Scottish independence lack clear public support and an agreed avenue to deliver a recognised state. Nationalist leaders have not done enough – in tone or substance – to listen and engage with the two million voters who rejected their project. Independence requires tough negotiations in a harsh economic environment and constructing complex institutions of state. It is dangerously naive to believe that a narrowly contested referendum victory sets foundations for a successful Scottish state. This requires long-term hard work on persuasion and consensus. Few on the pro-independence side have confidently taken responsibility for this task.

Constitutional gradualism also challenges complacent unionism. Pro-union leaders portrayed widespread enthusiasm for constitutional change as a conclusively rejected 'obsession'. In reality the 1.6 million votes for independence was the third largest democratic mandate ever received in Scotland. A serious form of unionism would engage with why so many fellow citizens rejected the union and seek to change their minds to preserve it. Wholesale reform of the UK state was never taken seriously in the face of this challenge.

As Scotland's constitutional future dominates our democratic life for the decade to come, fostering a culture beyond political entrenchment will be a challenge for us all. Yet we also face an even greater challenge to expand Scottish democracy beyond liberal electoral politics.

Expanding Scottish Democracy

For many devolution and democracy are synonymous. No wonder. It was hard fought for over a century. An elected parliament with significant powers was a step towards a more democratic country. At a point where Holyrood is now the central institution of democratic life, a reappraisal is required.

The conventional devolution story is the triumph of a national civic movement. So-called Civic Scotland, the Constitutional Convention and campaigners unite to deliver a 'better politics' in the face of Thatcherism. This narrow account is comfortable and self-serving for its architects.

Fresh accounts of devolution criticise its embrace of liberal, retail politics and the narrowing of alternate democratic horizons. Rather than meet its high democratic rhetoric, Holyrood is complicit in a great political and cultural stagnation – with key questions of economic democracy excluded to its margins.

The authors of *Roch Winds: A Treacherous Guide to the State of Scotland* (Gallagher, Westwell, Scothorne, 2016) take aim at the 'Scottish Ideology', the language of our national elite that subverts the politics of conflicting interests and class behind a facade of parliamentary consensus. 'Devolution politics were the politics of an elite,' they state, with its design a form of 'devolved Blairism'.

It's true that the Scotland Act's Schedule 5 Reserved Matters legally prevents significant Scottish divergence from the UK economic model – even if any of Holyrood's five administrations had demonstrated such an appetite. The exclusion of economic democracy is rooted in the building. *The Literary Politics of Scottish Devolution: Voice, Class, Nation* (Hames, 2019) explains that devolved politics followed the culture of its creation. The 'Dream' of creating devolution aspired to a forum for a Scottish democratic voice – 'seeking no more than recognition and visibility' at the expense of a detailed political programme.

Too often Holyrood and Scotland's democratic pedigree is measured against Westminster rather than international best practice. In Edinburgh the Executive dominates the Parliament, the Cabinet dominates the Executive and the Leader dominates the Cabinet. Thirty-two giant authorities exist under the misnomer of 'local government'. The warnings of President Michael D Higgins are worth heeding, on why Ireland mimicked flaws from British governance and failed to embolden democratic culture outwith parliament.

The trade union movement, traditionally an institution of worker education and economic democracy, has withered. Collective bargaining and the withdrawal of labour has reduced as a consequence. Tenants' union Living Rent and community land owners aim to rebalance economic power through collective organisation. Climate divestment campaigns have redirected the portfolios of major Scottish institutions. These positive influences, however, remain at the margins. Devolution's managers – despite vast resources at their disposal – will not embolden any form of economic democracy for fear of the resulting clash with capital.

Scotland's democratic future lies beyond parliament and the constitution. How democratic is our economy, our housing, our jobs, our land, our energy, our wealth? Where are our 21st century institutions of public ownership? If the architecture of devolution is unfit for these purposes then we must redesign the system and grow organisations outwith parliament that will do that work. Such aspiration, however, is only possible if advocates of greater democracy can work together.

Avoiding the Culture War Cul-de-Sac

The spectre of the 'culture war' is haunting Scotland. The phrase can be nebulous, so here's a clear definition. The 'culture war' is the manufactured divide between specific American liberals and conservatives over identities, language and culture.

Deployed effectively by both the Vote Leave and Trump campaigns, it caricatures the 'liberal metropolitan elite' as holding alien values to 'ordinary working people'. In the West many are falling into this trap.

In 'Why does England vote Tory?', Adam Ramsay (2020) concludes that war, Empire, and monarchy are the cultural epitaphs on which Tory England repeatedly triumphs. The response, says Alex Hochuli, has been retreat. The 'young, liberal, instinctively cosmopolitan' have 'turned [their] back on the nation, in abhorrence of its working-class majority' to instead entrench their politics in a language of liberal 'American idealism' (2020).

This American liberalism, however, is economically impotent by design. It's a husk following 20th century suppressions from Debs and the IWW, COINTELPRO and McCarthyite purges. So instead a 'social radicalism' against bad words, symbols, or behaviour in defence of certain identities becomes a progressive crusade. Mark Fisher warned that this culture milieu combined 'a priest's desire to excommunicate and condemn, an academic-pedant's desire to be the first to be seen to spot a mistake, and a hipster's desire to be one of the in-crowd' (2013). It is intensely unattractive. What could be a vanguard for greater democracy instead detaches itself from popular concerns in favour of divisive and irrelevant moralising. It seeks 'personal repentance, rather than institutional reform' (Lewis, 2020). Such liberal politics, devoid of class analysis, is withdrawn, elitist and judgemental.

Mainstream Scottish politics, so far, has remained largely immune to this culture war trap. Unlike in much of the West, the bare bones of social democracy remain electorally successful. The SNP's remarkable broad tent and driving purpose has made it a resilient democratic project that manages to combine a type of liberalism and grassroots populism presented as being irreconcilable elsewhere. Ex-MP George Kerevan, however, warns of a growing cultural gulf between its party apparatus and supporters (2020). A politics of perpetual offence and retaliation appears to be an oath of passage among a new cadre of aspiring apparatchiks. Immunity may not last forever.

Democrats, both in Scotland and across the world, must never abandon populism to the suffocating sneer of those who look down on their fellow citizens. As Fisher put it:

> We need to learn, or relearn, how to build comradeship and solidarity instead of doing capital's work for it by condemning and abusing each other (2013).

Actions for a More Democratic Future

Deeds not words. Here are some examples:

i. Build a Constitutional Convention on Scotland's future. Hold 32 simultaneous citizens' assemblies. Establish a SNP–Labour–Green parliamentary working group on constitutional change. Workers' representatives (trade unions) should take a central role in developing these bodies. Popularise a target (albeit non-legally binding) of 60 per cent public support for constitutional change.

Advocates of federalism must publish detailed proposals. Pro-independence and pro-union organisations should focus on understanding those who disagree with them, including inviting speakers with different viewpoints. Hostility to different constitutional views must be challenged in all forums.

ii. Rapid expansion, with state support, of trade unions, tenants' unions and community ownership must be a national priority. Establish public ownership of key resources. Revive workplace cooperatives. Promote worker roles on company boards. Gradually decentralise mega-councils towards town and village level control. Tax land. Launch a teacher-led expansion of citizenship education. Resource maximum electoral registration, particularly for the young and marginalised. Diversify entry into the professions.

iii. Prioritise material public concerns of poverty, services and jobs. Reject identity essentialism, a philosophy of innate and irredeemable segregation of peoples, in favour of stories of collective progress and benefit. End derision directed at grassroots political expression. Accept the reality of working with people we disagree with on certain issues. Don't look to American liberals and corporate institutions for cultural or political leadership.

How much of this will be achieved directly due to the COVID-19 crisis? Very little. Yet its experience demonstrates that we can rapidly change the priorities of our democracy with intense political will. All engaged in this type of work understand that such progress can be frustratingly incremental. However health, economic and constitutional shocks prove that we must prepare far-reaching programmes of democratic change for the decade ahead. The threat of climate extinction means that economic transformation is necessary for our survival and a better democracy. As citizens, together, we have a heavy burden to future generations to deliver nothing less.

References

Fisher, M, 24 November 2013, 'Exiting the Vampire Castle', *openDemocracy*, accessed at: www.opendemocracy.net/en/opendemocracyuk/exiting-vampire-castle/

Gallagher, C, Westwell, A and Scothorne, R, 2016, *Roch Winds: A Treacherous Guide to the State of Scotland*, Edinburgh, Luath Press.

Hames, S, 2019, *The Literary Politics of Scottish Devolution: Voice, Class, Nation*, Edinburgh, Edinburgh University Press.

Hochuli, A, 17 June 2020, 'The Triumph of American Idealism', *Damage*, accessed at: www.damagemag.com/2020/06/17/the-triumph-of-american-idealism/

Kerevan, G, 7 July 2020, 'SNP at the Crossroads', *Conter*, accessed at: www.conter.co.uk/blog/2020/7/7/snp-at-the-crossroads

Lewis, H, 14 July 2020, 'How Capitalism Drives Cancel Culture', *The Atlantic*, accessed at: www.theatlantic.com/international/archive/2020/07/cancel-culture-and-problem-woke-capitalism/614086/

Ramsay, A, 21 June 2020, 'Why does England vote Tory?', *openDemocracy*, accessed at: www.opendemocracy.net/en/opendemocracyuk/why-does-england-vote-tory/

CHAPTER 12

Leadership, Learning and Knowledge: Lessons from COVID-19

James Mitchell

*Meeting them [leadership challenges] is an essential re-
quirement for effective crisis management, but there is no
rulebook for doing so. Nor is it always clear that each of
these challenges is to be met by one or a small set of 'top
dogs' high up in the food chain.*
PAUL 'T HART & LARS TUMMERS, *Understanding Public
Leadership*, 2014: 136.

Introduction

THERE ARE FOUR stages in any crisis. First, there is the pre-crisis stage
during which leaders and public bodies try to anticipate, prepare and
seek to prevent or limit its potential negative impacts. Second, comes
the immediate onset and build-up of the crisis when the speed and
nature of response can be important with long-term implications.
Third, steadfastness, legitimacy and retaining public support is required for the duration of the crisis. And fourth, there are the lessons
learned and action taken in the aftermath. Crises, by definition, are
extraordinary and require nimble and flexible leadership.

Leadership is not the same as 'the leader'. Notions of collective
or distributed leadership are well established. The temptation to cen-
tralise power and adopt a command-and-control form of leadership,
not least to ensure speedy responses, is understandable but account
needs to be taken of the nature of the crisis and the limited knowledge
and expertise held at the centre. A key challenge is to mobilise without
clumsy interventions.

But there are wider leadership roles that are often overlooked that
can assist or undermine responses to a crisis. Those with influence and
authority in opposition parties and the media should not be ignored.

Normal party politics is usually suspended. But suspending normal party politics should not mean suspending constructive critical opposition. The timing of this crisis has been challenging from the perspective of opposition parties with Scottish Parliament elections due in May 2021. An emphasis on constructive over opposition might give the governing party an electoral advantage. An emphasis on opposition over constructive can undermine efforts to tackle the crisis and can appear opportunistic.

Anticipatory Policy-making

Anticipating and preparing for likely crises get little attention. Preparing for unknown unknowns or known unknowns is difficult. The US Government's vast spending (*c.* $9 billion) in preparation for the potential adverse impact of the Y2K millennium bug remains controversial. Some argue that it was money well spent and averted crises while others insist it was wasted on a non-existent or exaggerated problem. Anticipatory policies are like insurance policies. It would be foolish not to have them but unclear as to just how much preparation will be needed. The likelihood of a crisis occurring, its course and severity cannot be predicted with accuracy.

The extent to which public bodies were prepared for the pandemic can be best be judged by how successful preparations were in tackling the crisis as it unfolded. Endless resources might be invested in preparing for events that never occur. And a serious crisis can have multiple consequences with vast implications. The impact of COVID-19 has affected every citizen, every community and every public service creating the ultimate test. What may have started as a public health crisis soon spread across all sectors and aspects of society and the economy.

No amount of planning and preparation can ever cover all scenarios. The tendency to assume that the virus had a localised impact, even when it reached Europe, meant that public services were slow to react losing precious time.

Evidence and Knowledge
The Niagara of Advice and Information

Politicians, formally the key decision-makers, are not expert in pandemics. They rely on others for advice and guidance. Information flows rapidly and demands for immediate responses are high. In a crisis, it is not surprising that leaders follow advice that appears to be uniform and sourced by established experts. This is no excuse for passing the buck but COVID-19 raises crucial questions about advice and advisers. Networks of knowledge-based experts exist at international, state and sub-state levels in the field of health as in other areas. But evidence is political, often plural, partial, contested and contradictory. It would be odd to expect experts to agree on everything, and this adds to the challenge for leaders.

Fred Greenstein, a leading scholar on political leadership, notes that politicians need to be able to process the 'Niagara of advice and information' that comes their way, and this becomes more challenging during a crisis. In the early stages, information may be sparse and difficult to interpret. Choosing who to listen to is not as simple as might be imagined. Some commentators have pointed to expert advice that was ignored but have not always put this into perspective.

Many will alight on warnings from *Lancet* editor Richard Horton as someone who ought to have been heeded. Horton was certainly early in identifying a potential pandemic. He published a paper on January 24 reporting a recent cluster of pneumonia cases in Wuhan caused by a novel virus (then referred to as 2019-nCOV). He became a vocal critic of UK Government policy, but Horton had a major credibility problem; his reputation having been damaged when he published a paper by Andrew Wakefield, later discredited and struck off the UK medical register, back in 1998 which falsely purported to show a link between the MMR vaccine and autism. Horton's association with the MMR publication was not dishonest, only mistaken, but had significant negative consequences. It is too easy, too comfortable to say that his voice ought to have been inside government.

The Niagara of advice and information requires sifting, assessing and choosing. The claim that expert advice was ignored may really mean that it was not deemed to be as credible as competing alternative advice. The role of formal advisers is important. The credibility of Scotland's Chief Medical Officer was damaged when she herself ignored the advice that she had given to the First Minister that directly shaped instructions given to everyone in Scotland. But we need to distinguish between the loss of credibility due to behaviour inconsistent with advice given – which undermined the public health message – and poor advice. The advice proffered appears to have been consistent.

Communication

Even her harshest critics would concede that First Minister Sturgeon has exceptional communication skills. Throughout the crisis she led daily briefings remarkable for their clarity and conciseness, and this has been also true of others involved. Public information affects behaviour and can help control the pandemic. The wider political community also played an important part in the early stage of the crisis. Opposition leaders, local politicians, public and community leaders across the board contributing in getting key, consistent messages across to the wider population.

It is, however, valid to ask whether it was appropriate for a politician to take the lead in news conferences. On the one hand, the presence of the First Minister conveyed the seriousness of the crisis and her office gave her an authority that nobody else had. But as a public information exercise, it might have made sense to have had these events fronted by officials. Had she failed to appear she would have been criticised and it is notable that criticism arose after Boris Johnson abandoned his daily news conferences. Criticisms of these daily First Ministerial conferences as 'party-political' should have focused on the format with often ill-equipped journalists scrutinising the First Minister with little opportunity to develop a line of questioning.

Over time, consistency in messaging across parties, politicians and interest groups broke down as disagreement occurred on the message. Sections of business – with different attitudes to risk and reward – along with the associated lobbying community agitated for a different approach suggesting that business interests had been side-lined. The test of this claim will become clear after the pandemic is over, although it is unlikely that opinion will change as there will no agreement on the bottom line: lost profits or lives lost.

Debate latterly has been framed around public health vs economy, seen in some quarters as a trade-off but as a false binary by others. As a trade-off it came down to an assessment of risk. Lifting restrictions might have benefited sections of the economy at least in the short-term but had this had negative public health consequences, it would have been the responsibility of formal decision-makers alone. They would have been unable to hide behind the demands made by business or opposition politicians who had been making such demands.

Government as Multi-Organisation

Governments consist of numerous organisations, often pushing and pulling in different directions. Many organisations operate as silos with insufficient integration. Leadership requires an oversight and ensuring that due attention is paid to all parts of this complex machinery. Health led on the reaction to the crisis, which makes it all the more worrying that one of the gravest errors occurred in our care homes where infections rapidly spread and will be remembered as a most egregious part of the crisis.

The emphasis on health effectively meant a focus on the NHS, and protecting the NHS, in the early stages of the crisis. Efforts had to be made to ensure that support was given to 'carers' understood more inclusively than the NHS. Far less attention has been paid to wider public services, most notably local authorities, for their important leadership role in ensuring flexible responses, delivery of essential services in our communities and facilitating and supporting (where they have done so) remarkable levels of community-led support networks. A key lesson from this pandemic should be recognition of the bottom-up approach without which most services would have ground to a halt.

Challenges in the relationship between health and social care are not new, but the pandemic has highlighted the need for more integration – and not just at an organisational level. Closeting vulnerable groups together only makes sense if they are isolated and fully resourced and supported. Once more, the silo-based and narrow focus on the NHS proved costly.

Drawing Lessons

Whenever something goes wrong, we always look to attribute blame. Blame should be apportioned appropriately but we also need to learn and that requires openness. Blame games close down honesty and make people hide mistakes. What we require, but is in danger of being lost as crass party politics kick in, is a willingness to be open and reflective.

The likelihood is that we will be better prepared for a future pandemic but care needs to be taken to avoid 'fighting the last war'. The danger is that we will be blinded by what has already happened and lose sight of other pressing problems and impending crises, not least those affecting our environment.

Conclusion

No leader can emerge from this crisis with a perfect record. Lessons will be learned not least from what has happened elsewhere. Turning adversity into opportunity – 'don't waste a good crisis' – will be a mark of good leadership. That will be made much easier if this approached with a seriousness and maturity that has sadly not been in abundance in UK and Scottish politics in recent times.

CHAPTER 13

How a Small Country Might Just Be Able to Lead a Big Change

Katherine Trebeck

Introduction

2020 IS SET to be a year characterised by masks. As Scottish people woke up on Hogmanay morning, Australians were going to bed to the latest news of bushfires spreading across the east of the country – taking people's homes, wildlife and acres and acres of native vegetation with them. The hills surrounding Australia's capital city, Canberra (my hometown) meant smoke from nearby blazes settled in the city streets, endangering the lungs of locals. Many sought out facemasks, and the type able to filter out carcinogenic particles quickly sold out.

Now, as I write, multiple governments worldwide are telling their citizens that wearing masks in shops and on public transport is necessary to control transmission of COVID-19. That's masks in the literal sense.

But masks – or perhaps more accurately, blinkers – have been donned in a more metaphorical sense as many policy-makers and commentators turn a blind eye to the damage that the pre-COVID-19 economic system was doing to people and the planet, and wheel out policies that risk taking us back to business as usual in the pursuit of a 'V-shaped recovery'.

This wilful or perhaps just lazily convenient downplaying of the problems of the pre-COVID-19 economic system has generated a paradox. We are living in the richest time in global history, yet in cities around the world, homeless people sleep in doorways of vacant properties that are earning investors millions. Slum dwellers live alongside some of the most expensive real estate in the world. Women might be more educated than ever, but face violence, everyday sexism and penalties for taking on care work and having babies. Awareness of climate change might be high, yet we are pushing well beyond planetary boundaries while failing to ensure that everyone's minimal social needs are met, all the while ostensibly accepting the extent to which over the decades (and as part of COVID-19 responses) governments have pledged huge sums of money to support the fossil fuel industry.

The economic set up prior to COVID-19 in places like Scotland, the UK and most other countries was not delivering for enough people, nor was it protecting the planet. As a result, humanity faces extraordinary and interlocking challenges that pose an existential threat to thousands of species and to the realisation of human rights for hundreds of millions. On top of a pandemic.

COVID-19 and the Economy

The spread of COVID-19 shines a light on this economy – its inequalities, power structures and absurdities. It lays bare the divide between those who can readily work from their kitchen tables and those forced to deliver to them. COVID-19 reveals an economic system that depends on an army of low paid workers. These are the workers Guy Standing described as the 'precariat': without decent security in their work, let alone sufficient pay. They are on zero-hour contracts in the gig economy or eking out a living as self-employed.

The precariat are the frontline staff of our hyper-flexible economy where humans are treated as just-in-time inventory in the same way that oat milk is ordered on demand for the salariat's flat whites. The precariat were the first to lose their hours and their jobs as businesses shut to enable people to shelter from the virus – as bars closed, as people delayed haircuts and as events were cancelled. Without savings, they are amongst the hardest hit.

Beyond the GDP Era?

Why did such an economy emerge, an economy so misaligned with what people and the planet need? A complex suite of dynamics is at play, but among them is the gross domestic product blinkers constricting the view of so many politicians, their advisers and many in the media. The status of GDP as a proxy not only for economic health but national success far exceeds the function envisaged by its creator, but today the goal of economic growth shapes political priorities, many business models and even notions of welfare and success.

The dominance of the concept of economic growth has meant that GDP-defined institutions of global governance – notably the G7 and later the G20 – have become centres of power in global relations. A de facto GDP-meritocracy, except its merit is ill-founded given the disconnect between GDP and collective wellbeing in rich countries and the looming environmental breakdown. It is a configuration of global governance that is anachronistic in a world where nations are also pursuing the Sustainable Development Goals (SDGs).

Yet, the entrenched growth-based economy is what many post-COVID-19 recovery plans hang their suggestions and recommendations on. GDP is a measure created, in part, to assess the economic impact of Roosevelt's New Deal some 90 years ago, a time before humanity had pushed the planet to the brink. It is hardly a useful metric to gauge the extent to which economies are built back *truly* better today.

Fortunately, despite macro-policy regimes acting against them, some communities, businesses and policy-makers have been forging alternative paths and starting to build a wellbeing economy that is environmentally sustainable and socially just. The challenge is that these approaches often exist *despite* the system, rather than because of it.

Scotland's Efforts in Global Context

This is the global context in which Scotland sits – a world economy and supranational institutions largely wedded to outdated assumptions and yet again relying on old principles. In contrast, Scotland is showing signs of enlightenment – and preparedness to recognise new ideas and practices in the economy are necessary. It is all too easy to forget how far the debate in Scotland has moved when we only compare it to where it needs to be: it is worth recognising how far it has come when it is compared to other countries.

Scotland already has the talk and the templates for building a wellbeing economy. In policy terms there have been tentative moves in the direction of what is necessary and in that sense it is further down the path than many other economies where the conversation about new priorities is not even happening.

Now is the time to breathe life into them, roll them out, to scale them out and up, rather than ditching them in a misplaced deference to old way of doing things which don't require too much prodding to be revealed as inadequate.

The beginnings of mechanisms conducive to building a wellbeing economy include the Business Pledge and the Scottish Enterprise shift to making 'job-related grants contingent on fair work practices, including job security and payment of the real living wage'. Other mechanisms with potential, were they undertaken with more vigour, include the Sustainable Procurement duty, the Community Empowerment Act and community wealth building efforts. Perhaps the best role of a post-COVID-19 state is to underwrite community-led solutions? Again, there are the glimmers of existing practice to build on – not least in the form of the Climate Challenge Fund and nascent participatory budgeting projects.

On the environmental side of the ledger, here too Scotland has some form: ambitious climate targets and the work of the Just Transition Commission to map support for communities while powering down those industries incompatible with a low carbon economy. The existence of Zero Waste Scotland is something to celebrate – a post-COVID-19 economy needs to be a circular one.

Implicitly underpinning such tentative steps are the National Performance Framework and the First Minister's TED talk of July 2019 which elevate collective wellbeing as the goal of the economy. More *explicitly*, uptake of the wellbeing economy agenda has seen Scotland lead creation of a new group of governments – one with potential to nudge the GDP dominance of global governance and policy-making off its ill-deserved pedestal and open up the global conversation in a way that can go beyond 20th century orthodoxy towards policy-making better suited for the realities of the 21st.

'A Light in the Darkness'?

The Wellbeing Economy Governments (WEGO) partnership is a new partnership that has potential to chart a course away from business as usual towards a wellbeing economy. 'A light in the darkness' was how the Prime Minister of Iceland described the WEGO at the opening of its first policy lab in May 2019. She was referring to its collaborative mode of working in contrast to global politics often dominated by national self-interest, trade wars and competition.

Prime Minister Katrín Jakobsdóttir could just have easily been referring to WEGO's potential to normalise previously ostensibly radical ideas – the sort necessary to transition away from economic systems riddled with inequalities and unsustainability.

Impetus

Addressing the challenges facing humanity requires more than tweaking the current configurations of multilateralism. The world is striving to achieve SDGs, but with global governance based on other, often contrary, indicators. A few years before the signing of the SDGs, the UN's 2012 High-Level Panel on a New Development Paradigm suggested an awareness that economic models need to change. Yet its impact is hard to discern, not least when the influence of the WTO and the IMF continues to entrench growth-oriented economic models. Other institutions are criticised for their remoteness: the European Parliament is dubbed 'the European Spaceship', while the G20 is condemned for lack of participation of low-income countries and a propensity to favour photo-opportunities over substance.

Ecological economists have charted the disconnect between GDP and measures of 'genuine progress', a gap that has expanded since the late 1970s. In the face of such evidence, some in officialdom have stepped into the terrain. The OECD was one of the first international institutions to recognise the limitations of GDP as an indicator of progress, proposing alternatives based on quality of life and wellbeing. The UN has constructed indicators of human development, inclusive wealth and welfare and of course the SDGs, flawed though they are, point to wider priorities. World Bank efforts include the Economics of Ecosystems and Biodiversity and the Natural Capital Declaration.

These moves are welcome and significant in their own right. What desperately needs to catch up is the state of the world's governance – both within and between states. What if the world could see the bar raised by a courageous coalition of governments committed to testing an alternative vision of development and undertaking collaboration to create wellbeing economies?

This is the possibility of WEGO, launched in 2018 at the OECD's global wellbeing forum. It is led by Scotland (who provide secretariat functions), New Zealand and Iceland, and recently welcomed Wales. WEGO enables participating governments to share, exchange, collaborate and support each other in efforts to orientate economic policy-making around collective wellbeing: challenging and learning from each other to push boundaries and forge new approaches.

Possibility

Instead of waiting for global consensus – which is too often based on unambitious compromise – the WEGO mode of governance can be about leading by example and demonstrating what is possible.

As it builds its profile and reach, WEGO will spread good practice: modelling, testing and showcasing pioneering efforts in policy-making for wellbeing. States invariably model each other – learning from other's experience and mistakes, so WEGO's impact will likely emanate from influence, inspiration and collaboration to steer the world in the pursuit of wellbeing economies. It can bring the possibility of a new form of global governance via:

- *Showing*: modelling, testing and showcasing new ways of doing policy-making for wellbeing;

- *Sharing*: continually improving policy-making via policy exchanges;

- *Suggesting*: exerting influence as a like-minded block on existing mechanisms of international governance.

Membership of WEGO is about aspiration, rather than waiting for comprehensive attainment. What matters is members' willingness to undertake policy innovation for wellbeing, and commitment to demonstrable, continuous improvement.

Significance

WEGO brings impetus for change via soft power rather than economic might. The effectiveness of this route has been seen before via the impact of the Climate Vulnerable Forum; the ability of countries such as Sweden or Finland to achieve change by leading efforts in gender equality; the influence on the Paris Agreement of sub-state actors, who made bold commitments which opened space for others to act; or Brazil's pioneering of the 'zero hunger' programme, which it 'exported' to other parts of the world.

As an alliance, WEGO can foster 'power with': collective strength borne of acting out a new future together. As a collaboration, it can strengthen members' 'power to': their capacity to act and influence and consolidating their transition to a wellbeing economy. Scotland's leadership of it is a mode of so-called paradiplomacy –

international relations undertaken by sub-state regions.

WEGO has been created despite the belief in growth as universally beneficial remaining largely entrenched as an established economic order, the only concessions in recognition of its flaws coming in the form of qualifying adjectives such as 'inclusive', 'shared' or 'green'. For now, WEGO thus sits in the 'end of the bell curve territory' where innovation happens most readily amongst smaller actors unencumbered by as strong path dependencies and where players have courage to experiment.

But if it remains here, its impact will be inadequate.

Conclusions
Disappointment is Nigh?

Scotland's instigation of WEGO has given it another platform by which it can be significant beyond its size or constitutional status. As more governments join WEGO and as its profile rises, the collaborative potential will increase – and the will to chart a different course to that defined by GDP will be bolstered.

Yet until then, while small is beautiful, small is also often overlooked. Current relations of power between actors in global-level institutions cannot be swept aside overnight and it will take more than WEGO as currently configured to begin the task (hence why the wider Wellbeing Economy Alliance was created). Scotland's response to COVID-19 so far and much of the debate about what 'recovery' entails suggests that old, outdated recipes are still being reached for.

While Scotland's attention to the wellbeing economy agenda is growing, this is offset by a very real possibility to disappoint all those daring to hope that a different economic system will be built post-COVID-19. Scotland's tentative efforts might just as easily be overwhelmed by orthodox voices and the confines of blinkered, masked prescriptions.

In these difficult times when conventional approaches are being discredited, WEGO embodies the possibility of doing things differently. If it can live up to its potential, WEGO also brings the possibility of small country leading a big change – at a time when big change is sorely needed.

CHAPTER 14

Breaking with Growth:
Creating an Economy of Life

Bronagh Gallagher and Mike Small

Introduction

EMERGING FROM COVID-19, Scotland is not short of 'recovery plans'. All of these plans however are predicated on an economic model which demands always increasing levels of production, consumption and accumulation to be measured as successful. This is the model of economic growth. To fuel this growth, plans involve 'dirty bailouts' that prop-up the fossil fuel, aviation and car economy in a race to get 'back to normal' and ignore the reality of climate breakdown. This is an approach to recovery in which the treatment is the same as the illness. It will simply not be sufficient to 'respond' to the multiple, overlapping systemic crises we now face, which are crises of capitalism. If we are truly a society seeking recovery, we must acknowledge that it is also a recovery from our addiction to growth-at-all costs capitalism. It is only by breaking with this logic can we hope to carve out a meaningful recovery and a sustainable future.

Clung to and heralded by its champions, a growth economy is characterised by disfiguring poverty and obscene inequality, spiralling mental health problems and an inability to meet the most basic human needs in terms of access to housing and healthy food. Indeed, our current economic system is defined by stress and breakdown at every level. The definition of 'precarity' – the new(ish) term for radical job insecurity – is this:

Precarity is a precarious existence, lacking in predictability, job security, material or psychological welfare. The social class defined by this condition has been termed the precariat.

The experience of a lack of safety and security is now felt by us all – way beyond a certain social sector. Post-COVID-19, it is now an almost universal reality. The concept of precarity has come to name 'the politically induced condition in which certain populations suffer from failing social and economic networks... becoming differentially exposed to injury, violence, and death' (Butler, 2009). This is now you, me, us. We are the precariat.

But if we are all precarious now, so too is the basis of our world. This is because a growth economy not only demands inhumane work and living, it also drives extractivism and working beyond the natural carrying capacities of the Earth. We know this, yet all of the recovery plans presented rest on the idea of 'inclusive growth': the illusion of eradicating poverty while growing the economy. This rationale is not fit for the purpose of driving a recovery that needs to go beyond simply COVID-19 and into a future of Brexit, climate breakdown and global insecurity. The belief in the distributive altruism of the status quo is based on a chimera. Growth does not help alleviate poverty; it is dependent on its existence.

Degrowth offers an alternative path forward. While degrowth thinking has flourished recently, the idea can be dated to the year 1972 when the philosopher André Gorz asked:

Is the earth's balance, for which no-growth – or even degrowth – of material production is a necessary condition, compatible with the survival of the capitalist system? (Gorz et al., 1980)

Degrowth is a 'democratically planned yet adaptive, sustainable, and equitable downscaling of the economy,' leading to a future where we can live better with less. This requires transforming the current profit-oriented capitalist system. It opposes blind faith in market forces and dismisses the pursuit of 'green growth' and decoupling as main strategies to solve environmental and social problems. This does mean that the focus of society is no longer our contribution to growing the economy. It does not mean recession and enforced austerity. Rather, it is nurturing that which is life-giving and reducing the output of that which is destroying us. It is less for some and enough for everyone.

In this essay, we explore three key areas: the purpose of the economy, our work lives and our democracy as ways of understanding our current experience, reflecting on/exploring how degrowth alternatives could look and feel for us all.

What is Our Economy For?

Getting up for work on a Monday morning, most of us are not reflecting on the value we are creating for the country. We are thinking about the commute, the deadlines, the dream of getting away from it all, the bills we need to pay. The work we do – in the form of Scotland's biggest employment sectors – are business and financial services (banking, recruitment, advertising) and the retail and food sectors. We work for wages that enable us to meet our basic needs with what is left each month to secure a standard of living, in the form of consumer goods and experiences, that puts the average Scot amongst the most well-off when compared globally according to the OECD Better Life Index.

When we look at where so much of our collective effort and energy goes, as seen in our main employment areas, it is striking to observe that this is work which, largely, does not improve our collective experience. This is a model of employment with monetary value but very little social value.

The paucity of the economic argument that monetary value 'trickles down,' lifting all boats, is laid bare by the world we see around us and is utterly destroyed by UN Special Rapporteur Philip Alston's 2020 report, 'The Parlous State of Poverty Eradication'. Further, as COVID-19 proved so simply, the essential work that has real value for society, away from having a wage to survive, is not what our economy or culture encourages. We need a different compass to guide the value that we create together.

An economy which embeds care and collective contribution as its core logic would create an entirely new value system, placing significance on work beyond simply monetary value. It would mean being able to look after your children, your parents, your chosen family because it is both financially viable as well as socially desirable. A care economy recognises that what creates social value is the work that is often currently invisible – ie low paid or unpaid work – the work most often of women (Dengler and Strunk, 2017). A focus on collective contribution elevates what we now recognise as essential work – transport workers, the shelf stackers – as dignified work. A care economy lifts up the mundane and everyday, recognising that this is the work of creating a healthy whole, even if it is not glamorous. This shifts our story of 'success' away from individual professional achievement to that of contribution and cooperation.

A care economy would recognise that the best way to achieve collective wellbeing is not by placing primary value on our ability to earn money through any type of job in the hope that redistribution is effective. It would instead do things like actively grow those sectors of employment which are collectively-oriented, creating strong public services and meaningful social security systems. It would go beyond living wages to pay ratios between highest and lowest earners. It is the pre-distribution of resources so they are shared more fairly in the first place (Trebeck and Williams, 2019).

Without doubt, this would need to be a cultural, as well as economic, transformation, but the strong traditions of solidarity and fairness which continue to run through Scotland suggests that what people value most is not GDP, but how we look after each other. This is what our economy should enable. Rather than the endless consumption and production talismanic of growth, an economy that is oriented towards valuing and creating collective care and with less focus on material goods is a society and a country which looks and feels fair, healthy and contented.

Our Working Lives

As we brace ourselves for a potentially devastating economic depression, look ahead to climate disruption and take lessons on home-working from lockdown, the shibboleths of our working lives are primed to be reimagined.

Shorter working weeks are central to this (Kallis, 2018). Perceived as both radical and risible, it is worth remembering we live an inherited legacy of an industrial approach to work designed to maximise manufacturing productivity (or simply growth). Our working patterns are a norm from a different time, not a truth. If the Great Depression, less than 100 years ago, can institutionalise our five-day working week in an effort to offset mass unemployment, then our COVID-19 recovery presents no better time to ask fresh questions of our working lives divorced from the growth mantra of *more*.

Instituting shorter working weeks must go beyond the growth economy intentions of increasing individual productivity. To be truly transformative, its ambition and the reality must be about creating more good work to share. Decoupling significant portions of our time from doing paid work frees us up to create value in other ways, and enables us to move away from many of the toxic signifiers of modern life – the congested commute, unsustainable on-the-go consumption, a life lived at an inhuman and illness-inducing pace as we all juggle work, family and personal commitments.

It's not only *how we work* but the *work that we do* that demands reimagining. In Scotland, some of our most significant employers are large chains, multinationals and highly centralised public organisations. These jobs are often cog-in-the-wheel experiences with little autonomy or individual creativity needed – and which continue to reinforce class lines of services and professionals, skilled and unskilled. Worker co-ops, like Green City, and a culture of start-ups based on resilience and climate realities point to an alternative model: one in which there are more small-sized employers providing more localised services.

Shifting scale as well as different ownership models also creates opportunity for more localised responses to our needs. A growth economy demands economies of scale and just-in-time supply chains. This logic drives public policy decisions, meaning procurement favours large providers, our food is largely imported, and our health and care sectors are driven by profit motivations. Shifting from growth logic would crack open the viability of alternatives. We could be a workforce of makerspaces and fab labs, artisans, and community enterprises, crofts, worker co-ops and urban growing – making, growing and creating for ourselves. Locally-owned provision of social and community services based on the idea of the commons and peer-to-peer models (Bollier and Helfrich, 2019) feels imminently more human, practical and economically sound, than, for example, the significant number of Scottish Care Homes which are businesses with registered addresses in tax havens that we currently have.

Many of these alternatives already exist, but struggle in our current system. This is not an indictment of the credibility of alternatives, but of an economic system which depends on excess production, consumption and accumulation to survive. More small businesses, worker co-ops, more good jobs for everyone, localised need and localised production, would value the creativity and contribution we all have, in different ways. This is what an economy and working life freed from the relentless pursuit of GDP would feel like. Meaningful work for us all. Life lived at a slower pace.

Participation and Radical Local Democracy not Representation and Centralisation

Our economy and governance evolved together to create these systems and structures which shape our lives. If capitalism predicated on endless growth means globalisation filtered through nation states and corporate power, its antithesis is an anti-capitalist economy based on degrowth with increased localisation and decentralised power.

If growth-based capitalism means we are defined as one-dimensional consumers, a degrowth society means we can become multi-dimensional citizens in charge of a viable future. In the immediate sense this will mean changes about how cities are run and understood. Groups like Plan C have developed ideas on Radical Municipalism and Directional Demands, to help us explore the following hypotheses:

- First, that the 'municipal' – whether we're talking about towns, cities or city-regions – might be a fundamentally important scale at which, and through which, to generate progressive movements towards post-capitalism;

- Second, that certain types of political demands might be crucial in organising powerful social movements, helping us both improve material conditions while orientating us towards new understandings of what is possible.

They have stated:

'Municipalism' is both the practices of self-government by towns, cities, and city-regions – municipalities of different sizes – and any perspective that advocates for such forms of government. Taken on its own, municipalism appears as a politically neutral concept. It's just as possible to advocate a municipalist strategy as a way of fuelling capitalist accumulation – which is what partially underpins the logic of the UK's current devolution policy – as it is to advocate a municipal strategy that is based upon promoting the expansion of commons and social solidarity.

At its most basic, a radical municipal strategy is thus one that recognises the municipal scale – both in terms of the way that people's lives are organised in these spaces, and the institutions that govern them – as a space of contestation. Rather than a de-politicised administrative unit 'nestled' under the nation-state, and thus of relatively 'less' political importance, a radical municipalist perspective asks whether there is unique revolutionary potential in organising at the municipal level (Russell and Plan C, 2017).

This agenda has a long lineage but can be seen most recently in the work of the founder of Social Ecology Murray Bookchin – whose ideas have become influential in Rojava, and the Marxist geographer David Harvey who has argued that 'rebel cities' will become a privileged site for revolutionary movements, and that the 'right to the city' would become a clarion call for progressive movements (Harvey, 2012).

This is not an abstract academic notion. We can see radical urban experiments in:

- *Riace, Italy* – the small Italian town that has received global recognition for its successful open-door policy towards refugees.

- *Paris* – where the idea of the '15 Minute City' suggests the 'core of human activity' in cities must move away from oil-era priorities of roads and car ownership. To do this they argue we need to reinvent the idea of urban proximity. 'We know it is better for people to work near to where they live, and if they can go shopping nearby and have the leisure and services they need around them too, it allows them to have a more tranquil existence.'

- *Jackson, MI* – the American city where predominantly black working-class communities are looking to create a cooperative solidarity economy through a combination of direct action and electoral strategies under the banner of Cooperation Jackson.

- *Rosario, Argentina* – where the social movement Ciudad Futura, which has its roots in a network of different types of social reproduction, have also successfully listed a number of candidates for election to the city council.

All of these experiments point to real-world innovation in scale and purpose marking a demarcation from conventional economics and a new way forward.

Conclusion

Scotland sits at a unique and pivotal juncture. The tracks laid while leaving lockdown will chart a course that it will be hard to move away from once set. Given the reality of climate breakdown, the significance of this moment is only magnified. In this essay, we have argued that the changes required to meet this moment will not come from the logic that has brought us to this point, but rather demand a new orientation to how we live our lives. We have explored how we can rethink the purpose of our economy, how our work lives can be reorganised and how we can create viable participatory cities as part of new democratic structures and systems if we pursue an economic model which does not prioritise growth-at-all costs.

Nothing happens overnight. As radical as these ideas may seem, it is important to acknowledge that a world beyond growth is a direction of travel, not a defined destination. Getting there will be a process of discovery and adjustment, needing both consistent small choices on the part of each of us to do differently, as well as struggle and sweeping changes. The positive is that this is a future that is *already here* in many small ways. Scotland hums with alternatives. Stretching the length and breadth of this country are initiatives which speak to community energy, community ownership, alternative work models, alternative housing options. The scale of change might seem daunting, maybe even unimaginable, but we already have much we can build from.

We seek to inspire and imagine different yet credible futures and to outline the contours of a future Scotland which is fair, just, sustainable and balanced – a future which makes you want to live there, and, more importantly makes you want to be part of building it.

Too often alternatives and activists are painted as utopian as a way of dismissing ideas, as if trying to imagine the best world possible and then figuring out how to get there isn't what the work of the best governance should be. We have lived a reality shaped by logic of economic growth for 40 years. It has simply not delivered. Imagining a world beyond growth can no longer be dismissed as utopian; it is the most pragmatic response we have to a planet teetering on the edge.

References

Bollier, D and Helfrich, S, 2019, *Free, Fair, and Alive: The Insurgent Power of the Commons,* Gabriola Island, British Columbia, Canada, New Society Publishers.

Butler, J, 2009, *Frames of War: When is Life Grievable?,* London, Verso.

Dengler, C and Strunk, B, 2017, *The Monetized Economy Versus Care and the Environment: Degrowth Perspectives On Reconciling an Antagonism, Feminist Economics,* vol.24, issue 3.

Gorz, A, Vigderman, P and Cloud, J, 1980, *Ecology as Politics,* Montreal, Quebec, Canada, Black Rose Books.

Harvey, D, 2012, *Rebel Cities: From the Right to the City to the Urban Revolution,* London, Verso Books.

Kallis, G, 2018, *Degrowth,* Newcastle, Agenda Publishing.

Russell, B and Plan C, 24 June 2017, 'Radical Municipalism: Demanding the Future', *openDemocracy,* accessed at: www.opendemocracy.net/en/ radical-municipalism-demanding-future/

Trebeck, K and Williams, J, 2019, *The Economics of Arrival: Ideas for a Grown-Up Economy,* Bristol, Policy Press.

Section Three – Public Spaces

CHAPTER 15

Hairdresser

Cheryl Follon

I'm convinced that a new hairdo can be the difference
between absolute shutdown and living life to the full.
I believe a new hairdo is the portal –
like a door between heaven and hell. Amongst the smell
of grass and fruit and the volumising mousse and spray
people come in and sit down and ask for sweeping curves
and hair that floats up to the sky.
I press my hands together and set to it.
Once I woke in the middle of the night and my hands were quivering.
Someone wants me to set a galleon in the midst of a sea of blonde curls.
And I can do it, amongst the smell of grass and flowers.

CHAPTER 16

Futures in Common:
Democratic Life Beyond the Crisis

Oliver Escobar

THIS CHAPTER ARGUES that democratic life must be expanded in order to tackle the challenges of the century ahead. Let me start by unpacking this proposition. By 'democratic life' I mean the range of practices and assets that are the foundation for active citizenship: education, resources, wellbeing, inclusion, participation, deliberation, influence. In a nutshell: the kind of things that a person needs to be part of life in democracy.

By 'the challenges of the century ahead' I mean those challenges driven by epochal forces like the climate emergency, rapid ecological decline, the biotech and infotech revolutions, welfare state reforms, robotisation, population displacements and an intricate net of in-equalities and economic failures. Our chances of governing desirable futures rest on developing an expanded form of democratic life.

We have come to think about politics as party politics and democracy as electoral democracy. This narrow scope given to democratic life overlooks how the economy provides (or hinders) the foundations for active citizenship. It also ignores how current political institutions often struggle to provide the public goods that citizens expect from a democratic system.

The last decade has seen a democratic recession worldwide, only 5 per cent of the global population lives in a 'full democracy' (The Economist Intelligence Unit, 2016; 2018) and levels of public dissatis-faction have reached record highs in countries like the UK (Foa et al., 2020). Yet, support for democracy remains popular across the world: people still love the idea of democracy but despise many of its current practices (Escobar and Elstub, 2019a). Currently dominant versions of democracy and the economy are long due an upgrade. Both the institutions of the state and the market have shown their strengths and limitations, highlighting the need for a strong civil society capable of democratising existing processes and generating new ones.

Pandemic times have thrown into relief the cracks in the foundations of economic and political life. COVID-19 has been a shared event, but certainly not a shared experience. Everyone's situation has been unique, and we must pay attention to differences and inequalities across communities of place, interest and identity. Complex solidarity is the best antidote to bogus unity or destructive populism.

What are we learning from the public health crisis? It is clearly magnifying pre-existing crises. A recent report by Scotland's Urban Regeneration Forum (SURF) concludes:

> The evidence is that the crisis has increased the gap between the haves and have-nots and laid bare the fragility of social and economic mores. If wealth is the greatest shield from infection and serious illness, then disadvantaged communities are the most exposed (2020).

There has been early research into how communities have responded to the current public health crisis. For example, reports by SURF, the Scottish Community Alliance and the Scottish Community Development Centre have mapped the landscape of experiences at the frontline of community life, including a wide range of initiatives to address fundamental challenges: food insecurity, mental health, social exclusion, poverty, homelessness, unemployment, substance abuse, digital illiteracy, etc.

The frontline of civil society, the community sector, has shown what it can do with limited resources. It is creative and resilient, but also under siege: constantly plugging the gaps generated by the state-market combo (Henderson et al., 2018). Growing economic inequalities are mirrored – and indeed fed – by growing power inequalities and, as a global study by Dalton (2017) has shown, there is a growing gap between 'the politically rich' and 'the politically poor' across the world. The result is a range of democracies that struggle to be democratic, and economies that struggle to be economic, especially for the long-term.

Reimagining and Remaking

Transforming the institutions of political and economic life is a long-term enterprise that requires urgent short-term action. Fortunately, some work is already under way. There are various fields of practice founded on the notion that reimagining democracy entails a remaking of society, politics, culture and the economy. In this piece, I would like to highlight two such fields, namely democratic innovations and the social commons.

Democratic innovations are processes or institutions where politics and policy-making are conducted directly by citizens rather than only by intermediaries or representatives (Elstub and Escobar, 2019b). There are various types of democratic innovations, including some now entering mainstream politics and governance – ie mini-publics, participatory budgeting, digital crowdsourcing. These processes all embody a transition from a democracy where citizens are mainly occasional voters or protesters, to one where they are also decision-makers and co-producers. Let's briefly unpack some examples for illustration.

Scotland has been increasingly experimenting with mini-publics and participatory budgeting over the last decade. Mini-publics are processes where citizens are selected through civic lottery (hence reducing the self-selection bias that reinforces political inequalities) and supported to deliberate in an informed manner in order to produce a considered judgement or recommendation. Citizens' juries and citizens' assemblies are amongst the most popular forms of mini-public (Escobar and Elstub, 2017).

Scotland has for example hosted citizens' juries on wind farm development, health inequalities, realistic medicine, land management and public service reform (What Works Scotland, 2017). More recently, the Citizens' Assembly on the Future of Scotland has been brought together to consider how to tackle constitutional challenges such as Brexit and now also the recovery after the pandemic. In the winter of 2020, another mini-public will get under way: the Climate Citizens' Assembly legislated for by the Scottish Parliament to put citizens at the centre of public deliberation on how to tackle the climate emergency.

There are great hopes for these new processes, as imperfect as they are bound to be, given that they are embryonic institutions that will need development and refinement. The role of citizens' assemblies in unlocking key political issues in Ireland (eg equal marriage, abortion) is often offered as an example of how mini-publics can play a crucial role in democratic decision-making. There are other remarkable cases across the world (see www.participedia.net) but also evidence that mini-publics can lose their transformative potential when they are badly designed or misused.

Participatory budgeting (PB) is another democratic innovation that has gained momentum in Scotland in the last decade. Originating in Brazil as it transitioned from dictatorship to democracy, PB spread quickly across the Global South, before becoming mainstream in the Global North. The idea is deceptively simple: PB is a process where citizens decide how to spend public funds. But there is more to it: PB is an innovation that forces a disruption in established forms of governance, opening space to change the power dynamics and redefine the relationship between citizens, communities and institutions (Escobar, 2020).

After 30 years travelling the world (over 11,000 localities have engaged in PB), some countries are seeking to institutionalise PB. Scotland is a pioneer in this area. After hosting over 200 PB processes since 2010, there is now an agreement between the Scottish Government and COSLA (Convention of Scottish Local Authorities) that by 2021 all local authorities will allocate at least 1 per cent of their budgets through PB. It's too early to take stock of the actual impact of PB in Scotland. But there is currently a sense that we are at a crossroads: PB could fizzle out under the hospices of local authorities, becoming formulaic and transactional, rather than transformational (O'Hagan et al., 2019); or PB could become a trojan horse for participatory democracy to remake our institutions from the bottom-up and the inside-out (Escobar et al., 2018).

Beyond these examples there are myriad other democratic innovations, particularly in the new digital public sphere. We now approach the capacity to create more complex, engaging and deliberative online spaces. Everyone is now a digital citizen, wittingly or unwittingly: either an active citizen navigating the troubled waters of online life, or as a passive subject to the commodification and use of personal data to inform how you are governed and marketed.

We have now seen digital innovations across the world, from the constitution-making process in Iceland, to parliamentary innovations in Finland and crowdsourcing policy in Madrid. We now also know that the quality of dialogue and deliberation online can be designed for. The potential is remarkable. Take for example the case of Virtual Taiwan (vTaiwan), which is co-led by the government of Taiwan and civil society. Amongst other things, vTaiwan has developed the capacity to crowdsource legislation and enable public deliberation at scale (through an algorithm that maps key arguments). This has been deployed with some success on relatively small policy areas, but it's now moving to the mainstream and the capacity developed through these platforms is credited with helping to manage the pandemic swiftly and effectively.

Democratic innovations operate mainly in the spheres of political life. To affect economic life, we must also pay attention to another strand of contemporary transformative practice: the social commons (Henderson et al., 2020a). The paradigm of the commons originated in historical arrangements based on the shared ownership and management of assets such as common pastures, waters and other natural resources. They were held in common, and this community-based form of governance thus became known as the commons.

The crucial contribution of the commons is that they provide an alternative form of social organisation that goes beyond the dualism between state and market. This has inspired a revival of the ideals and practices of the commons across a range of social domains (hence the social commons label) from culture to energy, from digital space to land management and education and from physical assets to intellectual capital. These are all assets and activities held in common, that is, community-own and community-managed.

In Scotland, there has seen some foundational work done over the last few decades, growing the space for a mutualist-social economy, increasing community ownership, fostering social enterprises, supporting community development trusts and, to a lesser extent, experimenting with workplace democracy and cooperatives. Some of our recent studies (Henderson et al., 2018; Henderson and Escobar, 2019) show how community anchor organisations provide a range of social and democratic goods, from public services to environmental action, from housing to transport and from anti-poverty work to renewable energy.

Community anchors therefore show the potential for an economy of the commons that expands to counterbalance the economies of the state and the market. This would go some way towards changing undemocratic economies and practising the 'economics of arrival' proposed by Trebeck and Williams (2019). Beyond community ownership and empowerment, developing a 'wellbeing economy' also entails giving citizens new roles in the construction of markets and finances: not just as consumers and employees, but also as co-producers and decision makers through innovations in employee ownership and workplace democracy.

There is much potential for Scotland to invest in strengthening its community economy (Henderson et al., 2020b). There is a growing network of community development trusts running everything from housing to renewables, transport services and various land and urban assets. There is also a vibrant social enterprise sector and an incipient set of mutualist institutions for community-led finance. With some protection from the hostilities of operating on an unequal footing with public sector and private companies, the community sector could contribute to transform our economy while doing a lot of good at the heart of communities. Augmenting their infrastructure, investment, capacity and coordination can help to generate micro-networks with potential macro-economic power (ie local-transnational, digitally-enabled, democracies and economies).

In sum, democratic innovations and the social commons can make powerful contributions to reimagining and remaking public governance and the economic system. They are important scaffolding for a broader programme of large-scale reform comparable to the advent of the welfare state a century ago. That is the generational challenge faced by those who care about collectively governing towards desirable futures.

Desirable Futures

The beginning of this new century has been marked by global upheaval and contention, but also by new solidarities and visions for democratic life. History does seldom repeat itself, but certain patterns do. The subversion of power inequalities represents one of the greatest historical drivers of change.

Change sometimes is only possible in testing times. As Roberto Unger puts it, our societies have become addicted to change through crisis. We need to build a system that can change in ordinary times and break the pattern of change through shock. Those who suffer the most in such transitions tend to be those who most need the change.

If policies and decisions fall short from meeting the challenges of our time, let's not assume that other decisions and policies will do. Instead, let's change institutions and decision-making processes so that they are more inclusive, diverse, informed and effective. Otherwise, power inequalities will keep (re)producing entrenched inequalities in health, wealth, education and income. Institutional reform may sound boring, but it contains the seeds of desirable futures.

We must reform politics so that it's not just about party politics; and we must expand democracy so that it's more than electoral democracy. We must also shift from economies of scale and accumulation to economies of scope and imagination, while democratising workplaces and economies.

We are currently undergoing a period of both challenge and renewal on a global scale. In this context, Scotland has the potential to become a strong democratic polity. There are foundations laid across the country, albeit many are under siege. A switch in this direction is not contingent upon independence or the union – the case for democratic innovation and the social commons remains urgent regardless. The challenge of governing democratically in the next few decades requires an enlarged, deeper form of democratic life.

References

Dalton, RJ, 2017, *The Participation Gap: Social Status and Political Inequality*, Oxford, Oxford University Press.

Elstub, S and Escobar, O (eds), 2019b, *The Handbook of Democratic Innovation and Governance*, Cheltenham, Edward Elgar.

Escobar, O, 2020, 'Transforming Lives, Communities and Systems? Co-production Through Participatory Budgeting', in Loeffler, E and Bovaird, T (eds), *Handbook of Co-Production of Public Services and Outcomes*, London, Palgrave.

Escobar, O and Elstub, S, 2017, 'Forms of Mini-Publics: An Introduction to Deliberative Innovations in Democratic Practice', Research and Development Note 4, *newDemocracy Foundation*, accessed at: www.newdemocracy.com.au/2017/05/08/forms-of-mini-publics/

Escobar, O and Elstub, S, 2019a, 'The Field of Democratic Innovation', in Elstub, S and Escobar, O (eds), *The Handbook of Democratic Innovation and Governance*, Cheltenham, Edward Elgar.

Escobar, O, Garven, F, Harkins, C, Glazik, K, Cameron, S and Stoddart, A, 2018, 'Participatory Budgeting in Scotland: The Interplay of Public Service Reform, Community Empowerment and Social Justice', in Dias, N (ed.), *Hope for Democracy: 30 Years of Participatory Budgeting Worldwide*, Portugal, Epopeia Records and Oficina.

Foa, RS, Klassen, A, Slade, M, Rand, A and Williams, R, 2020, *Global Satisfaction with Democracy*, Bennett Institute for Public Policy, Cambridge, University of Cambridge.

Henderson, J and Escobar, O, 2019, *Supporting Smart Urban Intermediation*, Scottish Policy Brief Supplement, Edinburgh, University of Edinburgh.

Henderson, J, Escobar, O and Revell, P, 2020a, 'Public value governance meets social commons: community anchor organisations as catalysts for public service reform and social change?', *Local Government Studies*, 1–23.

Henderson, J, Revell, P and Escobar, O, 2018, *Transforming Communities? Exploring the Roles of Community Anchor Organisations in Engaging With, Leading and Challenging Public Service Reform*, Glasgow, What Works Scotland.

Henderson, J, Revell, P and Escobar, O, 2020b, *Building the Community Economy in Scotland*, Glasgow, What Works Scotland and Policy Scotland.

O'Hagan, A, Hill-O'Connor, C, Macrae, C and Teedon, P, 2019, *Evaluation of Participatory Budgeting Activity in Scotland 2016-2018*, Edinburgh, Scottish Government Social Research.

SURF (2020), *COVID-19: Lessons From the Frontline*, Scottish Urban Regeneration Forum.

The Economist Intelligence Unit, 2016, *Democracy Index 2016. Revenge of the 'Deplorables'*, London, The Economist.

The Economist Intelligence Unit, 2018, *Democracy Index 2018: Me Too? Political Participation, Protest and Democracy*, London, The Economist.

Trebeck, K and Williams, J, 2019, *The Economics of Arrival: Ideas for a Grown-Up Economy*, Bristol, Policy Press.

What Works Scotland, 2017, *Mini-publics: examples and resources*, accessed at: www.whatworksscotland.ac.uk/topics/mini-publics/

CHAPTER 17

Lessons in Civics: What Do We Do About the Rise and Fall of Civil Society in Scotland?

Gerry Hassan

LAST YEAR IN the US in the town of Williamstown, Massachusetts, I got into a conversation with a complete stranger who followed politics avidly. I naturally asked him about the outcome of the 2020 presidential election, to which he responded that even more important than defeating Trump was the vibrancy and health of civil society. It struck me as a perceptive remark in seeing past the debris of the Trump Presidency and looking at something deeper, more long-term and centred on the health of the republic and public engagement.

This insight got me thinking then and there about the health of civil society in Scotland – something that I have ruminated on since; even more so as we have witnessed the tragedy of the COVID-19, with thousands of citizens dying and falling ill, and the stress and tension points inflicted on so many people, services and society.

What is Civil Society and Why Does It Matter?

First, what is this thing called civil society which sounds on the surface so attractive? Civil society has had many different interpretations but one broad one is that it is neither 'state' or 'market': in the words of Craig Calhoun providing 'a social realm which in neither dominated by state power nor simply responsive to the systematic features of capitalism' (Calhoun, 1993). It has come to be associated with inter-mediate institutions which give meaning and sustenance to sociability, connectedness and being civil to each other – what the Indian intellectual Sudipta Kaviraj calls 'collective projects against the state'; the state that claims to act in your name (2001).

Second, the origins of the term can be found in the Scottish Enlightenment, articulated by Adam Ferguson in his *An Essay on the History of Civil Society* first published in 1767. It subsequently disappeared from use for a long time until re-emerging in the 1970s in a host of left-wing circles across the West, drawing from the ideas and writings of the Italian revolutionary Antonio Gramsci.

Then in the 1980s it gained new impetus in debates around the slow implosion of the Soviet bloc and in places such as Poland and East Germany where opposition leaders in their respective regimes tried to make sense of facing dictatorships that were in terminal decline. And at the same time, and in a much less dramatic way, Scotland turned to the term to give rigour to the debate around autonomy and home rule.

Scottish civil society is one of the distinctive strands that contributes to who we are collectively as a society and nation, and underpins our experiences and everyday lives. In 1707 large parts of Scotland were left to be run by elites and professional authorities, contributing to the maintenance of a semi-autonomous civil society which was to a degree self-governing and self-administering.

Tom Nairn, writing originally in 1975 in *The Red Paper on Scotland*, put this in typically Nairnesque style. The terms of 1707 were 'a peculiarly patrician bargain between two ruling classes' which resulted in a compact with regard to Scotland whereby

> a nationality which resigned statehood but preserved an extraordinary amount of the institutional and psychological baggage normally associated with independence: a decapitated national state, as it were, rather than an ordinary 'assimilated' nationality (Nairn, 1975).

The Rise of Civil Society in 1980s Scotland

Civil society has at times been over-romanticised and, connected to this, there has been a vagueness about what its membership and characteristics were. For example, historian Chris Harvie writing in the 1970s sketched the following definition of civil society in Scotland made up of 'the kirk, law, local government and education' (Harvie, 1977). This is a commonplace definition but one that is content to include elements of the state (local government) and what became state-run (education). And in this it taps a myopia that has long existed on the left and liberal opinion about the extent of government power and the reach of the state in Scotland which continues to this day.

The role of civil society became one of the distinctive stories of 1980s Scotland and the opposition to Thatcherism, seen in the language of 'civic Scotland' and the 'alphabet soup' of bodies such as the STUC, SCVO and SCDI – and in William McIlvanney's notion of Scotland as a 'mongrel nation' comfortable and proud of its diversity and different voices.

Fast-forward to pre-COVID-19 and we find civil society not exactly in the best of health, often forgotten about and not mentioned in most dispatches. What became the traditional institutions of civil society – trade unions, churches, older, paternalist charities and benevolent associations, and related to this the role of independent, print media – have experienced significant decline and retrenchment and now speak for smaller, older constituencies with less clout and legitimacy.

Added to this, one of the powerful strands of post-war civil society – the voluntary sector and NGOs – have increasingly become less distinguishable from the state and reliant on central, and to an extent local, government for funding. Big national NGOs have often ended up in the invidious trap of delivering key government policies on welfare, employment and health, and hence having their once cherished independence compromised.

Pre-pandemic, a civil society – weakened by the lack of powerful intermediate institutions between state and citizens, and the hollowing out of alternative centres of power to the state and corporate power – has significant negative consequences which affects all of us.

This decline has had a concomitant impact on political and civic debate and discussion. For example, the retreat of trade unions, churches and even local government (which is part of the state) have decreased the settings where political talent and experience used to be identified and nurtured. These were nurseries of politically learning on the job how to be leaders, shapers and initiators – on public speaking, influencing, organising, creating effective change, delivering services and building alliances with colleagues and defeating opponents.

If one looks at the 20 years of the Scottish Parliament, two of Labour's three First Ministers ran local authorities – Henry McLeish (Fife) and Jack McConnell (Stirling) – whereas today not one Cabinet minister pre-MSP made their name and reputation having done so; Keith Brown who left the Cabinet in 2018 being the last example (having been leader of Clackmannanshire council). The same is even more true of senior members of the Tories, Labour, Lib Dems and Greens.

If you think this does not really matter, local government in the 1980s became a place of political innovation and experimentation, of new, younger voices emerging through the involvement of more women and communities who had previously not been heard, leading to a host of emergent policy areas including LGBT issues, gender equality and anti-racism that Scotland had previously avoided. And it was a place which developed rich supportive relationships with civil society organisations to the general betterment; no more is that really true.

What Do We Do After the Fall of Civil Society?

This leaves us with big challenges about who enters public life, what kind of debates are held and what even qualifies as debatable, the extent of pluralism and competing views, and how power is held to account – whether political, economic, civic or cultural. Scotland has not historically been very good at power and accountability – pre-devolution there was an absence of political power here; but something more was at work about a self-denying ordinance of asking too penetrating questions which peered behind the veil.

Take a couple of examples. Between the time that the Scottish Arts Council was established in 1967 and the 1997 referendum, on not one occasion was it called to appear before a parliamentary committee to give evidence; the first time this occurred was December 1997. Then there was the implosion of what was Scotland's biggest football club, Rangers FC, in 2012, with the football authorities, media and politicians asleep at the wheel, and the authorities desperate to prevent any systematic review and instead wanting to return as quickly as possible to 'business as usual' and 'normalcy'. Now where have we heard that recently?

There have been positives in emergent social organisations. Football fans self-organised against the usual stitch-up with regard to Rangers and forced them post-liquidation to begin again in the fourth league tier. Similarly, in the summer of 2020, pupil power forced the Scottish Government to retract the decision of the Scottish Qualifications Authority who, in relying on assessments in place of exams, had systematically disadvantaged working-class children.

These are welcome victories but what they show is the power of episodic self-organisation in times of major crisis where the system can on occasion concede. This doesn't replace the need for sustainable long-term organisations which can demand to be treated as equal parties. These new forms of fluid participation and liquid democracy have yet to find forms and ways of organising, mobilising and financing which can make them permanent features on the landscape. And that leaves us with a major imbalance.

Adding COVID-19 to this mix merely accelerates the existing order before with the Parliament acting increasingly as the locus of national political power, while corporate capitalism moves inexorably towards monopoly capitalism here and globally with grotesque concentrations of power, alongside a set of weak institutions in between.

This poses questions not just for politics but for public life and society. It forces the unpalatable thought that maybe the over-told over-romanticised story of civil society was a little bit dewy-eyed in places and shorn of the limitations and inadequacies in public life. Yet even allowing for this, how do we deal with the present predicament of the state of civil society and look at how we can best uphold pluralism, hold power to account and facilitate wider engagement?

Where and when will the next generation of politicians and wider leaders emerge – who can hopefully draw from a richer tapestry of experience and skills? And how – with the retreat of trade unions, churches and incorporation of NGOs – do we avoid being governed by a political class with little experience of anything beyond talking politics, and who sit alongside a nomenklatura of administrators who represent the same insider language and interests?

Even more so, how in a Scotland where political power has become focused on the Parliament and there are few radical initiatives and voices, do we aid new platforms, spaces and places? The Scottish Government-backed Citizens' Assembly pre-COVID-19 has been a valuable, rich experiment but like many such interventions it cannot sit on its own and in order to aid change it has to sit in a rich ecology of other such projects, living and practising a culture of participation and changing society and the system in the process. A political environment reduced to the cautious centralism of the Scottish Government and a few isolated radical voices will always work in favour of the former and to the detriment of the latter.

Tom Nairn over the years has written much about the vice-like hold of Scotland's conservative culture and the ossified tendencies of too many in authority. But he also maintained a deep-seated faith that a post-independence civil society would spring to life and be reborn with energy and verve. What Nairn never ever did, even when questioned by myself, was explain how this reassertion of civil society purpose would arise; it was in a real sense an article of faith about the redemptive powers of independence which was not founded on hard-headed analysis.

The state of civil society is as momentous an issue as how we judge and do conventional politics, as who comes out top in the 2021 Scottish Parliament elections and the politics of a future indyref. The condition of civil society will play an enormous role in the choices we have in the 2021 elections, in any future indyref and in the future. This might be heresy to some but, to return to the insight of my American acquaintance, the vibrancy of this part of Scotland and what it represents might be of more importance than who wins in 2021 or gets over the line in a future indyref because it will determine how real are the choices and consequences of those and other contests.

We should really start considering how we can nurture public life, pluralism and holding power to account more effectively. How can we start thinking about public life – which isn't just about state and market? And how do we do justice to those campaigners and protesters who gave succour to the idea of Scotland as William McIlvanney's 'mongrel nation'?

We have lived through many changes in Scotland and the UK in the last 40 years. One is the rise and fall of civil society, that should lead us to ask how do we really want to organise and live in the world between the state and market? How can we avoid a Scotland of monopolies and machine politics, of robber baron capitalism and identikit politicians?

In the course of those past four decades we have lived through the weakening of that ossified culture that Tom Nairn described, and the passing of what seemed to some of us as we grew up a society of male elders – whether of the church or non-church kind – who felt they knew best and that the rest of us should know our place and be thankful for their benevolence.

Their passing gave us what now appears a brief window and opening which has now mostly closed. Such a retrenchment is a story of power and elites acting in their own self-interest, but if this is to be defeated we have to ask: who speaks and even cares for civil society? And it goes to the core of what Scotland is – beyond being a 'nation' and distinctive society: namely a set of ideas which are made and remade by being a communicative, social and political space of competing actors and agencies (Hassan, 2014).

One cause for hope (as well as concern) is the chasm between the 'official Scotland' of the Scottish Government, local authorities and national public bodies and the society of voluntarism, activism and self-help – the everyday, lived experience of self-government. The divide between these two Scotlands has been obvious for decades: pre-devolution, with the Scottish Parliament, in the indyref debate of 2014 and now dramatically accelerated under COVID-19.

What has been alarming in recent years has been how the politics of centralisation and top-down in Scotland seem to have little understanding or interest in this 'third Scotland' and because of this have not adequately supported such community and grassroots initiatives. This has become, under the pressures of this pandemic, an even more critical issue, and when we eventually emerge from this crisis we need to have a different kind of take on the limits of the centre, local democracy – and the role and make-up of what constitutes civil society beyond polite, respectable middle-class opinion.

A very different and pluralist vision of self-government is tantalisingly on offer in this: one which is not fixated on a parliament and politicians but on a rich mosaic of communities and people making decisions on issues that matter locally – and which has the potential to change how we see and govern Scotland for the better.

References

Calhoun, C, 1993, *Habermas and the Public Sphere*, Massachussets, US, MIT Press.

Harvie, C, 1977, *Scotland and Nationalism: Scottish Society and Politics, 1707–1977*, Crows Nest, Australia, George Allen and Unwin.

Hassan, G, 2014, *Independence of the Scottish Mind: Elite Narratives, Public Spaces and the Making of a Modern Nation*, London, Palgrave Macmillan.

Kaviraj, S, 2001, 'In Search of Civil Society', in Kaviraj, S and Khilnani, S (eds), *Civil Society: History and Possibilities*, Cambridge, Cambridge University Press, 287–323.

Nairn, T, 1975, 'Old Nationalism and New Nationalism', in Brown,

G (ed.), *The Red Paper on Scotland*, Edinburgh, Edinburgh University Student Publications Board, 22–57.

CHAPTER 18

How Parks Got Our Attention
Willie Sullivan

LIKE MOST PEOPLE I have spent a lot of time in local greenspaces over the COVID-19 period. I visited Victoria Park in Glasgow most days for a period of weeks, having only been there half a dozen times before that despite living only a few hundred metres from it. Now I have returned to work and can travel much further. I still try to go there every few days.

Lockdown happened as winter changed to spring. The parks came to life, different flowers and leaves appeared almost daily. Too often almost everyone seemed like a suspicious stranger, but the textures and colours of new foliage soothed our avoidance of each other.

I have grown to appreciate this park in a way I never knew was possible. This surprised me. My first job after leaving school at 16 was as an Apprentice Gardener in Dunfermline's beautiful Pittencrieff Park, known around those parts as 'The Glen'. I went on to be a Landscape Officer in the local council before switching careers. I knew but forgot the importance of these places. Now, I seem to have rediscovered that value and more. The period of COVID-19 has allowed whole communities to do the same, and this is something important from this time that we need to hold on to.

In August 2020 an *Observer* journalist spoke to parks managers across the UK, who highlighted what we know of the massive increase in the use of parks (Shabi, 2020). The place to take your daily walk and then as lockdown eased, of where to hold often too big parties and of overwhelming levels of littering. But also places of a newfound connection and of ownership, as local people took it on themselves to tidy up with their own litter-pickers, alongside an upturn in public reporting of required repairs and maintenance. This demonstrates simply that people caring much more about parks – and about more besides.

Why Public Parks?

Victoria Park as the name suggests was made by the Victorians, acquired by the Burgh of Partick and opened by the Provost of Glasgow in 1887. This is the period when most of the great British Parks were created. They were thought necessary to relieve workers from the cacophony, toxic air and molten heat of workplaces like steel mills and shipyards and to draw them away from less helpful forms of release such as alcohol or political rioting. It was a motivational cross-over of Christian charity, capitalist control and, one hopes, some part kindness.

It is probably not a revelation to lots of people that going to green spaces makes you feel better. And maybe it is not surprising that having been confined to my flat for most of the time getting to the local park was such a source of joy for me. Judging by my own experience and comments on Facebook and Instagram I was surprised by the level of happiness and comfort these places gave us at a time of high anxiety, when we were starved of so many other sources of human sustenance. Physical community, touch of loved ones and at least a fair chance that we knew what was coming next. Parks seemed to compensate a bit for these deprivations or at least make them more bearable.

I'm sure people with gardens appreciated them in a similar way but for me there is something additional about a 'public' park, a green place provided by us and for us. They hold many of the elements of private gardens, wild places and countryside – particularly the shared greenness, trees, flowers and the ecosystem of plants and animals. Like private gardens, and as parts of cities, they are also made by design and planning. Landscape and parks design as a discipline has a history at least as long as architecture and town planning.

For weeks I had to go to the park alone, but it was always clear to me that it is a people's space. Myself, the guy downstairs that works up in Clydebank docks; the people that do Tai Chi there; those checking their run on Strava or more recently families having a barbecue, we all own Victoria Park. I don't need to understand the details of collective provision allowed by the existence of Glasgow City Council Parks Department. By instinct we knew, every one of us, that this is our park, together.

Despite us not 'all being in this together' in the way Dominic Cummings wanted us to believe, lots of us longed to be there for each other, especially at times like the start of the lockdown. Forced apart, not sure if ourselves or our loved ones might get ill and die, wondering if society would breakdown like in the disaster movies, hopeful that the food supply chain would hold up. It might all feel a bit silly looking back now but I am sure even the most resilient of us had dark, doubtful moments.

How well a society is set up to deal with upheavals like COVID-19 seems be a lot about how much we feel we can depend upon each other and our public institutions. When that is not the case people go buy guns or toilet roll.

Parks are the places where nature becomes at least as important as the design and where its public provision is so clear. The balance of this trinity – nature, purpose and community – is what makes public parks so special and what became obvious during COVID-19 lockdown.

High Value Low Cost

Many past studies of public spaces have included parks in with other parts of the built environment, such as streets and markets. This is useful to show what these spaces share in value and methods of provision but downplays many of the special things about parks. The growing, living and changing quality of a park is different from the built environment and importantly we do not go there to buy things and particularly not in the spring of 2020.

Cheap to construct compared to other kinds of public provision, parks are also relatively cheap to look after. The cost of museums, sports centres, libraries or theatres are many times more costly. Parks seem hugely undervalued by many architects, town planners and city managers and up until now taken for granted by many citizens. Parks are designed, laid out and looked after by people but other forces are just as important. Plants and trees are shaped by their species, by their interrelationship and by the weather. Parks are both in and out of control. Humans and nature co-create them. An architect can't claim credit for the beauty of a tree, and this is another reason why they are not valued as highly as buildings.

An economic system that syphons value away from the local and deposits it high up in social and financial pyramids has left us confused about the value of parks. They are almost impossible to price in pounds. How to show them as an asset on a balance sheet, where do they fit into GDP, as potential real estate? Thinking about parks hits you with the blunt dumbness of allowing markets to tell us what everything is worth. Parks are free to enter yet seem priceless.

Almost entirely our taxes pay for municipal parks. When they were established it was a straight up case of public money given to Partick Burgh Council to run Victoria Park. Up until the 1980s few people thought it was a good idea to try and make profits from parks. Yet this public model of provision has now been severely undermined, with massive cuts to budgets, tries at outsourcing and creation of internal markets.

This has not proved easy, even for the most committed market makers, especially where there has been political and public resistance. Many aspects of these services have been privatised, low profit activity such as craft gardening and horticulture often devalued into contracts labelled 'grounds maintenance'. Particularly where local authorities were politically supportive of this approach. Party control was no guarantee of resistance. Conservative, New Labour and SNP have been equally seduced by the story of market efficiencies and private innovation.

As often happens in the operation of large council contracts, over-time there is a consolidation of firms into a smaller number of bigger public service companies. This results in local councils moving value to financial players and investors and naively aiding the flow of value out of the parks and local communities.

This same system may now look at ways of commodifying and selling these spaces. Concerts, festivals and events in parks can add value to them and ticket sales may be justified but this balance between private profit and public good is so often got wrong. The controversy over the use of Princes Street Gardens in Edinburgh for Christmas markets shows why people that love the parks, and there are many more of them now, need to be included in any decisions in how money is raised from them (Ward, 2020). Maybe we are happy enough now with a simpler no-frills experience of our parks.

Parks are both a point of resistance and perhaps 'just too difficult' in the trend to push the blood-sucking funnel of private profit ever deeper into the barely warm public body. The people's expectation of free public parks at once loved and yet still taken for granted, made it a difficult place to turn a profit. Their resilience and timescales are that of trees so it may be that it just takes a long time for the damage to be noticed or it may be that they have bent with the wind of neoliberalism only to stand up again once it has blown over.

A Golden Age of Public Parks

COVID-19 constraints lighten for now and I walk through the Arboretum in Victoria Park on a sunshine filled August evening. A light breeze vibrating the leaves of maples, beech and pines needles; now giants they were there as saplings when the Lord Provost of Glasgow opened the park nearly 150 years ago.

Old and new communities make old and new uses of the space between the trees. Barbecues smoking, the occasional whiff of weed, community picnics, kids playing in the play area, altletes doing bootcamp training, dog walkers and women in Hijabs feeding the ducks on the pond. The park is alive in a thousand ways. It is not an exaggeration to say I love this place and I don't think I am the only one. These are strong feelings; they are feelings for nature but they are also feeling for my community. A community I barely felt part of only a few months ago. Such strong feeling could be put to good use.

Glasgow and many parks departments across Scotland are a story of survival and success in the face of sustained adversity. They have resisted privatisation, struggled against austerity, and often been ignored because of the low tech, less than glamorous, slow and steady nature of their work.

It seems we never knew of this success. It takes something like COVID-19 to show it to us. Because of the practical and philosophical difficulty of commodifying and privatising parks they have largely maintained a model of public provision and public service that is simple and that works.

Yuval Harari wrote in the *Financial Times* in March 2020 that emergencies such as COVID-19 accelerate history (Harari, 2020). History will roll on. Pandemics and technology will continue to change our society. What direction it rolls has never had greater consequences. We can see that privatisation and profit seeking from public goods are something we should veer away from. Local jobs in local institutions taking care of local assets are part of why our parks are good and why ideas such as 'Community Wealth Building' and the Preston Model of local municipalism show the way to go as a means to circulate wealth around in local economies allowing for costs like the provision and development of parks to be comfortably met (Preston City Council, 2019).

We can see from turnouts at local elections that voting is not the best or only way to involve people in how we plan and run the public places for our citizens. Our own work at Electoral Reform Society along with Coalfield Regeneration Trust show that, given the structures and the opportunities afforded to people by citizens' assembles, people are very able and more than happy to develop plans for how parks can be developed and protected for future generations (Electoral Reform Society Scotland, 2019).

Public parks have flourished in often difficult political and cultural weather for over 150 years but it took an emergency like COVID-19 to bring our love for them to the surface. Hariri again reminded us that as a historian his focus of study is not merely the past but of change. Human society has some big changes to make. Not only the pandemic and that's big enough but adapting to and reducing climate change and managing technologies such as Artificial Intelligence combining ever more closely with our own instincts and human behaviours.

If we live in towns and cities, it is a basic need for a good life that we have public parks in which we can wonder and wander, meet up and play with others – or just know that together we allow these places to exist. In a time of endless complexity this is beautifully simple. Parks are not something that a corporation could or would provide, rediscovering our parks told us deep inside that humans create some wonderful things when we work with and for each other and nature. This is more real and long-lasting than clapping for the NHS. It gives us the opportunity to make sure parks are at least as good and hopefully better in another 150 years. Trees take a long time to grow.

References

Electoral Reform Society Scotland, 2019, *Reclaiming our Coalfield Communities: Deliberating Local Democracy*, Electoral Society Scotland.

Harari, YN, 19 March 2020, 'The World After Coronavirus', *Financial Times*, accessed at: www.ft.com/content/19d90308-6858-11ea-a3c9-1fe6fedcca75

Preston City Council, 2019, *Community Wealth Building*, accessed at: www.preston.gov.uk/communitywealthbuilding

Shabi, R, 9 August 2020, 'Sanctuary in the City: How Urban Parks Saved Our Summer', *The Observer Online*, accessed at: www.pressreader.com/uk/the-observer-magazine/20200809/282084869145040

Ward, S, 11 January 2020, 'Fury after Edinburgh Xmas Market Turns Princes Street Garden into Mud Bath', *Daily Record*, accessed at: www.pressreader.com/uk/daily-record/20200111/282076278808767

Section Four – Relational Scotland
Care, Life and Wellbeing

CHAPTER 19

The New Old Age
Hugh McMillan

I am looking at the contents
of my coat pocket:
a train ticket, a pencil
plucked from the playground,
a receipt for a steak pie

and large glass
of Sauvignon blanc,
and I think I should put
these on a shelf as symbols
of a lost and easy age

of innocence.
It is enough almost
to make you weep
this sacred detritus,
rubbish pregnant now

with such meaning.
When we emerge
blinking into the future
with our long hair,
our chipped teeth,

our bandaged specs,
will those months
of self-help, yoga,
soda bread and scrabble
swell our brains

to the size of a new world?
Will poetry have seen us through?
I think, jealous
of their high-fiving freedom
through our long days

of want and envy,
we will swarm out to find a rook
to strangle while nature
scatters with a collective sigh
of here's this lot on the piss again.

CHAPTER 20

Towards a Caring Economy
Angela O'Hagan

FROM MARCH TO MAY 2020 the public and politicians stood on their doorsteps on Thursday evenings at 8.00pm to 'clap for carers'. While people gathered to honour and show their appreciation for health workers and then carers across our social care system, those same workers were struggling to access proper PPE and elderly people were being discharged into residential care homes without being tested for COVID-19. While the 'battle' against the virus continued, the 'heroes' of the NHS 'fought' to save life amidst political slogans and public health messages.

In the strangled military language that dominated reporting and commentary as the pandemic peaked, the 'collateral damage' was revealed to be black and minority ethnic workers and other disadvantaged members of the community, mainly older people and low-income workers. Among those dying from the virus and its complications, and among those working to protect and provide for the general population, significant inequalities were immediately revealed. This chapter considers some of those inequalities of experience, with a particular focus on the gendered dimensions of paid and unpaid care.

The experience of COVID-19 at the individual, household, community and country level has revealed and reaffirmed our social and economic reliance on care. We have all, to different degrees, been engaged in providing and receiving care while many among us, especially disabled people, have been overlooked and left on the margins.

Public policy and public attitudes have not been formulated around a practice of having care as a starting point or understanding that care forms the core structure of our social and economic life. Despite our complete reliance on the provision of care – as parents, kinship carers, unpaid carers for family and friends and accessing health and social care through our public services across our life courses – care has continually been undervalued economically and socially. Until now. As policy-makers, politicians, commentators, as well as everyone else, seek to carve a pathway through a new COVID-19 reality, we have an opportunity and a responsibility to shift our collective commitment to valuing care and supporting investment in care as integral to our social and economic wellbeing.

Care, inequality and COVID-19

The undervaluing of care and its over-provision by women are not new, and have been the focus of feminist economics analysis for many decades. They are of course entirely interlinked. Care is undervalued *because* it has been considered the domain of women – of women's work in the domestic and, increasingly in, the public sphere. The gendered dimensions that structure social behaviours have in turn shaped economic thinking. This has resulted in the significant contribution that care makes to economic activity and to shoring up the productive economy being ignored and instead perceived as a cost to public finance and a drag on economic participation. This perception of care constitutes core elements of the gender pay gap, including the labour market segregation that concentrates women across jobs and sectors in the care economy.

Gendered patterns of care provision were well established before the pandemic shook their foundations. According to Engender, 'between 59 per cent and 70 per cent of unpaid care is delivered by women in Scotland, worth approximately £10.8 billion to the economy per annum, and women are twice as likely to give up work to carry out unpaid care' (2020a). Women, on average, carry out 60 per cent more unpaid work than men (ONS, 2016) a reality which was exacerbated during lockdown with women taking on additional childcare and housework as schools and nurseries closed (IFS, 2020).

While more men have died from COVID-19, there were more confirmed cases among women, as women's overrepresentation as unpaid carers and in health and social care jobs put them at higher risk. The imbalance in caring responsibilities can also make it harder to take on or maintain paid employment. For example, the majority of lone parents are women (92 per cent), with three-quarters of lone parent households already financially vulnerable in 2016–18 (73 per cent), and more likely than average to be in unmanageable debt.

During the pandemic women were in the majority of designated keyworker jobs in health and social care, cleaning and the majority employed in many 'shut down' sectors, such as retail (60 per cent), accommodation (58 per cent) and food and beverage service activities (53 per cent). In addition, Close the Gap reminded us of the persistence of the gender pay gap, and that 'all sectors designated high risk have a gender pay gap. In some cases, the gender pay gap is significantly higher than the national figure of 13.3 per cent, 11 including health and social care (27.8 per cent), manufacturing (18 per cent) and retail and wholesale (16 per cent)' (2020).

In its graphic depiction of 'spirals of inequality' the Commission for a Gender Equal Economy highlighted how the crises of gender inequality and COVID-19 collided, combining established patterns of gendered inequality that had created conditions for the gendered economic and social impacts of the pandemic. These conditions include the consequences of 'austerity' such as the underfunding of social care, the withdrawal of services and funding from local authorities across the UK and the massive reduction in household income – as social security benefits have been cut to fund tax giveaways by the Westminster government (2020).

The global pandemic exposed the underlying inequalities and structural inadequacies that exist at individual, household, sectoral and country levels in Scotland as well as many other countries. Political choices to reduce public spending and dismantle public infrastructure have weakened public services, leaving supply chains and workforces ill-prepared for responding to the scale needed. Underlying the frantic response to COVID-19 were the everyday inequalities and realities of poverty, poor housing, violence against women and girls and hunger. As reported in *The Guardian* in March 2020, over 1.5 million people in the UK were already missing at least one meal every day before lockdown, and economic collapse precipitated the escalation of access to food banks and prevalence of hunger in Scotland and the UK (Lawrence, 2020). These

> pre-existing social and economic inequalities in the midst of 'plenty' should shame the countries and societies where political choices – by voters and politicians – have permitted these 'lived effects' to be the daily realities of millions (O'Hagan, 2020a; 2020b).

Among those most affected have been disabled people, already marginalised from public services and paid employment, with social security income lost to government cuts. Black and minority ethnic people have been dying in greater numbers, exposed to higher risks in low paid jobs in key worker occupations, alongside higher paid but still vulnerable healthcare professionals.

Evidence from multiple sources, including Inclusion Scotland and Glasgow Disability Alliance (GDA), demonstrated both the distance from decision-making and participation that disabled people and households continue to experience and the limitations of local services. GDA described the pandemic and lockdown measures as having 'supercharged' the inequalities experienced by disabled people, as their members expressed worry and anxiety about accessing food, medicine and money (GDA, 2020). Pressures on community-level social care, community pharmacies, access to food and personal care all reveal structural weaknesses that need to be addressed, in relation to resources and organisational structures and relations.

In a highly personal account, disability rights advocate and former senior social worker Dr Jim Elder-Woodward recounted his experience of service withdrawal and the inadequacies of the current funding and management of adult social care in Scotland. He concluded that the principal lesson for public care service funding and management is that:

> Disabled people and their directly accountable organisations must be not just at the centre, but at the heart and mind of any economic, social and civic decision-making within society...If not, I fear we will be squeezed even farther to the edge of society. They're there to be terrorised even further by the tyranny of the non-disabled majority (Elder-Woodward, 2020).

As we resurface from the emergency of the first experiences of COVID-19, amidst the calls for building back better to a new normal, constant and sustained voices are calling for participation of disabled people, people of colour, people on low incomes and those otherwise marginalised from decision-making in shaping the future of services and spending priorities. A consistent demand from civil society organisations has been for policy-makers not to make assumptions, but to fund and use robust equalities data and evidence of the lived effects of inequality and discrimination, particularly as a politics of care is developed. This means that the promises of empowerment, participation and engagement whether from the Scottish Government, in the provisions of the Community Empowerment Act (2015), or in the emerging ways of working on community wealth building, or even the limited commitments to participation in budget decisions, have to be more than promises.

Care as Investment

From a feminist economics perspective, care has long-since been regarded as central not only to economic and social justice, but to a well-functioning economy. Our reliance on care whether through public services, private care homes or unpaid carers, and the provision of health care in hospitals or elsewhere, has underscored its personal value and our economic dependence.

In addition to overlooking the value of care economically and politically, while maintaining a sentimentality about care, the contribution of the care economy is also underplayed in general economic models and the description of an economy. Looking closely, the Scottish Government estimates the value of care economy in Scotland to be in the region of £3.4 billion, employing some 200,000 people (Scottish Government). Annie Gunnar Logan of Coalition of Care and Support Providers Scotland (CCPS) reminds us that the

> combined membership of CCPS employ around 45–46,000 people, the majority of whom will be care and support workers. They manage a total combined income of about 1.2 billion. So quite a big economic force in terms of economic activity and work force and they support, anything up to 200,000 people and families in Scotland' (Alliance, 2020).

Calls for investment in care as essential social and economic infrastructure are not new, and have characterised the work of feminist academics such as the WISE Centre for Economic Justice (WISE), and civil society organisations such as the UK and Scottish Women's Budget Groups, Engender and Close the Gap in Scotland, alongside social care advocacy organisations including the Alliance for Health and Social Care. Consistent arguments have been made for investing public money in adult social care and childcare as essential to economic development policy as a means of generating sustained employment in care, as well as allowing parents and carers in paid employment to access jobs or increase their hours, generating a series of multiplier effects, including increased tax revenue.

Investment in care has consistently been demonstrated to generate significant economic return, exceeding investment in other sectors. Research by Susan Himmelweit and Jerome de Henau, among others, across OECD countries with different economic structures and contexts has repeatedly found that the economic benefits of investing in care as public infrastructure surpass investment in other sectors. They confirm that 'investment in care continues to outperform investment in construction in total employment creation by at least 60 per cent in all European countries' (2020). In the current context of economic recovery and renewal, they emphasise that:

> Economic recovery from COVID-19 will require stimulus through public expenditure… a greater employment stimulus could be made in any recovery plan by investing in care than in construction, the conventional object of stimulus programs… investment in it still produces more jobs overall. Investment in care also yields far more employment for women… The gender employment gap would fall, whereas investment in construction would increase it, while creating very few jobs for women (2020).

Care, and the need for investment in care, as central to our economic and social infrastructure was the principal focus of the WISE submission to the Advisory Group on Economic Recovery (AGER), convened by the Scottish Government, and drawing heavily on the evidence from Himmelweit, de Henau et al. WISE highlighted the significant economic contribution that investing in social care infrastructure delivers, joining the research with the calls for investment in care from civil society organisations in Scotland and the 'Nine Principles for Economic Recovery' (Engender, 2020b). These principles framed demands for investment in care as consistent with the Scottish Government pursuit of 'inclusive growth', emphasising the essential nature of care, the economic returns and the need to remedy undervaluing of paid work in care, and the role of unpaid carers.

The report from the AGER, led by the commercial banker Benny

Higgins, was disappointing in its treatment of care, most notably because of the failure to join warm words on the acknowledged reliance on care to firm commitments on investment supported by mechanisms such as the Scottish National Investment Bank that can be drawn upon by other key sectors (Scottish Government, 2020a).

The Higgins' report met considerable criticism from a range of advocates for alternative economic policy, including feminist and care advocates and advocates for a wellbeing economy. While Higgins resorted to insult, the Scottish Government have responded with greater clarity on their intentions to invest in care and remedy poor working conditions and wages in the sector in their detailed responses to the AGER (Horne, 2020; Scottish Government, 2020b).

Towards a Caring Economy for Scotland

A caring economy is not such a far-flung idea and is the central focus of the Commission for a Gender Equal Economy. If the vision of a wellbeing economy is to be realised in Scotland, and the fairer and more inclusive society that is the aspiration of SNP governments is to be secured, then investment in care as a key economic sector is imperative. The frameworks are already in place. In 2019, the Scottish Government's vision for Social Care Support and the reform of adult social care was framed as 'An investment in Scotland's people, society, and economy', confirming the 'way we value and understand social care support – social care support is an investment in Scotland's people, society, and economy' (Scottish Government, 2019).

In its response to the AGER, the Scottish Government has reaffirmed its commitment to this principle, stressing that: 'Investment in care as infrastructure yields significant economic return and must be valued as a key part of our economy'. Furthermore, it commits to exploring 'how social care support is understood and valued, how it is funded and paid for, and what models of care we need in Scotland and how they are delivered'. The social care sector is also calling for a review of funding and the models of management and delivery, including commissioning processes and the central involvement of service users in shaping services and how funds are managed.

The necessary challenge now for the Scottish Government and its delivery partners is to join the narrative with political and public spend commitment. The conceptual framing of the National Performance

Framework, the regulatory structures of the national care standards and the commitment to human rights are embedded in political rhetoric and public policy, and public management. Recent work on human rights budgeting (Scottish Human Rights Commission, 2019) provides guidance and structure to augmenting long-standing commitments and direction to integrate equalities analysis in the Scottish budget process and spending decisions. These combine to provide the elements of a structure for quality care with uniformity of dignity, and fit with the 'provocations' from the Alliance (2017).

These principles, produced through a collaborative and deliberative process to frame health and social care reform, focus on integrating a human rights approach, by moving away from the 'fix-it' model delivering on targets, and engaging in the organisational reform that cedes institutional power and engages in the humanity of care. In its response to AGER, WISE echoed this same approach, advocating that

> as part of a care-led economic renewal, the development and investment in universal care services will require a revisiting and re-visioning of the institutional structures to deliver and sustain social care provision (O'Hagan, 2020b).

In Scotland after the virus, we need to move from slogans to meaningful and sustained commitment and to act on and not clothe policy in the language of wellbeing but to turn that phrase around to become the principal frame for public policy.

References

Alliance, 2020, 'ALLIANCE Live podcast with Annie Gunner Logan', accessed at: www.alliance-scotland.org.uk/blog/resources/alliance-live-podcast-with-annie-gunnar-logan-transcript/

Alliance, 2017, 'Five Provocations for the Future of Health and Social Care', accessed at: www.alliance-scotland.org.uk/people-and-networks/wp-content/uploads/2017/10/Five-Provocations.pdf

Close the Gap, 2020, 'Disproportionate disruption: The impact of COVID-19 on women's labour market equality', Briefing 4, accessed at: www.closethegap.org.uk/content/resources/Disproportionate-Disruption---The-impact-of-COVID-19-on-womens-labour-market-equality.pdf

Commission for a Gender Equal Economy, 2020, 'Spirals of inequality', UK Women's Budget Group, accessed at: wbg.org.uk/analysis/spirals-of-inequality/

Elder-Woodward, J, 2020, 'Personal experiences of managing an Option 1 support package', accessed at: www.iriss.org.uk/news/features/2020/07/08/personal-experiences-managing-option-1-support-package

Engender, 2020a, 'Women and Covid', accessed at www.engender.org.uk/content/publications/Engender-Briefing---Women-and-COVID-19.pdf

Engender, 2020b, 'Gender and Economic Recovery', accessed at: www.engender.org.uk/content/publications/Gender--Economic-Recovery---Engender-and-Close-the-Gap.pdf

Glasgow Disability Alliance, 2020, 'GDA's Covid-Resilience Engagement and Response. Interim Report', accessed at: www.gda.scot//content/publications/GDAs-Covid-Resilience-Interim-report-27April_alt-text.pdf

Himmelweit, S and de Henau, J, 2020, 'Stimulating OECD economies post-COVID by investing in care', IKD Working Paper No. 85, accessed at: www.open.ac.uk/ikd/sites/www.open.ac.uk.ikd/files/files/working-papers/COVID%20care-led%20recovery_IKD_WP85_2020_06_12%20%28003%29.pdf

Horne, M, 5 August 2020, 'Coronavirus in Scotland: Green 'zealots' risk wrecking recovery, top economic adviser warns', *The Times*, accessed at: www.thetimes.co.uk/article/coronavirus-in-scotland-green-zealots-risk-wrecking-recovery-top-economic-adviser-warns-lhd22m3ql

Institute for Fiscal Studies (IFS), 2020, 'COVID-19: the impacts of the pandemic on inequality', accessed at: www.ifs.org.uk/publications/14879

Lawrence, S, 28 March 2020, 'Families borrowing to buy food a week into UK lockdown', *The Guardian*, accessed at: www.theguardian.com/society/2020/mar/28/families-borrowing-buy-food-week-of-lockdown

Office of National Statistics (ONS), 2016, 'Women shoulder the responsibility of "unpaid work"', accessed at: bit.ly/2KBdnG9

O'Hagan, A, 2020a, '"A critical practice of thinking otherwise": Bacchi, gender and public policy analysis', *Feminismo/s*, vol.35, 13–15.

O'Hagan, A, 2020b, 'Without care "front and centre" of economic recovery, how can we create a robust, resilient, wellbeing economy?', WISE Centre for Economic Justice blog series, accessed at: www.caledonianblogs.net/wise/2020/06/26/without-care-front-and-centre-of-economic-recovery-how-can-we-create-a-robust-resilient-wellbeing-economy/

Scottish Government, 2019, 'Social Care Support: An investment in Scotland's people, society, and economy', accessed at: www.gov.scot/publications/social-care-support-investment-scotlands-people-society-economy-shared-vision-adult-social-care-support-including-support-carers-partnership-programme-support-local-reform-adult-social-care/

Scottish Government, 2020a, 'Towards a Robust, Resilient Wellbeing Economy for Scotland: Report of the Advisory Group on Economic Recovery', accessed at: www.gov.scot/publications/towards-robust-resilient-wellbeing-economy-scotland-report-advisory-group-economic-recovery/

Scottish Government, 2020b, 'Economic Recovery Implementation Plan: Scottish Government response to the Advisory Group on Economic Recovery', accessed at: www.gov.scot/publications/economic-recovery-implementation-plan-scottish-government-response-to-the-advisory-group-on-economic-recovery/

Scottish Human Rights Commission, 2019, Human Rights Budgeting, accessed at: www.scottishhumanrights.com/projects-and-programmes/human-rights-budget-work/

CHAPTER 21

Death in the Time of COVID-19
Dani Garavelli

ON THE DAY BEFORE her mother Margaret's cremation, Karen Murdoch arrived at the funeral home where her remains lay, clutching small bags of lavender. She knew she wouldn't be allowed to see her body – at peace, at last, after COVID-19 left her paper-skinned and coughing; or to carry her coffin. She knew the funeral service would be sparsely attended: just Murdoch's sister, brother, daughter and a few friends; that they would be unable to sit together or touch each other; and that after the committal, they would take their socially distanced leave of one another, and make their way to their separate homes.

So the lavender – an ancient symbol of serenity and grace, and Margaret's favourite flower – had assumed a symbolic significance. It was one of the few ways Murdoch could say goodbye: a small personal gesture at a time of enforced detachment.

She was already in her car, having dropped the bags off, when the funeral director ran from the building and knocked on her window. 'He said: "Why don't we tie these on together?" So we went back inside and we attached them with ribbon all around the willow casket. It was a nice thing to do, and so unexpected.'

Mourning rituals: they are part of what makes us human. Long before we had the language to express complex emotions such as loss, we were honouring our dead. The first undisputed evidence of ritual burial dates back 100,000 years to Qafzeh in Israel where bones stained with red ochre were found, the use of dye suggesting ceremony. But skeletons discovered in a pit in a cave in Atapuerca in Spain mean that it is possible that humans were being laid to rest in the Middle Pleistocene period – 350,000 years ago.

Different religions, different cultures have different rites. For Muslims there is Ghusl, the ritual washing of the body by family members, followed by Kafan, the wrapping of the body in a series of sheets or shroud. For Jews, there is shiva – a seven-day mourning period where friends normally gather to say prayers at the home of the bereaved. Nor has the secularisation of society diminished the desire for formality. Today, funerals are increasingly customised: wreaths in the shape of guitars, football teams forming guards of honour, motorcycle sidecars converted into hearses. But they all cater to the same hunger: for shape, spirituality, and 'closure'.

'Human beings crave certainty,' says Simon Stuart, a clinical psychologist working in adult mental health. 'We like to feel there is meaning, some kind of coherence to our existence, and the rituals we use to mark key points in that existence are very important. Death is a huge part of that. We want to celebrate, commemorate, to mark it in some way. Then, along comes COVID-19 and everything is blown out of the water.'

The pandemic transformed our relationship to death overnight. Suddenly, husbands, wives, children, parents, brothers, sisters, lovers of the very ill were told they could no longer spend their last precious days holding their hands.

When they were allowed to visit, in hospitals and care homes, it was because death was imminent; and they had to do so wearing PPE. Faces, once familiar, became alien. Touch – that profound form of human communication – was transformed from a source of comfort to a source of potential contagion.

Murdoch's mother Margaret, who had dementia, was in a care home which was locked down in early March. Visitors were banned. For eight weeks, Murdoch worried about her. Was she eating? Was she agitated? Margaret was one of many care home residents who contracted COVID-19. When it was clear she was close to the end, Murdoch was allowed in to see her one last time.

'She looked ravaged,' Murdoch says. 'I spent an hour with her, talking to her up close because you have to be. I was wearing a paper mask and an apron. At one point, she moved her hand up my arm and we had skin to skin contact. I was conscious this was not a good thing, but also that this was not what I should have been thinking about.'

Sarah Drummond's mother Heather Black, a prominent HIV campaigner in Edinburgh in the 1980s, did not succumb to COVID-19; she died of oesophageal cancer. Yet the virus infected every moment of her final weeks. Heather was an energetic, outgoing woman, happiest in the pub surrounded by her friends and family. When she received the diagnosis, she wanted to take her extended family away on one last foreign holiday, and to throw a living wake. Why miss out on the party, after all? Instead – from her diagnosis in March to her death in May – she was stuck at home.

She missed out on the chance to go into a hospice too. The offer was there – but the hospice's rules were two named visitors only, and she was not going to forego the company of one of her three daughters. So Sarah, Zoe and Tora cared for her at home, and it was a terrible experience. Scared, wracked with pain, and vomiting brown foam, Heather begged to be allowed to die. Her daughters try not to dwell too much on that time. 'F***, it was hard,' says Drummond. 'If we allow ourselves to think about it too much it would hurt even more.'

***

'To every thing there is a season, and a time to every purpose under heaven' – Ecclesiastes 3:1. Humanist celebrant Professor Maggie Kinloch is not religious, but she saw COVID-19 turn a time to dance into a time to mourn. 'Usually the period of the year from April through to about October is wedding season,' she says. 'We work our backsides off, travelling across the country helping lovely couples get married. But what happened [as the pandemic took hold] was that all those couples had to delay their weddings. There was a moment when we went "blimey," and then we realised it had to be like that because celebrants' diaries were filling up with funerals.'

Between the end of March and the beginning of July, Kinloch led 34 funeral ceremonies. Some of her fellow celebrants did more; up to seven a week. They witnessed great resilience and a willingness to adapt, but also great anguish.

'It was grief upon grief upon grief,' Kinloch says. 'There was the generalised grieving we were all doing for the life we couldn't have because of the coronavirus.

'But then, if a family was told "Your loved one has died of COVID-19" that was a terrible grief because bereavement is always awful, but there's something particularly awful about having died of this virus at this time. Then on top of that, they were being told "The funeral is going to be strange because your loved one was so well-known, and in normal circumstances there might have been 300 people there, but you can only have ten, and you can't all travel in a family car, and you can't carry the coffin. Oh, and you can't have people back for refreshments afterwards.'"

It was distressing for the celebrants too, not being able to offer physical gestures of emotional solidarity: a pat on the shoulder; a hug. 'Every instinct in our body says give people a cuddle, shake their hand, touch them on their arm, but of course we couldn't do that,' Kinloch says. The whole event was more clinical. 'We were wearing rubber gloves and having to make sure the lectern had been sanitised.'

Pre-pandemic, celebrants would spend a couple of hours at the home of the bereaved so, by the time of the ceremony, they had a real feel for the life being mourned. Now – like so much else in our lives – this was being carried out via FaceTime or Zoom. 'It was fine, but it meant we weren't meeting in the flesh until the day of the funeral and at a time of grief that feels odd because you want to be in the same space as the people you are looking after.'

Technology has been a boon. Most funerals conducted during lockdown were live streamed so relatives unable to attend in person could do so virtually, with mourners tuning in from across the world.

In Giffnock, Scotland's largest Jewish community, Ephraim Borowski, director of the Scottish Council of Jewish Communities, says the pandemic has brought people closer together; but it also made traditional rites like shiva more difficult.

Some Jewish mourning prayers cannot be said without a minyan (a quorum of ten) present. This might be manageable at the graveside where there is space for people to socially distance, but it is likely to be impossible in the front room of someone's home.

Then there is Yizkor, prayers for the dead recited in the synagogue four times a year, including Shavuot (Pentecost). This year Pentecost fell during the pandemic. On May 28 – the eve of the festival – I joined a Zoom Yizkor led by Rabbi Moshe Rubin from his kitchen. The service was followed by social chit-chat, then everyone said, 'Happy Shavuot' and went off to eat the traditional cheesecake in their own homes.

Borowski says technology has its benefits. When the actress Ida Schuster died in April, more than 100 people from all over the UK, the Netherlands and Israel tuned in to pay their respects.

But it also has its limits. People on webcams cannot hold you. Without a 'purvey', there is no opportunity to decompress; to share funny stories and intimate moments. Conscious of this, Kinloch has been asking those watching online to get in touch after the ceremony. 'I say, "If you had been here, you would have hugged them, you would have told them of your love. It would be good if you could communicate with them in the next few hours. Phone, email, text: let them feel you close to them."'

Mourners have found other ways to show respect, standing out on the streets to watch the hearse go by. It was the first thing families would tell Kinloch when she greeted them on the steps of the crematorium. 'They would say, "Oh, Maggie, there were about 100 people out when we left" and they would be so touched by that.'

Such displays of solidarity are beautiful; little shards of light cutting through the darkness, but are they enough to offset the distress of having our traditional grieving process disrupted?

'When we are under extreme stress our focus changes: we zoom in, we focus on that stress, on what we need to get done. And that's a useful adaptive position for humans to have,' says Stuart.

'But it is possible people who have experienced the tragedy of bereavement at this time may have tried to compartmentalise their grief – "I will put it over there and deal with it in due course." How is that going to work out?'

Kinloch fears there will be a legacy of PTSD in many of the families of people who have died during the pandemic.

'Almost everyone seemed traumatised,' she says. 'There was anger with a lot of people because they couldn't be with their loved one near the end, and they couldn't carry their coffin.

'When people have lost someone their emotions are already all over the place, they don't know what day it is. So add to that state they are in, the annoyance they can't do the things they usually do, or the confusion because things are different, and that's a high level of distress.'

Two months on, Murdoch says she is at peace with her mother's death, but acknowledges there is 'a potential black hole' around the eight weeks she was unable to visit her. She also feels guilty about not being able to offer her brother, who is mentally vulnerable, the physical comfort he craved. 'I am not allowing myself to think about that period,' she says. 'Perhaps I am shoving something under the rug that will appear in the future. Time will tell.'

However, in common with many other people I have spoken to,

Murdoch has plans for a more intimate family ritual after the worst of the pandemic is over.

All going well, she will travel to Tighnabruaich with her brother and sister and scatter her mother's ashes there. 'Mum went there as a child on holiday – it was where she was always at her happiest,' she says. 'And I spent my childhood summers there too in a tiny caravan – it's a safe and comforting place to be.'

When I speak to Drummond, she has just arrived back from a few days in a cabin in East Lothian with her sisters and their children. 'It was somewhere we had been several times before,' she says. 'Mum used to give it to the kids as a present. She wouldn't go herself – she liked her home comforts too much. But she would pack us all off and tell us to have fun. We went the first weekend it was open again, and we have had a lovely, healing time.'

We human beings are an adaptable species. Deprived of one set of rituals, we come up with alternatives. We are always seeking fresh ways to invest life's random cruelties with form and meaning.

This is something Jeremy Hamilton has thought about a lot. He designed Clyde Coast and Garnock Valley Crematorium – a light-filled, timber-clad building in Clyde Muirshiel Regional Park – as a direct result of attending a funeral so awful it compounded his sense of loss.

It was 2011. A family member had died in tragic circumstances. At the crematorium, ceremonies over-lapped, the car park was jam-packed, everyone was competing for space and there was condensation running down the walls. Later, in the grips of a breakdown, he became obsessed with these bad memories. With no experience in the funeral industry, he decided to build an alternative: a building that was the antithesis of the brutalist monstrosities he loathed, and where the needs of the families were paramount.

At the height of the pandemic, Clyde Coast crematorium was operating 12-hour days, six days a week. But Hamilton's dream had always been to provide a comforting, holistic experience, so the restrictions hit him hard. He offered a free webcast to anyone who wanted it, with the business bearing the cost. But was there anything more he could do?

Hamilton found the answer in a local social enterprise Eadha, which is Gaelic for aspen. The crematorium was already involved in tree-planting as part of its carbon offset programme. But, since early March, Eadha has planted a sapling for every person cremated at

Clyde Coast. The trees include aspen, birch, alder, willow, juniper and the rare Arran Whitebeam. 'We expect to plant 800–1,000 by the end of the year,' Hamilton says. Every family receives a certificate and a map showing where the saplings planted in a particular month are sited.

It's a touching thought: that something so enduring should be born of something so destructive; that one day, the trees planted in the time of COVID-19 will stand tall, their branches giving shelter to a post-pandemic world.

CHAPTER 22

A Fable for Today
Kapka Kassabova

What lingers most in my memory of Chernobyl is life afterwards: the possessions without owners, the landscapes without people. The roads going nowhere, the cables leading nowhere. It sometimes felt as if I were recording the future. SVETLANA ALEXIEVICH, *Chernobyl Prayer*

THERE WAS ONCE a glen in the Highlands of Scotland *where all life seemed to live in harmony with its surroundings.* The river, later to be named Beauly, from the French for 'beau lieu', sprang from three sources and joined up into the Strathglass, Gaelic for 'grey-green valley'. The valley whispered with oaks and Caledonian pines. Cattle drovers rode over the hills to the Great Glen, retracing the paths of early Christian missionaries. The forest floor was covered in blueberry bushes that turned dark purple in autumn. Wolves, golden eagles, red deer and wildcat roamed. Springs bubbled up from the hillside and waterfalls thundered in springtime. The springs had names and healing properties – St Ignatius, St Ninian, Morag, Mary – and stories were told of entities and encounters by the springs.

Then a strange blight crept over the area and everything began to change. It was the era of dam-building to bring 'power to the glens' whose remote parts were without electricity. Thousands of engineers and labourers came to live and work by the river, including former prisoners of war. A local laird opened up a gravel quarry on his estate, to supply the dams with material. New roads and infrastructure were built. The dams turned out an engineering marvel. True, a waterfall or two had to be sacrificed, and houses had to be flooded, but their owners were promised jobs on the dams and free 'power' in perpetuity. The hills where only the outlines of wild animals and chimney smoke touched the skyline were now studded with pylons and power lines. New lochs appeared, the river was altered.

Soon, every river of Western Europe would be impounded until the only wild rivers left on the continent would be in the Balkans. But it was the way of the future, it was just after the Second World War when life was kindled from the ashes of apocalypse. You couldn't argue with it. Just as you couldn't argue, earlier, with the felling of ancient forests for the empire's ship-building and, later, the coffins made to bury the generation of young men sacrificed in the last throes of Empire. The original mixed forests were replaced with a monoculture of pine. Earlier yet, crofting Gaeldom had been terminated by clearing the land of people and replacing it with a monoculture of heather moor and sheep. The moor was made for recreational deer hunting, and in time deer became a dominant monoculture. A pattern was emerging. Over time, people would become accustomed to seeing the body of the land shorn, mown, grazed, subjugated. They would even consider it beautiful, and they would no longer distinguish blueberries from poisonous fruit. A day would come when dog turds would be picked up for health and safety reasons, and placed in plastic bags then deposited in the forest or in the oceans, in perpetuity.

Decades passed, people didn't get the free power they were promised by the Electricity Board, but they did get used to the changed landscape. Golden eagles still roamed, if not wolves and wildcat, and salmon jumped in the river.

Then a strange blight crept over the area and everything began to change. Some evil spell had settled on the community. I saw it close-up from our house by the river. It was the era of green energy. There was a lot of money in it for large corporations and large land owners. A new mega-power line was built across the Highlands. The first pylon went up by the banks of the river. It was three times bigger than any pylon seen before. At 70 metres, the new pylons were the Eiffel Towers of the Highlands, and the construction company commissioned to build them promised that they would soon 'blend' with the landscape. New roads and infrastructure were built. The pylons, the profitable windfarms that came on their heels, the expanded substation the size of a town – it was a marvel of industry. True, ancient landscape had to be eviscerated, more trees were lost, birds were electrocuted, and many were forced to sell their houses and leave, while the remaining locals who now lived in the shadow of the pylons, the substation, the ghosts of the forest, didn't get any of the electricity because it was exported to the cities in the south, but green energy was the way of the future, you couldn't argue with it. You didn't want a return to nuclear power, did you?

True, the invasion of the pylons also brought the arrival of a construction company with almost a billion pounds revenue who bought the old small quarry started for the dams by the well-meaning lord, and began to expand. For this, they needed to fell more of the woodland, and remove ancient burial cairns. The forest was replaced with a hole until ground water was reached, then it was replanted with monoculture pine. No birds sang in the broom and gorse weedland that sprang up among the stunted pine. But we all needed gravel and sand, the construction company pointed out when we complained. We needed it for our houses, for our driveways, for the ever-expanding roads. We were all complicit in it, they pointed out, besides there had always been a quarry here.

Years passed, we got used to the changed landscape, the tinnitus caused by the electricity lines, the migrating pain in our bodies and hearts, the sight of pylon towers everywhere we looked, the thunder of diggers extracting the earth where the woodland once stood with its purple blueberry floor. Our walking path was now on the edge of the extraction pit: on one side was an abyss, on the other – the remaining wood of the river whose name means beautiful. The natural landscape looked dwarfed by the industrial landscape: the billion-pound corporations, the vehicles that came to fell the trees, the lorries to carry away the trees, the vehicles that came to extract the earth, the vehicles that carried away the earth, the roads that had to be expanded to accommodate the vehicles, the vehicles in which representatives of industry arrived, wearing health and safety helmets and avoiding eye contact. The dams looked small and quiet now.

Then a strange blight crept over the area and everything began to change. Some evil spell had settled on the community: mysterious maladies swept... Everywhere was a shadow of death. But this time, it had a name: COVID-19. What a relief to have a name for it! For too long our affliction had been nameless. So we stayed home, tried not to do any further damage, and pondered the meaning of our condition.

Truth be told, we had been expecting it. We knew that we had gone too far in colluding with the extraction, extermination and extinction of all that is natural, abundant and alive in our earth and bodies, the two being the same thing (this too, we have forgotten). We know that *something* should be done when Australia burns, when the great Amazon is pulped and its cadaver dismembered into pastural monoculture, when Europe's last wild rivers in the Balkans are impounded by mafia states with EU funds, when politicians with white smiles build walls and prisons for people they tell us are *others*, when humans with all their worldly possessions in a plastic bag run from the ashes of their homelands only to be put in prisons – we felt it in our bones that something had to change. And that we would have to give something up for that change to happen. That if we don't do it voluntarily, it will happen to us. And it is. The earth is shutting us down, just as we have tried to shut it down, because *seldom if ever does nature operate in closed and separate compartments.*

So when this season the salmon stopped jumping in the river and went into sharp decline, we were struck with sorrow, but not surprised. True, we had thought that salmon would be there forever, we had assumed that *we* would be there forever.

During the first silent weeks of the quarantine, when the people of the glen were being good and staying inside like grounded children, a noise was heard. The nearly-billion-pound construction company was felling the remaining forest. It was preparing to expand, again, all the way to the river this time. Nesting birds came to houses and fields, looking for a home. Deer ran across fields and roads. When we came out of our quarantine and walked along the edge of the abyss, on the other side was another abyss in the making.

Grief is felt in the area of the chest. When we are heart-broken, we can't breathe.

We can't breathe because there aren't enough trees left to make oxygen.

We can't breathe because we see on the news that sea creatures choke to death on the health and safety plastic in which our food is wrapped, and the coral reefs we dream of seeing one day are also dying.

We can't breathe because the pain of others increasingly feels like our pain and we begin to suspect that we are the others.

We can't breathe because we know: *no witchcraft, no enemy action has silenced the rebirth of new life in this stricken world. The people have done it themselves.*

We can't breathe because the earth's atmosphere is polluted by the construction companies that felled the trees, and their businessmen cousins that you couldn't argue with, because the water is pesticide-toxic and our blood awash with pharmaceutical residue, because the nuclear fallout of Chernobyl and Fukushima is in our endocrine systems and we have pre-existing conditions. We feel divided between and within ourselves, like the split atom that gives nuclear power and in turn splits the human genome because *radiation is an uncoupler and the death of cells exposed to radiation is thought... to be brought about in this way,* we are the children of the nuclear age whose aim is self-extinction – and we can't breathe.

We can't breathe because we want to awaken from this nightmare and start again, make amends, say sorry, give us another chance, refill the hole and replant it, demolish the wall and the prison built at our expense by Plutocratic horsemen of the apocalypse. A woman who was raped during a recent war asked her rapist, a teenaged soldier, why he was doing this. 'Because I am already dead,' he replied.

We can't breathe because we want to say sorry even though we have done nothing wrong. We used to worry that we're running out of time, and now we see that there's nothing personal about it – the world as we know it is running out of time.

We can't breathe because truths are surfacing as the glaciers melt, ancestral memories surge, the earth's ancient places call us and we suddenly yearn to reconnect with it all, we yearn for intimacy, meaning, justice, for a sacred place, just as the sacred forests are being felled and the sacred mountains extracted, and it feels like our own bodies.

And until we change our ways we will be compelled to wear a health and safety mask, as if under sedation. Under sedation, you can't speak or think clearly. Not because the mask protects us – nothing can protect us against ourselves – but out of fear, shame and grief. The primitive mask is an apt symbol and end-result of our primitive, split-atom handling of our Earth.

A memory remains of how one woman from Strathglass had heard hammering noises and men's voices by the river where a massive dam would be built thirty years later. Another woman had heard 'witches singing' where the first electricity lines and pylons would be built – the small ones. They were publicly derided by the Board at the official launch of the first dam, but over the decades, employees of the Board regularly heard voices, singing and laughing in the empty tunnels that the 'Tunnel Tigers' had dynamited, many perishing in the process. When I walk by my thrice-dammed river whose name means beautiful, on the edge between two crashing abysses, under the pylons – the big ones – and the electricity wires buzz above me like an evil spell that once signalled a fast-track to the future, what do I hear?

I hear that the future has arrived. We repeatedly did not take *the other road* that was available to us, as the mother of the ecological movement, Rachel Carson, saw it in her pioneering work on how the health of the Earth and the health of the human being are the same thing. I have woven my words here with words from her master-piece *Silent Spring* (1962). Its opening chapter is called 'A Fable for Tomorrow'.

The crossroad where we found ourselves a generation ago, or two generations ago when Carson saw it all, is now behind us, like the ancient woodland. What is ahead of us? Why do I feel strangely drugged? I wake up and tear off the mask.

CHAPTER 23

Casting Long Shadows:
Children and Young People and the
Importance of Trust in a COVID-19 World

Suzanne Zeedyk

IN THE WINTER of 1944, Nazi forces cut off food supplies to the Netherlands. Famine ensued, with people reduced to eating tulip bulbs, including mothers-to-be carrying babies yet unborn. Luckily, the famine was short-lived, although not before 20,000 people died. It ended when Allied troops freed occupied Holland in May 1945. Those short six months cast a long shadow. Once the babies were born and grew into adults, a surprising number went on to develop cardiovascular disease, obesity, type 2 diabetes and schizophrenia (Paul, 2010).

In 2001, the Twin Towers of New York City were obliterated in a terrorist attack. Hundreds of pregnant women were in the vicinity. Some could not shake the terror they felt, resulting in post-traumatic stress disorder, with its heightened sensitivity to danger. What happened to their babies? Research shows that a number carried the consequences of that day within their biology. At 12 months of age, their baseline levels of cortisol remained abnormally low. Their ability to handle stress had been permanently altered by experiences their mothers had had while they were still in the womb (Paul, 2010).

If you are wondering whether this essay is about pregnancy, it isn't. I'm simply trying to find a way to talk about the remarkable ways in which, as human beings, our present is woven from strands of our past.

The Connection Between Past and Present

I don't think we fully appreciate the connection between past and present. We tend to think of the past as a place. It's a place with edges and boundaries. It's a place we move on from. It's a place we think we *can* move beyond precisely because we conceive of it as having boundaries. The past is a place we tell stories about – because we don't live there anymore. Except, the thing is, that's not quite true. The past still lives within us.

We need to think more deeply about the threads that connect the past and present. We need to do that right now, as Scotland leaves our national lockdown and steps into the COVID-19 world that follows. The decisions we take in these weeks and months will do more than get us through this unprecedented period. Those decisions will shape our future, and especially our children's futures. That's going to happen whether we intend it or not. I would prefer that we are thoughtful and creative and wise in the choices we make.

The past lives within each of us because it moulds our biology. The neural pathways in our brains, the blood vessels in our vascular system, the sinews in our muscle fibres were all sculpted by experiences of threat and safety. They are threads, both literally and metaphorically. Long and thin, those threads stretch not only through the spaces of our bodies, but back through time, even to the generations before we were conceived. Scientific studies of trauma and adverse childhood experiences have revealed that children's distress casts a much longer shadow than our culture has reckoned on. We now know that childhood suffering incubates adult health conditions like heart disease, liver cirrhosis, obesity, drug use, alcoholism, diabetes and dementia (Felitti, 2002).

Getting Curious About What Causes Distress

If we are wise, this knowledge about trauma will prompt us to greater curiosity about the sources of childhood distress. What stresses do children and young people carry? Asking that question takes courage, for it generates unexpected and uncomfortable insights. You begin to see that adults cause more loss and fear than we recognise.

We trust in our good intentions. We hold them close, alongside our beliefs and expectations. But when we look candidly, we see that children's emotional realities do not automatically match up with our adult intentions. Children and young people feel things that make us uncomfortable. In particular, they feel things about us, about the adults in their lives – about things we did, things we decided for them, things we couldn't protect them from. When we've stopped to look at ourselves through their eyes, and what we see is too discomforting, it is easy to resort to denial. Denial protects our sense of ourselves as good people, saving us from shame and guilt.

Here's the problem. There have been all sorts of well-intentioned policies and practices put in place by policy-makers, professionals and ordinary mums and dads in Scotland's past, which we now know caused long-lasting harm to children in their care. If we don't ramp up our courage and curiosity in this time of COVID-19, we risk casting long shadows on our children's futures, as did our well-meaning predecessors in their time. Let me illustrate by telling more stories.

- In Scotland of 1939, children living in cities were in danger of dying from bombs. Anxious social workers evacuated them to safety in the countryside. We now know that many evacuees, especially the youngest and older ones who received poor placements, experienced significant emotional and mental health difficulties. This affected their marriages and their health throughout adulthood, and their relationships with their own children (Rusby and Tasker, 2009).

- In Scotland of the 1950s, policy-makers overseeing shiny new NHS hospitals prevented parents from staying with their children. Parents were allowed to visit once a week because medical staff viewed parental fussing as an obstacle to children settling into the routine of the ward. Campaigners argued vehemently that this policy caused emotional deterioration and developmental regression, especially for the youngest children. Anecdotal evidence now shows they were right. A large number of those children have gone on to suffer lifelong relational struggles, psychiatric problems and health conditions as a result of their hospital stay (Robertson and Robertson, 1989).

- In Scotland of the 1970s, many upper-class families continued (as they do today) the tradition of sending their children away to boarding school. So many revelations have emerged from those adult children of the damage done by their warped sense of 'privileged abandonment' that mental health professionals have developed the concept of 'boarding school survivor syndrome' (Schaverien, 2015).

- In Scotland of the 1980s, teaching unions defended the legal right of teachers to belt children and adolescents using the time-honoured leather taws. 'Belting' turned out to be slang for 'institutionalised violence'. Carol Craig argues that it is time for Scotland to face up to the consequences of our history as a 'belt happy culture' that has left a national legacy of low confidence and a fear of mistakes (Craig, 2018).

Unless you believe that any of the policy-makers, professionals or parents of those eras set out to harm, then you have to accept they believed their actions would serve children and young people for the good. They trusted in their own intentions. Yet, they were mistaken, and their actions cast long shadows over their children's lives. We face the same risk today.

There are a growing number of voices who agree. They fear unintended consequences of COVID-19 policies. For example, in July 2020, Scotland's NHS Child Health Commissioners called publicly for a rights-based, trauma-informed response, declaring that 'success will be determined by the quality of all our relationships' (2020). Jackie Brock, representing the Children's Sector Strategic Forum, reasserted that 'the rights of children and young people need to be absolutely central to decisions [around COVID-19]' (2020). Bruce Adamson, Scotland's Children and Young People's Commissioner, announced a comprehensive review of the pandemic's impact on children's rights, the first of its kind published anywhere in the world, because he viewed lockdown measures as 'catastrophic' for children's mental health (Brooks, 2020).

I draw hope from this choir of voices, and hold to that hope despite knowing that many harbour the same concerns I do. Bruce Adamson's words were frank:

In Scotland we've got a well-developed civil society that is good at supporting [children and young people] to be involved... [But that involvement] went out the window as soon as lockdown came along... That sends a very negative message that they are a luxury or an addition rather than an integral part of the decision-making process (Brooks, 2020).

What Adamson means is that, in 2020, we adults still aren't good at listening. COVID-19 gives us an opportunity to face up to that.

When Children Pay Prices

Children and young people pay biological and emotional prices when adults and systems can't offer enough attention, time, curiosity or self-awareness to listen to their feelings. Interestingly, the problem is rarely lack of knowledge of the risks. It turns out that, for each of the historic stories I told earlier, champions were already warning of the dangers of the policy. Yet it proved immensely difficult to alter those policies, due to cultural norms, systemic structures and sometimes imperative world events. James Robertson, who campaigned relentlessly for two decades for parents to be allowed to stay with their children in hospital, concluded in 1970:

> The major obstacle to suitable care of children is neither practical difficulty nor lack of knowledge. It is that, whatever level of intellectual understanding may obtain throughout the professions, the appropriate sense of urgency and alarm is missing. There is a tendency for even the best-educated and best-motivated of people working with children to become to some extent habituated to [their] states of distress and deviant behaviour (Robertson, 1970).

Robertson was shining a light on the ways that we become inured to children's pain. He was trying to get us to see ourselves. Our concern is 'blunted', even when we have 'good will and good intention', because the pressures exerted by professional systems and by ordinary psychological defences allow adults' perceptions of the 'acuteness of children's problems' to become 'dulled as by a tranquilliser'.

That capacity for 'dulling' our attention to children's misery did not cease in 1970, when Robertson gave his pointed lecture. That is why Scotland needed to embark in 2017 on an Independent Care Review that revealed how extensively children and young people's needs are failed by our current care system. That is why the grassroots campaigning organisation Give Them Time emerged in 2018, driven by Scottish parents who have found local authorities obstructive when they seek to defer entry of their four-year-old children into formal schooling if they feel they are not yet developmentally ready. That is why Darren McGarvey needed to film his 2019 BBC series 'Darren McGarvey's Scotland', which confronted viewers with the rampant rise in poverty.

That is why we should all be troubled that, as Scotland spends £900 million per year of taxpayers' money on expanding childcare provision (Nursery World, 2018), it is still not mandatory for those seeking early years qualifications via a standard SVQ route to undertake modules in child development, attachment or trauma. These modules remain at best optional, despite the emphasis on attachment within the latest government practice guidance. That is why, as I write this essay, young people are holding public protests outside the national headquarters of the Scottish Qualifications Authority. They are angry that, after five months of disrupted education due to COVID-19 lockdown, the decision has been taken to downgrade marks using a formula that entrenches the social inequalities they already face growing up in deprived communities (Davidson, 2020). These all count as examples of our systems and society 'dulling' themselves to children's misery. It is almost inevitable that we will see more of it as we embark on further COVID-19-related policies.

Staying Alert to Children's Needs

Is it really inevitable? Is it not possible that we could be alert to the needs of children and young people in the COVID-19 world we are entering? Is it not possible we could design creative, emotionally attuned solutions?

Yes, it is entirely possible. The question is whether we will choose to do that. Here are two key steps leaders can take to facilitate that. When I use the word 'leader', I don't mean people holding power in formal roles; I mean individuals who want change and are willing to take action to bring it about.

1. Nurture Trust

Trust lies at the heart of healthy societies and healthy systems. Get that right and a whole range of problems are solved because they never arise in the first place. Our society is suffering because trust in each other and in systems has become fragile. The lack of trust makes us anxious, angry and suspicious – and it makes us ill. For the human body, trust feels like safety – relaxed, comfortable, reassured. Even if danger arrives, you know you will not be tackling the threat alone because you are confident that there are others who will come to help. Trust comes from a confidence that you belong. When people feel unheard for long enough, they become hypervigilant, and their body moves into the stress responses of fight, flight or freeze. Increasingly, we have a hypervigilant society, with division, blame and dehumanisation following close behind.

The counter to this situation begins in nurturing relationships where trust can grow. An increase in the sense of belonging was palpable at the beginning of COVID-19 lockdown – ironically, given the requirement for physical distancing. Clapping on a Thursday night didn't benefit only keyworkers, it also strengthened neighbourhoods. If we focused on finding ways to retain that sense of community cohesion, that would be healthy for adults and children alike as we step out into a COVID-19 world. I accept that may sound simple, even naive: 'just nurture trust'. If it were so easy, I wouldn't need to write about it. I wouldn't have found enough instances of contrasting policies to fill up this essay.

2. Be Fiercely Curious

Curiosity is the gateway to change. We are going to need much more of it if we are to meet children and young people's needs. COVID-19 has made adults anxious and has made systems anxious. We are as yet uncertain how to meet the challenges that COVID-19 has landed us with. When human beings are anxious, they resort to default patterns. They become controlling, because that reduces the sense of uncertainty. They become less able to hear others. The uncertainties wrought by COVID-19 are likely to close us down. Curiosity will help us stay open.

Curiosity is an active state, not a passive one. It prompts questioning, rather than acceptance. It lets you get creative, seeing beyond the situation to new possibilities. Curiosity is what drives children to explore the world, discovering how it works, taking risks. Without curiosity, creativity is impossible. We are going to need creative solutions if we are to devise systems that can truly meet children's needs. And because systems are always reluctant to change, we will need more than ordinary levels of curiosity. We will need fierce curiosity. That state contains an energy that carries you through moments of doubt and resistance. Fierce curiosity is the polar opposite of blunted 'dulling'.

Making Choices

Like the Second World War, like the collapse of the Twin Towers, COVID-19 constitutes a global landmark in human history. In Scotland, we can, if we are wise, guard against some of the long shadows it threatens for our children and young people. Leaders of the past were presented with choices that shaped our world today. COVID-19 calls our generation of adults to make choices of their own.

References

Brock, J, 2020, 'Child rights or public health? There's no choice', *Children in Scotland blogsite,* accessed at: www.childreninscotland.org.uk/child-rights-or-public-health-theres-no-choice

Brooks, L, 16 July 2020, 'Scotland's children need post-COVID-19 mental health care, says report', *The Guardian,* accessed at: www.theguardian.com/society/2020/jul/16/scotlands-children-need-post-covid-19-mental-health-care-says-report

Craig, C, 2018, 'Scotland's addiction to the belt', *Sceptical Scot.* accessed at: www.sceptical.scot/2018/04/scotlands-addiction-belt/

Davidson, J, 2020, 'SQA chief to face Holyrood education committee over handling of exam results', *Holyrood Magazine,* accessed at: www.holyrood.com/news/view,sqa-chief-to-appear-before-holyrood-education-committee-over-exam-results

Felitti, V, 2002, 'The relation between adverse childhood experiences and adult health: Turning gold into lead', *The Permanente Journal,* vol.6 issue 1.

NHS Child Health Commissioners, 2020, 'Understanding and mitigating: Unintended consequences of COVID-19 for infants, children and young people', Scottish Government Child and Maternal Health blogsite, accessed at: www.blogs.gov.scot/child-maternal-health/2020/07/31/understanding-and-mitigating-unintended-consequences-of-covid-19-for-infants-children-and-young-people/

Nursery World, 2018, 'Scottish councils win extra funding for childcare expansion', accessed at www.nurseryworld.co.uk/news/article/scottish-councils-win-extra-funding-for-childcare-expansion

Paul, AM, 2010, *Origins: How the Nine Months Before Birth Shape the Rest of Our Lives,* New York, US, Free Pres.

Robertson, J, 1970, 'The problems of professional anxiety', unpublished lecture, accessed at: www.robertsonfilms.info/anxiety.htm

Robertson, J, and Robertson, J, 1989, *Separation and the Very Young*, London, Free Association Books.

Rusby, JSM and Tasker, F, 2009, 'Long-term effects of the British evacuation of children during ww2 on their adult mental health', *Journal of Aging and Mental Health*, vol.13 issue 3.

Schaverien, J, 2015, *Boarding School Syndrome: The Psychological Trauma of the Privileged Child*, Abingdon, Routledge.

CHAPTER 24

Mental Health, Wellbeing and the Psychological Challenge of COVID-19

Catherine Shea

AS I WRITE, I am picturing this book of essays as a kaleidoscope of perspectives or, better yet, a stained-glass window, in which each shard sheds its own coloured light upon Scotland's post-COVID-19 future. The place from which I refract what I hope will be light is the small interstitial node of a psychotherapy practice from which I offer clinical supervision to therapists/clinicians working in prison, in the NHS and in third sector services. I am also involved in the Scottish arm of the Association for Cognitive Analytic Therapy, a network of clinicians and service managers in the NHS Scotland (SNHS) from the Borders to Argyll, from Aberdeen to Inverness.

My perspective is also informed by the modality in which I work – Cognitive Analytic Therapy (CAT) with a specific focus on trauma. The creator of CAT, Dr Anthony Ryle, sought to understand and ameliorate the human tendency to repeat coping behaviours that once made sense in our earliest relational settings, but which have long passed their sell-by date and now limit the scope of our responses. CAT also helps us discern similar patterns of human behaviour and interaction at work at a team, organisational and societal level. Further, it recognises that the individual's wellbeing – and perhaps especially their mental health – is utterly inextricable from that of the society in which they live. In this way, it challenges the received neo-liberal habit of abdicating responsibility for the consequences of its policies, 'privatising' them as it were, locating them firmly with the individual and making failure to adapt to and thrive within its systems the individual's problem as if it arose *sui generis*.

Searching for a Better Reality

It was a similar understanding that informed support for independence in Scotland during the last referendum, when at least half a nation seemed to be crying out for the opportunity to work from the premise that we could only create a better life for all the people of Scotland by building on different values from the ones which increasingly dominated the UK. Subsequent years seem to have made this even more important, and yet have also undermined it. With austerity, Brexit and a reactionary UK Government, we are witnessing ever greater division and prejudice across Britain – and climate change is now threatening our very future on this planet.

On top of all this, we have COVID-19, which has sought out and amplified suffering wherever it was to be found – in homes where abuse reigned, in homes already suffering from poverty and unemployment, in BAME communities where all sorts of factors have led to disproportionate mortality rates, in hotels to which asylum seekers were removed and crammed in cheek-by-jowl with no money for months on end.

The pandemic has also brought anxiety to homes which previously felt relatively secure, destroying businesses and the livelihoods that depend on them. And this is to say nothing of the levels of cruel bereavement and loss, the existential challenge to people's sense of the worth of a human life, as they watched coffins stacked in temporary morgues and buried without witnesses in stupefying numbers.

In short, the advent of the virus has redoubled the threat to people's psychological wellbeing as much as their physical health, not least because it has revealed to us the underlying dynamics and values of the Westminster Government which still shapes so much of how we live – and they are not caring or pretty. Suicidal ideation has gone up across the board but especially among young people, who are particularly affected by the loss of opportunity, hope and expectation, with the suicide rate across the globe accelerating not far behind the growing death toll from COVID-19 itself.

Anxiety, grief, depression and even despair are appropriate responses in the face of such experiences: in what sense can they be called 'illness' and how should they be 'treated'? Some managers of SNHS psychological services are expecting a tsunami of referrals on the back of COVID-19 and there may, indeed, be more people seeking help who suffer what might be classically termed a breakdown. It is equally possible though that this surge in demand will not happen, because we are going through something that is clearly happening to us as a collective: we are indeed 'in this together'. Commonality and solidarity may make a difference. Experiences shared may not be so deleterious as ones suffered in isolation. We cannot pathologise, isolate or blame people for the consequences of a pandemic, so our current cultural habit of blaming the individual for expressing in their person the ill-health of their society holds less currency.

As we move forward as a nation, there is a big question to be addressed as to what mental health means and what kind of society creates it. In what kind of matrix does it flourish? One that encourages the atomisation of the individual and collective dissociation from the experience of others, or one that behaves in ways that recognise the interconnectedness of all beings, environmentally, inter-personally and intra-personally? One that makes developing 'resilience' the intra-psychic responsibility of the individual, or one that creates the living conditions which nourish it and/or tackles the social causes that undermine it – racism, poverty, unemployment, domestic violence and so on?

Rapid Response, Patient Perspectives

How we answer these questions reveals the values which inform and shape day-to-day praxis in all our institutions. So, looking at Scotland's response to this crisis, with reference to mental health provision, what do we discover that might inform our strategy for the future? The first response from SNHS was rapid and fleet-of-foot. Initially, many clinicians were on standby in case they were needed for practical duties on wards, so psychotherapy services were curtailed, with brief but regular phone support offered to many patients, with others more vulnerable being offered the option of therapy via an online platform or by telephone. Staff who were not redeployed (and very few were in the event) began to work from home. There were many glitches with out of date equipment and limited technical support, even in areas like NHS Highland which already used online platforms in order to provide for its far-flung population. But there was a global tidal wave of support in the form of Zoom making its platform more secure and offering its business functions free to NHS workers and, in response, a keen sense of everyone rising to the challenge, fulfilling the projections of 'heroism' so often visited upon the NHS.

The perspective of patients is also crucial as we think forwards from what we have learned. Some have been disenfranchised by the changes. Those who don't have Wi-Fi, tablets or laptops and those who don't have a private space within the home where they can speak in confidence have effectively been excluded from provision, at least temporarily. This needs to be factored in to any future vision of delivering more services remotely. Others miss the ritual of coming to a safe, familiar building, where they were made welcome by trusted staff and where they can do their inner work and leave it behind, perhaps using the journey to and from to prepare for and then process their sessions.

On the plus side however, there are also people who are glad to be spared an anxiety-provoking journey and who therefore have more head-space in sessions for other things that concern them. Some patients have felt able to reveal more than they had previously when speaking from the place where their lives are lived. There are those whose work has deepened now that they have the option of working by telephone, where they can be heard without being seen; while yet others still wish to be seen, even if they choose not to speak much during online sessions. All these permutations potentially reflect people's attachment behaviours and give new grist to the mill of therapeutic work.

The Impact on Clinicians

But before we get too gung-ho about a brave new world of virtual therapy, we need to reflect on the impact of these changes in the work on the clinicians, the service providers themselves. The groups I have consulted with have navigated the different stages of adaptation with goodwill, determination, reflexivity and no little stress. Initially, they were concerned for their patients and how they would adapt. They were concerned that the quality of the therapeutic relationship might suffer when eye contact was no longer possible, when both people could see only the head and shoulders of their interlocutor and might therefore miss the signals that come from whole-body presence.

Therapists were also working from home, dealing with work-related administration and receiving traumatic material in their own space, without being able to leave it behind in an office, without the support of other colleagues and while also home-schooling or caring for other dependents in the same space. They found themselves warding off a sense of chaos and un-containment, found their own personal vulnerabilities, usually shielded behind a working self-state, becoming activated. They were also under constant pressure to maintain services, to see urgent referrals, to live up to 'heroic' projections and to fulfil the targets placed on service managers.

It is a tribute to the strength of relational practice, in which anything that happens can become material for reflection, that many practitioners can now apprise the unexpected gains of the situation which has helpfully challenged assumptions about how therapy was formalised. They note that 'being in this together' with their patients, managing glitches together, the patients sometimes being more tech-savvy than the clinicians, and sharing, if not articulating, the vulnerability that, in a pandemic, we all have in common, has made the therapeutic relationship feel more equal and 'levelled the playing field' thus also enhancing the work. It is also significant that new online trainings and informal practitioner networks have arisen providing a forum for honest dialogue and mutual exploration and that, in this respect, COVID-19 is inspiring communities of reflection and growth.

The Importance of Relationality

But this is not without cost. These clinicians' manifest strength has been overtaxed. Like many NHS workers trying to live up to 'heroic' expectations – not just those of the public but of managers who are themselves under pressure – many clinicians have been working without breaks for months now and have been asked to take on more and more work. It is as if there is a forgetfulness that these are human beings who are also living through this pandemic, that they are subject to it and suffer from it just as their patients do. Implicit in the kind of budget- and target-driven culture in which we are all immersed is the danger of their being dehumanised into 'units of production'.

There is also a danger, moving forward, that SNHS managers, conscious of cost centres and of achieving targets for 'units of work', might embrace working remotely too readily, without considering some of the costs outlined above. What is possible in response to a crisis is not necessarily optimal or sustainable in the longer-term and it remains moot whether therapeutic outcomes will be the same. Yes, some clinical modalities are already manualised into online versions, and can be recommended by GPs, and certain aspects of therapy may be successfully delivered in that way.

But human beings are fundamentally both relational and, in a culture drowning in signs, more responsive to those which have been endowed with meaning: they are more likely to access a website if someone who has taken the time to get to know them points them in that direction for a reason specific to them. And not all aspects of healing can be translated into questions in boxes, nor achieved by two 'talking heads'. It is now known that resilience in the face of later traumatic events is affected by the quality of early attachment experiences: where these are also traumatic, where lack of safety and attunement has aroused survival terror and overwhelmed an infant's neurological systems, providing an embodied attuned relationship is key to effective treatment and reprocessing.

With more aversive patients, whose lead strategy for safety is avoidance, starting work on the phone or online might provide a helpful entry point. But as they progress there is no substitute for being present with another in a trusting relationship. Furthermore, many approaches to trauma therapy work directly on and with the body. It is not impossible to do some of this online but remote working limits what can be achieved. Therapy can and will adapt creatively to changing conditions and learn from doing so, but it must not lose sight of its essential task, which is to name and challenge threats to our humanness lurking in the shadow of shibboleths like efficiency and innovation and manifesting in personal distress.

The Reality of Inequality

COVID-19 has reiterated (yet again) that the link between health inequality, deprivation and poverty and poor mental health is undeniable. Moving forward we can no longer ignore this. As the project manager of a very successful trauma counselling service in the West of Scotland said recently, there is no point in trying to reduce people's activation when they don't know where the next meal is coming from for their children, when their current 'survival terror' is all too real. In one of the most deprived areas of Scotland (by any index you care to name), her project workers have long been aware that supporting their clients in understanding their traumatic past and achieving a greater measure of self-regulation was a fragile business. So many people were already living on the edge of catastrophe, with unemployment, poor housing, food poverty and, in consequence, poor educational attainment.

Regaining Ownership

Once the pandemic hit, the project rightly recognised that there was no point in trying to work higher up Maslow's hierarchy of needs when the very basics of survival were now palpably under threat. They threw the weight of their experience into supporting community initiatives to provide food and aid to vulnerable people and families; they staffed the helpline set up to support volunteers who suffered vicarious trauma from what they were witnessing and who were becoming burnt out. They were central to a joint project designed to encourage struggling people to seek help: in a culture where this was widely deemed a sign of weakness, the phone line was aptly named 'Sign of Strength'.

And they looked askance while top/down 'solutions' were dreamed up and delivered without dialogue with the local community activists who had knowledge about what was happening on the ground. But even when these misfired, the community worked around them creatively.

For example, when the local authority delivered food parcels to people which largely consisted of tins of food that no one wanted to eat, and the contents of which anyone with sight problems couldn't read, the community organised a food-swap tent so that people could get what they needed and not waste what they didn't. This community is already coming up with its own creative solutions for moving forward: these are rooted in local skills and knowledge. Despite their success, we cannot expect volunteer efforts to sustain this. Responsive funding is needed that aims to support what is proven to work on the ground, rather than some idea dreamed up without dialogue by a remote committee. And it needs to be done in the spirit of giving these people what they are owed, in the spirit of truth and reconciliation, of compensation for decades of neglect, rather than in the form of a few stems of patronage that wither and die because they aren't suited to the native soil. Communities can no longer be problematised as lacking in resilience: they need to be supported in using their considerable talents to create the conditions in which they can achieve it.

'No Return to Business as Usual'

Just as clinicians at the coal face of service delivery pulled out all the stops to engage with, adapt to and learn from this new situation, so too people in such communities have shown flexibility, strength and compassion in their care for one another. To support and build on this reservoir of good will, for new and sustainable learning to emerge from it, we need to understand that, at their heart, both these responses are founded in the human qualities of relationship, collaboration, dialogue and it is these qualities rather than economic arguments that should shape future strategy. If COVID-19 has taught us anything it is that this will not cost more; the health vs wealth argument has been demolished. Rather, we cannot afford to do otherwise. Brené Brown puts it well:

> We will not go back to normal. Normal never was. Our precorona existence was not normal other than we normalised greed, inequity, exhaustion, depletion, extraction, disconnection, confusion, rage, hoarding, hate and lack. We should not long to return, my friends. We are being given the opportunity to stitch a new garment. One that fits all of humanity and nature.

Section Five – Justice, Equality and Belief

CHAPTER 25

New Abnormal
Stephen Watt

From the outset, hills will be ticketed.
Mountains. Munros. Mole Mounds
will become the addict's seduction.
Lit by God rays – Aurora Borealis –
casino-flushed champagne sunbeams
will pledge airglows and comets.
The fruit machines of Scottish twilight.

    We must no longer sell our ghosts.

This country's focus must be rigid. Flesh and blood.
No stone; pull them all down.
Wallace. The Bruce. Desperate Dan.
Oor Wullie. Greyfriars Bobby.
Any known racists, offenders, or *probable killers*.
Universities will research and analyse
affiliations to Miss Hitler beauty contest winners.

    Scotland's second life will be glorious.

Butterfly wing-hearted, teachers must be honest
about numbers. Push desks into corridors,
then rewarded for composure.
Piles of hardbacks will reinforce walls
since the libraries closure, and galleries
become accessible upon Instagram sign-up.
Enjoy Mackintosh and Vettriano close-up.

    Zoos are of no use. Or football.

Indisputable centuries of sectarianism in Glasgow
means only one thing. Release giraffes,
rhino, flamingo, hippo and buffalo
into the green jungle of the east
and elephant, zebra, ostrich and wildebeest to graze on the grass
where its blue.
It is the humane thing to do.

Lest we not forget cultural value.

In nightshades where music lives
and thrives and love-lives swell, we will recompense you
with virtual Tinder dates
between matching profiles and lifestyles.
Nightclubs may restyle themselves
into clinics for fertilising cells
or simulate church bells if passions should surge.

It is a surprising uprising of the Saltire.

To breathe, only in yoga class. On tandem bikes, designed
to reduce footfall. Upon treadmill pavements
where our office is the kitchen.
In deserted shops, lined with soulless dummies,
discounted stock and limited rooms for fitting.
Sweden edified us with one-way floors.
Theatres remain in permanent intermission.

Then what is our zenith of social distancing?

All flute band parades are cancelled.
Medication is delivered by pharmacies.
Fish merchants will electrocute trespassers
if they dare enter Scottish territory
and Satanic death cult sanctuaries
can no longer practice in our cemeteries.
Isn't this the news we have waited centuries to hear?

If it is not, then let us hear your ideas.

CHAPTER 26

Changing Scottish Justice Will Take Courage and Cooperation

Hannah Graham

Scottish society has a problem with punishment, well documented over decades and different parties of government. It sits uncomfortably with national identities, how we see ourselves and our futures. Overall, recorded crime in Scotland is among the lowest seen in 45 years, since 1974 (Scottish Government, 2020a). Yet dominant responses to crime and those who commit it may not make us safer or better off. Emerging from the exceptional circumstances and adversity of the COVID-19 crisis offers opportunities for doing justice differently.

A Progressive Nation with a Punitive Streak?

Scotland has higher rates of punishment than most other European nations. This encompasses both incarceration (imprisonment rate of 146 per 100,000 of national population) and community sentencing (probation rate of 397 per 100,000) (Aebi and Tiago, 2020; Aebi and Hashimoto, 2020). It deviates from other small nations often considered counterparts, like Finland (imprisonment rate of 49 per 100,000; probation rate of 53 per 100,000), Norway (imprisonment rate of 60 per 100,000; probation rate of 45 per 100,000) and Ireland (imprisonment rate of 81 per 100,000; probation rate of 129 per 100,000). Wha's like us? Damn few this side of Europe.

Poverty and inequality entangle with control and punishment. Three examples illustrate this. Official statistics show that, in the eight years prior to the pandemic (2011–19), nearly 15,000 short prison sentences were imposed for the main crime of shoplifting. This is a recognised driver of women's criminalisation and imprisonment

(McIvor and Burman, 2011). Secondly, half (52 per cent) of the total Scottish prison population comes from the 20 per cent most deprived areas in Scotland (Scottish Government, 2020a) – Dundee, Glasgow, East and North Ayrshire, Inverclyde and Clackmannanshire among others. Finally, of the thousands of Scots sentenced to Community Payback Orders each year, only a quarter (26 per cent) are employed, in full time education or a government training scheme (Scottish Government, 2020b). Troubling prospects of mass unemployment and recession in the wake of COVID-19 and Brexit may make acute issues and inequalities more pronounced.

How we punish – and restrain punishment – speaks to who we are. Fellow criminologist Fergus McNeill and I have argued that the worst acts of individuals should not bring out the worst in us as a nation (2019). To take that stand is not to deny the frustration of persistent petty offending nor diminish the gravity of serious crimes as any less harmful or harrowing. What it does is contend that the act does not make its perpetrator any less human, any less one of us.

Escalations of vengeance and intensifications of punishment in the wake of crime won't produce fairness or safety nor bring back what was lost. There are few things that prison cannot make worse. Prison accelerates a person's return to crime and prison, at higher rates than if they had never been. It is life limiting and sometimes life ending; it mars health and job prospects. Prison is not an effective deterrent; it generates more victims in its wake. The Scottish Government and Scottish Parliament know this. The Scottish judiciary and procurators fiscal know this. The evidence and arguments are well-kent.

Uncertain Times and Emergency Measures

The COVID-19 crisis and lockdown restrictions have had potent impact across Scottish justice. In particular, the impact in Scottish prisons has been disruptive. Prisons went into lockdown to try to prevent infection. People were locked in a cell the size of a small bathroom for 23 hours a day, for over four months, eating insipid meals next to their toilet, if their cell has one. Emergency powers were used to change the Prison Rules. Ostensible solitary confinement en masse and heavy restrictions on those self-isolating prompted the Scottish Human Rights Commission to raise concerns with the Scottish Parliament and Scottish Government. To the Government's credit, things previously discussed for years – such as (restricted function) mobile phones and virtual family visits in prisons – were implemented in a short period.

Prisoner accounts of this time brim with human concerns. Feelings of boredom and emptiness, frustration, loneliness and craving human connection, fears for loved ones and an uncertain future, and cheers of thanks for the NHS and key workers. Men in Barlinnie (The Boys from Bar-L, 2020) and Edinburgh prisons (Saughton Sonnets 4, 2020) described life inside during lockdown:

'You know sometimes when you take your jumper off, you get sparks and static, and the hair on your skin stands up. Well that's how it feels here sometimes, only in here it can be like there's live electricity in the air. I was thinking that if someone switched the lights on with a big switch, this place could go on fire.'

'We have more time to lie and think, to ruminate all the news. Time locked down from our featureless views.'

'No more visitors come see me... the only human contact I get is from my television.'

Sadly, in the lockdown period between March and July 2020, six prisoners and one prison officer died of suspected coronavirus-related causes. There were other prisoner deaths during this time. Also, at one point, almost a quarter of Scottish prison staff were absent from work.

Early in the coronavirus crisis, former Cabinet Secretary for Justice and SNP MSP, now MP, Kenny MacAskill called for understanding and action in support of those in Scottish prisons and those living with addictions and at risk of drug deaths:

If we don't do something soon, we ain't seen nothing yet. If we want *Trainspotting* to remain a movie and not return to being a reality, we need to be bold (MacAskill, 2020).

Pressured times called for emergency measures. Scottish justice policy-makers and practitioners showed remarkable hard graft and co-operation, working long hours to develop and implement responses. In the Scottish Parliament, there was cross-party support for the Coronavirus (Scotland) Act 2020, authorising emergency powers for prisoner early release. To implement this, the Release of Prisoners (Coronavirus) (Scotland) Regulations 2020 were backed by members of the SNP, Labour, Greens and Lib Dems – the Conservatives chose to abstain rather than oppose it. The early release scheme was called for and welcomed by criminologists, lawyers, charities, families of prisoners, the Chief Inspector of Prisons, among others. According to the Scottish Prison Service, a total of 348 people were released from prison early during May 2020. Concurrent to this scheme, normal liberations also continued with an estimated 100–150 people released a week during lockdown. In the 12 weeks from 13 March to 5 June 2020, the Scottish prison population decreased by approximately 15 per cent, from 8,094 to 6,888 people. However, as courts have re-opened, numbers are rising. Time is of the essence.

A Menu of Strategies for Change – But is There the Appetite?

In considering potential futures after the virus, is there the appetite and courage to change Scottish justice? Some changes may not be popular with the public gallery. Commonweal and fellow feeling often prove conditional. Showing more humanity and mercy towards people with convictions may be suppressed or emboldened by the proximity or distance of an election, by news headlines, by the prospect of perceived leniency, by the proximity or distance of a prison and whether post-release destinations are next door, next week, or not.

With indications that the 2021 Scottish Parliament elections mean a fourth consecutive term in government, arguably the SNP can afford to spend some political capital. In doing so they can further differentiate themselves from the Conservatives, whose populist stances on punishment can be tediously predictable ('soft touch justice'/tough on crime). A high punishment society is not in keeping with the SNP's professed social democratic ideals, nor are the staggering fiscal and human costs easily justified in a wellbeing economy recovering from a pandemic. Revisiting Lesley McAra's observations of a 'de-tartanised' Scottish justice in the first years post-devolution, greater distinctiveness – a re-tartanisation – might be found in achieving a smaller, more proportionate penal system and a renewed commitment to enabling welfarism to flourish across civic and political cultures (2008).

Relatedly, Holyrood's 'consensus culture' characterises much of the deliberations of its Justice Committee, including during COVID-19. Their scrutiny activities are an intelligent choreography of collegiality and acumen. Yet, in the 2016–2021 parliamentary term, opposition parties have proposed few ideas and strategies regarding prisons and community justice. This needs to change.

In seeking to become a nation where punishment is more restrained, and prison is only used in the most serious and risky cases, research evidence and practice experience point to a range of strategies. Selected examples here are illustrative and credible, not exhaustive, nor quixotic hypotheses.

- *Decriminalisation and diversion.* In responding to low-level crimes and anti-social behaviour, better answers are often found before and beyond the realms of criminal justice. Official statistics show that out-of-court disposals by Police Scotland and the Crown Office and Procurator Fiscal Service have fallen significantly in recent years – a trend warranting exploration and reversal. With examples of drug use and drug and alcohol-related minor infractions, or poverty and debt-related fine defaulting, diversion to treatment and improved access to supports can help address issues without resorting to criminalisation and punishment. Similarly, uses of structured deferred sentences should be encouraged (ie after conviction but prior to sentencing, engaging with supervision and support (eg with housing, relationships, mental health, addictions), with the likely prospect of an admonishment if progress is made).

- *Bail and sentencing reform.* More progress is needed on reconciling the importance of the independence of the judiciary with the urgent need to change some patterns of bail and remand decision-making, sentencing and punishment. One of the sentencing reform discussions worth pursuing is whether some less serious crimes should be non-imprisonable and dealt with through community-based responses that better address underlying causes and conditions. Another discussion and course of action is to shorten prison sentences, including the time served for life sentences – again, internationally, Scotland is an outlier.

- *Reform breach rules.* Curb opportunities for risk-averse reactions by authorities of people being resentenced or recalled to custody for minor technical violations. Resist increasing requirements and conditionality of orders and licences where it is not stringently necessary.

- *Decarceration and early release.* There are more strategies than space to explain them here. Scottish authorities could improve on doing the fundamental basics well, on time and at scale. Ensure people have essentials needed to function in the community and sign-on for benefits: photo ID, a bank account, an email address, a GP registration and continuity of medication. Also, use technology (eg electronic monitoring tagging) wisely and well. Bold activism and decarceration strategies can yield results, like the American Civil Liberties Union taking governments to court to get tens of thousands released from custody during COVID-19.

- *Social justice and social solidarity.* Restraining punishment necessitates mending other safety nets and systems – the ones broken by austerity, marred by conditionality and stigma. As more powers over social security come to Scotland, dealing with the incivilities and hardships caused by Universal Credit and benefits sanctions are priorities. Improving access and availability of treatment and support for mental health and alcohol and drug use and drug law reform will likely have positive collateral consequences in Scottish justice, including reducing or diverting from police contact. Prioritising social justice necessitates investment in communities and access to goods, services and supports routinely afforded to citizens without convictions. Examples like community wealth building and progressive approaches to inclusive community justice in North Ayrshire appear promising (Weaver et al., 2019). Making substantive inroads with reducing poverty, social exclusion and inequality in Scotland will have effects on crime and punishment. Failure to do so will mean the same.

- *Diversity.* Justice leaders and decision-makers need to become more diverse. For example, at the time of writing, the Justice Spokespeople for all five parties as well as the Lord Advocate are men. With women making up only 22 per cent of sheriffs, lack of judicial diversity makes Scotland an outlier in Europe. Predominantly older white men from privileged backgrounds sentence predominantly younger white men from underprivileged backgrounds.

The COVID-19 pandemic is a landmark by which time will be marked as before and after; a time of rapid change and cooperation in Scottish justice. It is a public health and economic crisis that has weighed heavily on hearts and minds in homes and cells across the nation. What its legacy need not be is a crisis of our humanity. In emerging from it and pursuing a more just future, may our courage not be found wanting.

References

Aebi, MF and Hashimoto, YZ, 2020, *SPACE II – Council of Europe Annual Penal Statistics: Persons under the Supervision of Probation Agencies*, Strasbourg, France, Council of Europe.

Aebi, MF and Tiago, MM, 2020, *SPACE I – Council of Europe Annual Penal Statistics: Prison Populations*, Strasbourg, France, Council of Europe.

Graham, H and McNeill, F, 2019, 'Open Letter about Whole Life Custody Draft Proposal', accessed at: www.sccjr.ac.uk/publications/13428/

MacAskill, K, 8 April 2020, 'Scotland's prisons are a coronavirus hothouse. Here's what we must do,' *The Scotsman,* accessed at: www.scotsman.com/news/crime/scotlands-prisons-are-coronavirus-hothouse-heres-what-we-must-do-kenny-macaskill-2533018

McAra, L, 2008, 'Crime, Criminology and Criminal Justice in Scotland,' *European Journal of Criminology*, vol.5, issue 4, 481–504.

McIvor, G, and Burman, M, 2011, 'Understanding the Drivers of Female Imprisonment in Scotland', Glasgow: Scottish Centre for Crime and Justice Research.

'Saughton Sonnets 4', 29 June 2020, *First Time Inside,* accessed at: www.firsttimeinside.co.uk/hidden_voices/saughton-sonnets-4/

Scottish Government (2020a), 'Scottish Prison Population: Statistics 2019–2020', Edinburgh: Scottish Government.

Scottish Government (2020b), 'Criminal Justice Social Work Statistics in Scotland: 2018–2019', Edinburgh: Scottish Government.

'The Boys from Bar-L', 8 May 2020, *First Time Inside,* accessed at: www.firsttimeinside.co.uk/hidden_voices/the-boys-from-the-bar-l/

Weaver, B, Lightowler, C and Moodie, K, 2019, 'Inclusive Justice: Co-Producing Change', Glasgow: University of Strathclyde, accessed at: www.northayrshire.community/inclusive-justice-co-producing-change/33688/

CHAPTER 27

There is No Race Problem: Theorising the Absence of Racial and Ethnic Disparity Data in Scotland After COVID-19

Tommy J Curry

COVID-19 HAS LED to disproportionate rates of infection and death among racial and ethnic minority groups in the United States and the United Kingdom. Various social inequalities have always existed within modern democratic nations. However, COVID-19 has shown that the existing social inequalities in Western nations which are usually thought to pose no threat to democratic governance and practice within these societies have lethal consequences for the most marginalised populations (Curry, 2020). While the United Kingdom and the United States are trying to reconcile their ideology of humanism and colour-blindness with the growing evidence of anti-Black racism and racial discrimination throughout their various societies, Scotland remains exceptional (European Union Agency for Fundamental Rights, 2018). Whereas the US and the UK have made data disaggregated by race and sex publicly available, Scotland has not. This chapter asks policy and opinion makers in Scotland to consider how the ideological commitment to Scotland as a colour-blind and egalitarian society dictates the epistemological engagements the society has with race and racism, specifically anti-Blackness.

De-emphasising racism in the UK – because Britain and Scotland do not have the history of slavery or the institutional racism of the United States – is commonplace. While Black Americans have been victims of slavery and Jim Crow segregation, the UK claims no similar history, and consequently is thought not to have a similar racism. Colonialism is often thought to be different, more benevolent, and less dangerous, than American-style racism. The pandemic has highlighted, quite contrary to the pronouncements of racial equality by the leaders and citizens of the United States and England, that racism is alive and well in their respective countries. The data shows significant health disparities, economic obstacles to opportunity and discrimination across the board despite the pronouncements and deniability of the public (Heath and Richards, 2020). A post-COVID-19 Scotland should track and report racial and ethnic data to the public in an effort to create a truly equal democratic society.

Compared to Scotland
The Consequence of Racial and Ethnic
Minoritisation in the US and UK During COVID-19

Throughout various government reports produced in the United States and England, racial and ethnic data is disaggregated by age and sex. England has produced reports that look at racial and ethnic variation in infection rates and mortality by geographic location, socio-economic status and comorbidities (Office for National Statistics, 2020). Similarly, data from the Center for Disease Control and Prevention in the United States shows that Black and Hispanic groups have higher rates of COVID-19 incidences and mortality than whites (Center for Disease Control and Prevention, 2020). The data gives researchers and policy-makers the opportunity to inquire into the various interaction effects that racial and ethnic group membership has on infection rates and mortality. During a pandemic such as COVID-19, societies can expect increased rates of death across multiple age groups. What is worrisome however is when specific racial and ethnic minorities seem to be burdened disproportionately by these consequences. In a truly equal society that embraced social and political egalitarianism, racial and ethnic group membership should have no significant effect on mortality and infection incidences compared to the predominate white majority. This is unfortunately not the case.

The racial and ethnic variance in COVID-19 incidences are of no small consequence. In England, the Office of National Statistics found that 'after taking into account age, measures of self-reported health and disability and other socio-demographic characteristics, black people were still almost twice as likely as white people to die a COVID-19 related death' (Booth and Barr, 2020). Racism experienced by BME communities and more specifically by BME key workers affect health, exposure risk and disease progression (Lyle, 2017). In the United States, Black Americans experience the highest mortality rates of all racial groups and suffer a rate of death almost three times that of whites (74 per 100,000 compared to white American's rate of 30 per 100,000) (McCarthy, 2020). Racial disparities in the US are so great that Justin Hansford and Tasnim Motala (2020) have argued that 'Colour-blind solutions will not go far enough to address Black American's disparate experience of COVID-19, which are exacerbated by deeply entrenched inequities'.

Another major concern is the disproportionate mortality that COVID-19 has on racial and ethnic men in the United States and the United Kingdom. In the United States, COVID-19 has also been linked to higher rates of mortality for older men of racial and ethnic minority groups (Ford and Reeves, 2020). While men are infected at a lower rate than their female counterparts in England, their mortality rates are higher (Office of National Statistics, 2020); rates of mortality for racial and ethnic men are double that of their female counterparts with the exception of the Chinese male population (ibid.: Table 4). The Public Health England report found that the 'highest age standardised diagnosis rates of COVID-19 per 100,000 population were in people of Black ethnic groups (486 in females and 649 in males) and the lowest were in people of White ethnic groups (220 in females and 224 in males)' (Public Health England, 2020).

This data shows that COVID-19 trends in mortality have racial and gender components in the United States and the United Kingdom. Unfortunately, there are not the same kinds of resources available to make comparisons of race and sex breakdowns in Scottish datasets. Scotland refuses to make racial and ethnic breakdowns in COVID-19 incidences and mortality publicly available. *The Addressing Race Inequality in Scotland* study published in 2017 shows that BME communities continue to report racial discrimination and experiences of structural racism in housing and employment. The reports stated that BME populations have continued to be overrepresented in poor quality and overcrowded housing in Scotland (Lyle, 2017). In fact, homelessness affects BME communities 75 per cent more than across the population as a whole (ibid.). Even though members of BME communities tend to have the highest educational attainment in Scotland, people from BME backgrounds are still twice as likely to be unemployed compared to their white counterparts (ibid). Employment discrimination confines BME members to low wage jobs and results in poverty rates twice that of white communities (ibid.).

The latest Public Health Scotland reports do not provide race/ethnicity data disaggregated by age and sex. Data from other countries however such as the United States and England include data disaggregated by race/ethnicity, age and sex. The recent report, *Analysis of Deaths Involving Coronavirus (COVID-19) in Scotland, by Ethnic Group*, again provides no sex or age disaggregation. In fact, the report claims not only that no Black people in Scotland have died from COVID-19 related illness, but that the racial and ethnic groups most vulnerable in the US and the UK are among the safest (National Records of Scotland, 2020). Despite not having an official report outlining the breakdown of class depravation on COVID-19 cases or mortality in Scotland, there has been a publicly accepted narrative linking poverty and low-income status to COVID-19 transmission and infection rates (Sanders, 2020).

Fiating Racial Equality

Scotland's framing of social inequity and COVID-19 related deaths as a matter of socio-economic status and location is as much an epistemological issue as an ideological one. Scotland conceives of itself as a truly liberal democracy that has transcended the decadent folk mythology of racial inferiority and institutional racism. The progressive ideology behind this view suggests that colour-blindness and humanism are values that the society should strive towards and realise throughout all institutions. These values are commendable, but far too ideal and abstract to be realisable in Scotland's society. Rather than fiating racial inequality away, or simply *making racism* not exist by not collecting or explaining away evidence of racial disparities, Scottish opinion and policy-makers need to confront the reality of racial inequality and account for how racism operates within its society. Present health disparities are interpreted almost solely as effects of depravation, specifically poverty and housing.

Colour-blindness, or the idea that race is irrelevant to how democratic societies operate, is an ideology utilised to deny institutional racism and normalise whites being most of the powerbrokers within predominately white societies (Bonilla-Silva, 2001; 2003; Bonilla-Silva et al., 2006). A colour-blind perspective is also somewhat naive given the history of Scotland's participation in the slave trade and its pivotal role in the development of racialist thinking during the Enlightenment. Racism in Scotland, like that of Britain, was cultivated to justify colonialism and imperial ventures into Africa, the Caribbean and Asia. To imagine that the ideas generating the racial distinctions insisted upon by David Hume, or the hierarchy between civilised and primitive peoples in Adam Smith's *The Wealth of Nations*, are completely absent from the structure of Scottish societies is utopian (Sebastiani, 2011; 2013). These notions simply lack the ability to explain why members of racial and ethnic groups tend to be pulled downward despite education in Scotland. How one comes to know of an issue and interpret empirical evidence towards one explanation or the other is of significant epistemological concern.

Previous governmental reports have pointed out that racism in Scotland remains unencountered despite the relationship between racial and ethnic group membership and poverty. The Joseph Roundtree Foundation report *Poverty and Ethnicity: Key Messages for Scotland* found, in previous attempts to examine racism in Scotland, the

> Lack of adequate data and poor monitoring of ethnicity, whether of recruitment and progression by employers, of ethnic minority take-up of services by local authorities or insufficiently detailed data gathered at a national level, was a recurring theme (Kelly, 2016).

The *Addressing Race Inequality in Scotland: The Way Forward* report has similarly highlighted the lack of data collection surrounding race and ethnicity to adequately investigate the full extent of racism and its effect throughout Scottish society (Lyle, 2017). These reports not only demonstrate the inability of Scottish policy-makers to attend to racism in society but indicate that there is a resistance towards framing social inequality in Scotland as a racial or ethnic problem. Because governmental entities and power holders wish to see Scotland in non-racial terms, the interpretation of data as well as the kinds of data being collected ignore racial and ethnic markers. The effect of this epistemological commitment is to frame racial and ethnic discrimination and the disparities that arise from racism as having their origin in socio-economic status or being most accurately explained through class-based terms.

By de-emphasising racism and the prevalence of racial discrimina-

tion in employment, housing and everyday life, Scottish analyses of
COVID-19 infection and mortality are framed as disparities in opportunity. Marginalised racial and ethnic groups in this framework are
no different than marginalised white groups, since their marginalisa-
tion is economic and not political or racial. Consequently, the racial
discrimination that disproportionately tracks Black, Asian and other
racial and ethnic groups into poverty at twice the rate of whites is
interpreted as an economic issue remediable through social mobility
and education. As such, the society is not broken and in fact provides
a means through which all individuals despite their racial or ethnic
background can lessen their marginality. Opinionmakers can simulta-
neously celebrate a racially progressive white society that is unlike the
United States and the United Kingdom, while explaining any racial or
ethnic variation of COVID-19 infection and mortality as an economic
effect that affects all poor people, be they white, Black, Asian, etc,
equally. In short, this absence of data misrepresents the racial and
ethnic disparities of groups as progressive policy successes.

Conclusion

The COVID-19 virus has highlighted missing gaps in demographic data
and knowledge production concerning racism and discrimination in
Scottish society. This absence of evidence indicates a need for theorists
to conceptualise the effects such lacunae have for how we think about
democratic equality and social disparities. There is sufficient evidence
documenting the presence and consequences of racial and ethnic discrimination on minority groups. The current literature however asks
us to believe that while racism produces increased rates of poverty,
homelessness and downward mobility for educated minority groups,
none of the deleterious effects of racial and ethnic discrimination in
Scotland are linked to COVID-19 mortality as they are in the US and
the UK. Said differently, even the racism in Scotland is more progressive and less harmful than its American or British counterparts. These
hypotheses should give us pause and push us toward a deeper understanding of racial, ethnic and economic inequalities in Scotland after
COVID-19. The lack of evidence we have concerning how COVID-19
spreads and affects racial and ethnic minority groups means that there
are effects of the virus that are not known and can never be known
given the current data collection methods and publicly available
information.

References

Booth, R and Barr, C, 7 May 2020, 'Black People Four Times More Likely to Die from COVID-19, ONS Finds', *The Guardian.*

Bonilla-Silva, E, 2001, *White Supremacy and Racism in the Post-Civil Rights Era,* Boulder, Lynne Rienner Publishers.

Bonilla-Silva, E, 2003, *Racism without Racists: Colorblind Racism and the Persistence of Racial Inequality in the United States,* Boulder, Rowman and Littlefield.

Bonilla-Silva, E, Goar, C and Embrick, DG, 2006, 'When whites Flock Together: The Social Psychology of white Habitus', *Critical Sociology,* vol.32, issue 2–3, 229–253.

Center for Disease Control and Prevention, 2020, *Weekly Updates by Select Demographic and Geographic Characteristics,* accessed at: www.cdc.gov/nchs/nvss/vsrr/covid_weekly/index.htm#Race_Hispanic

Curry, TJ, 2020, 'Racist Democracies: The Role Demographies of Death and Dying have in Racializing Covid-19 Mortalities,' The Philosopher's Magazine: Special Issue: Thinking Through the Pandemic, 90.3, 36–43.

European Union Agency for Fundamental Right, 2018, *Being Black in the EU,* Luxembourg, Publications Office of the European Union.

Ford, T and Reeves, R, 15 May 2020, 'COVID-19 Much More Fatal for Men, Especially Taking Age Into Account', *Brookings.edu.*

Hansford, J and Motala, T, 2020, 'The Contradiction of Color-Blind Covid-19 Relief: Black America in the Age of Pandemic, Brown University. Accessed at: www.njjn.org/uploads/digital-library/The%20Contradiction%20of%20Colorblind%20COVID_19%20Relief_%20Black%20America%20in%20the%20Age%20of%20Pandemic%20.pdf

Heath, A and Richards, L, 1 July 2020, 'How Racist is Britain Today? What the Evidence Tells Us', *The Conversation.*

Kelly, M, 2016, *Poverty and Ethnicity: Key Messages for Scotland: 2016,* Joseph Roundtree Foundation.

Lyle, K, 2017, *Addressing Racial Inequality in Scotland: The Way Forward,* Edinburgh, St. Andrew's House.

McCarthy, N, 30 July 2020, 'Nearly Three Times as Many Black Americans are Dying from COVID-19 compared with white People as Pandemic Death Toll Surpasses 150,000', *Forbes.*

National Records of Scotland, 2020, *Analysis of Deaths Involving Coronavirus (COVID-19) in Scotland, by Ethnic Group*, Edinburgh, National Records of Scotland.

Public Health England, 2020, *Beyond the Data: Understanding the Impact of COVID-19 on BAME Groups*, London, Wellington House.

Sanders, R, 2020, *ESSS Outline: COVID-19, Low Incomes and Poverty*, Glasgow, Iriss.

Sebastiani, S, 2011, 'National Characters and Race: A Scottish Enlightenment Debate' in Ahnert, T and Manning, S (eds), *Character, Self, and Sociability in the Scottish Enlightenment*, New York, Palgrave MacMillan, 187–206.

Sebastiani, S, 2013, *The Scottish Enlightenment: Race, Gender, and the Limits of Progress*, New York, Palgrave MacMillan.

Statistics, OfN, 2020, *Coronoavirus (COVID-19) Related Death by Ethnic Group, England and Wales: 2 March to 15 May 2020*, accessed at: www.ons.gov.uk/peoplepopulationandcommunity/birthsdeathsandmarriages/deaths/articles/coronavirus-covid19relateddeathsbyethnicgroupenglandandwales/2march-2020to15may2020

CHAPTER 28

Spirituality:
Nurturing Life Before, Within
and Beyond COVID-19

*Alison Phipps, Alastair Mcintosh
and Simon Barrow*

SB: The first big question for both of you is how have we nurtured the human spirit in the context of COVID-19? What have been your observations?

AP: My first thought comes from Kathy Galloway of the Iona Community, when she spoke recently about the immediate need under lockdown to give one another space – spiritually, physically and socially. Nadia Bolz-Weber, the Lutheran minister and theologian, has elaborated the work of the Creator as 'making space'. Everybody is now doing that wherever they are, as best as they can. I think about asylum seekers in hotel detention, who were suddenly in a household of 90 created by the Home Office. It has been intolerable for some. But for others, it has been a time of ease and grace. Bound up in all that is the idea that we are trying to give one another space by making amends or by offering creative possibilities for people's lives to look different.

For some, this 'making space' has actually been experienced as a bereavement of sorts, because they have lost the immediacy of their family, their church or some other community. There's also an adjustment to caring under circumstances we've never had to care under before, which has involved being thrown on to the mercy of others unexpectedly. For me, that meant experiencing the care that was being given particularly by the refugee and asylum communities I have long served. When, suddenly, we went into lockdown, they knew immediately what this was – a kind of bodily habitus that involved clicking back into what it means to live under curfew. They instantly knew who to care for, and how, in those circumstances.

For me, that led spiritually into a really interesting place regarding justice, because the people who were lost in this were largely the powerful, whose power had been stripped from them. And the people who were 'found', you might say, were those for whom a form of lockdown had been their reality for a very long time. Also, we've had a bunch of refugee organisations in Glasgow being given money by the government for the first time. Because of injustice from the past, this has allowed them to balance the scales a little bit. It won't last, but it's Sabbath, a rest. And furlough is Jubilee, a forgiveness of debts and a kind of Universal Basic Income by stealth. But this is just for a period, seven months maybe. So we will need to look again to see where we are then.

SB: I had conversations with a number of people with autism and others with mental health challenges. They were saying that under lockdown some of the pressures they routinely face had been removed. So that was a sense of liberation. But then new concerns about financial survival emerged. So there was both a buoying of the spirit, and a crushing of it, both at the same time.

AP: At the start of lockdown, we didn't know what it would be like. We had some inkling. We knew that there would be an increase in domestic violence, say. And we knew that certain groups of people would be picked off by the government. And then we began to see the full horror, particularly what was happening with people seeking asylum. Then we began to see the story of care homes. But at the start of lockdown, the questions of spirituality were very much as Kathy put them – giving one another space for some sort of creative work to begin. Then there have been people on the front line, strung out and working 16- to 18-hour days, doing the exhausting reactive work. They now need to recharge and replenish. I'm just starting to see that around my friends who are medics or care workers. So there's almost a sense of turn-taking, I think, with some of this.

AM: There was a survey recently which suggested that something like a quarter of people had said that they noticed a deepening of their spiritual life during lockdown, while a quarter felt they had not felt that. But only 5 per cent said they felt less depth. It's difficult to know what to make of such surveys, but there is a sense that people have experienced some really interesting shifts in their lives. We need time to pay attention to this.

I've got two inflatable canoes, and on one of the trips I made with these, I took a neighbour's son, a 14-year-old lad from just a few doors away. We were fishing and he suddenly said, 'Do you know anything about Zen?' I said, 'Well, a little bit.' At that point he mentioned reading Alan Watts. Now, in Govan you don't expect exactly expect a 14-year-old suddenly to name probably the principal figure in opening up Eastern spirituality to America in the 1950s and 1960s. And it turned out he'd been watching all of these Alan Watts videos on YouTube, and we spent most of the time discussing this. I asked him if he kept a kind of spiritual journal to keep his thoughts in. He liked that idea, so I gave him a wee notebook to take with him. And I thought, well, that's probably just a one off, but then my wife too had something similar happening with a neighbour. So some people, young or old, really are taking the opportunity of this changed situation to reflect, in unexpected ways.

In terms of the survey, the sceptical side of me had come out, and I thought, well, the trouble with surveys and spirituality is that it's very difficult to map the numinous. Also, people tend to give responses according to what they think they should say. But then suddenly that story brought the opening to the spiritual to life. I trust such story, such experience. It too may be a picture of what's going on. We're in our bubbles and zones of activity. Things bubble up, there are pricks of light, windows opening onto new themes in life.

AP: When I went into academia, it was dried up and atheistic in a rather negative way, and I was told to publish my poetry and prayers under a different name if I wanted to stay safe and have a career. You couldn't really be open about being a practising person of faith, a person who prayed, with any department other than theology – and then you had a legitimacy, because you could talk about it in a very critical, quite secular way! But now I think I've really noticed a change, an openness to the larger questions of life. It hasn't come under COVID-19, it was coming before, but I really started to notice it in a younger generation around 2014. It was probably stirring before that, but it came up with the independence referendum in Scotland, and a bit later, post-Brexit, in England. So here we have a generation robbed of their futures, made symbolic by those two votes. And suddenly they're looking for answers.

At that time people were asking me questions, and there was no longer an awkward silence about having a spiritual conversation. In New Zealand, where I have spent some time, these were very welcome because there is a fertile culture of spirituality in that context, and in others across the global south. That said, I'm quite sceptical of the way in which southern American evangelicalism and Pentecostalism has promoted itself as a 'prosperity gospel' in the global south, for instance, so I might be pulling back from talking about it in those settings.

But under COVID-19, I've had more conversations about spirituality, people phoning me out of the blue and wanting to talk about life and death. They wouldn't call it spirituality, and they certainly wouldn't use church or religious language. So the language I'm tending to draw on in these exchanges is very translational. I will be speaking to people about my tradition, and then asking others how they see things. It's invitational, because it's looking openly at questions and not imposing something on people. It's saying, 'This is how it is for me, so how is it for you?' Maybe it feels and looks quite different. Also, under COVID-19, no questions are resolved. They're all wide open. So, ontologically, people are having to be open to more possibilities than we've ever lived with before. That's really interesting.

AM: Yes, I'm seeing this coming up strongly in the climate change movement. Arising out of Occupy, I've sensed younger people on a search for meaningful spirituality. Parker Palmer, the American Quaker, talks about the need to hold spaces that are hospitable to the soul – 'inviting as well as open, safe and trustworthy, as well as free'. So I suppose my big question is: 'Where are the spaces that are hospitable before and after lockdown?' We need to have very open conversations where we're very clear that we're not trying to be a religious organisation but spirituality is still part of it.

SB: In terms of hospitable spaces for nourishing of the soul, the tragedy is that so often churches and other formal religious spaces are not like that at all. By contrast, what you've both been saying is that exploratory conversation about nurturing ourselves and each other needs to be very open and textured. But there's another realm of 'the spiritual' which has been co-opted by the market to become a kind of shop-around 'self-improvement'. It's consumerist, very passive, disconnected from social justice, and uninterested the roots and traditions of something that the three of us might want to call spirituality – a real thirst for life in its fullness.

AP: Working with refugees, who are displaced indigenous peoples, we've needed to think about indigeneity, along with displacement, and we've found the only way to think that in a way that is safe for them, and to hold space, is to think it spiritually, and to hold it ritually and ceremonially. We've done that by calling it an arts practice. But it's been about the art of living, it's been about the ability to hold comedy and tragedy, to laugh together, to eat together, to sing together, to dance together, to engage in things that peoples of culture will do, rather than what our dried-up academic spaces will allow. That means drawing on indigenous traditions from Ghana, Zimbabwe, Gaza and so on.

When I think about it, that is close to Celtic spirituality. It is comes out of figures like Saint Brigid of Kildare – a tradition and understanding of hospitality and fostership. So it is a translational, interculturally transitional space that is not demanding everyone fits in the same box or has the same orthodoxy or the same language or the same discourse. But what I'm seeing happening as we practice that is an experience of what you might otherwise call (in my Christian language) repentance and confession and praise and gratitude – a re-emerging space for acknowledgement of one another, of the goodness of what we have made together; space for silence, possibly for song, or for the quiet passing round of a chosen ritual or of objects that we've made on our own or together, in whatever the group might be.

There is, at this moment, no pure place to stand. Black Lives Matters. Therefore, for me, the sin of the world sticks to me like glue, as Lee Fisher would have said. Expiation comes by us choosing to work together towards a better future, not by us dwelling constantly on what we got wrong in the past. So there needs to be a space to move on from the stuckness. That is a place of moving from knowing you need to repent, but you can't, into a place where the art of forgiveness can be enacted. It's what I've experienced when I've been in many indigenous spaces where I am a representation of the people who colonised and destroyed and killed and looted and stole and did all manner of unconscionable things that the British did under colonialism. In this new space there's an equal first on the other side of all of that – to be the people who are able to make peace with justice. I think Black Lives Matters offers that, and I think the questions around slavery in Scotland offers that too.

SB: That's taking us into difficult territory – the threatening shadow that we're dealing with in Trumpism, or in the kind of disaster capitalist project that hasn't simply gone away because of COVID-19. *So is there a life-force, or spirituality, of resistance we need to discover or recover? A way of being together that doesn't exhaust us in the midst of struggle, but impels us forward and energises us?*

AM: Maybe I can come in on that one, because I have spent most of the past 24 hours on issues related to land reform. Land reform in Scotland is very interesting. There's now over 400 community land trusts, and to the best of my knowledge, not one of them has gone bust yet. I had a BBC Alba reporter round, doing a bit of filming about climate change, but tying it in with Hebridean land reform. And the final question was about how spirituality tied in with both of those. I said that land reform is a counter-capitalist dynamic. It is about bringing the most fundamental resource back into the democratically accountable control of the people who live on a particular piece of ground. And it's working at multiple levels. Partly it's about agriculture, but it's also about renewable energy and having the benefits coming into communities instead of being exported. It's about small business, too. It's about socially affordable housing where the community controls it, instead of having it sold out of the community.

But in addition to all those, it is about the psychology and the spirituality of what it means to become a community. It's our membership of one another, based on interconnection in communities of place. So often the leading figures in land reform are people who are not just in it for themselves, they're doing it for the community, for others.

I'm wary when I hear knee jerk anti-capitalist stuff because usually it's not going deep enough. It's just looking at economic control. But it's not actually recognising the power of those market dynamics by which we are all bound up in consumer behaviour. And the principal antidote to that is to undercut the false 'wants' that consumerism tries to fulfil. So we start to cut down on the consumer behaviour that drives climate change. If we are serious about that, we've got to find our satisfaction in ways that are more than just being spoon-fed by marketing departments. If we ask our African friends how they deal with a social sickness, they'll probably say that they deal with it by calling back the soul. That's what we are doing with land reform in Scotland. We're calling back the soul of a people of place. And it is celebrated in culture: in dance and song and in so many aspects of our culture.

On Lewis I grew up amongst Harris Tweed weavers. Weaving teaches us a lot. When your life is going outwards at warp speed, you're not filling in with the weft. When that happens the warp spreads out more and more out, and becomes frazzled at the ends, and dissipates. It gets tangled and lost. So if we're looking at how Scotland is going to recover from COVID-19, and how it might respond in terms of both adaptation and mitigation terms to climate change, then I think we need to create a society that weaves the weft into the warp. That's about wellbeing economics. It's also the work of artists and creative people. It's about building meaning back into our communities and holding the basket of life. And why? So that our young people are then held in a basket of community. So they don't just become a lost generation to the 'pause' of COVID-19.

AP: Yes, to be a spiritual person of depth comes back to the holding of space, where we started. Some of the best gifts are baskets for things which are good and worth keeping through a lifetime. And then there may be another basket of things which are really bad and not worth keeping. I think we're in a moment where we are faced with the spiritual work of naming these things. Also, I remember my GP saying to me, with regard to some trauma I had taken on: 'I could give you beta blockers or you could take up embroidery or something.' So I took a bit I took up knitting and I've continued to do it ever since. It came at the same time as my understanding about the importance of renewing the human threads of our connectivity.

SB: We could have started with this, but let's finally turn to the question of what we mean by spirituality? We've let that emerge so far. But one of my favourite definitions is from liberation theology and Leonardo Boff. He simply says that 'spirit' means life, so spirituality is about nurturing, developing and sharing life in the face of (and in contest with) the forces of death. It's not about some rarefied activity for a group of people called religious, or reckoning themselves to be spiritual gurus. It's something we share and work at together.

AM: Absolutely. Alison mentioned Celtic spirituality. If you were to ask me what I mean by 'Celtic', I would basically say the part of you that was not colonised by the Romans and the Normans to the same extent as some others were. With St Columba, the sense of connectedness to community and the natural world got larger and larger. That is the vision that his biographer, Adomnan, described when an angel showed her a mantle before his birth, full of all the colours of the flowers. As the angel drew the mantle away, the mother reached out, only to see it expand to fill the whole world. This is what it means to open to spiritual awareness. The beauty by which our lives are deeply woven, no matter how "small" those lives might seem to be, gradually expands to fill the world. And that, to me is the importance of the weaving metaphor.

AP: Just before I left New Zealand I was doing work with a woman who's worked with masks as part of her post-trauma therapy. So she's done this both with the mosque shooting, and also with the Christchurch earthquake. She told me about it and I said to her that before I left I'd like to make my own trauma mask. It was incredibly powerful. And talking of weaving, at the moment the churches' clothes are pretty tatty. The institution has been pretty much stripped naked. So for the church and for other institutions, this is chance to look at ourselves. It's a chance for recovery. We will not look like we once did after COVID-19 if we do that. And that is no bad thing.

For me the understanding of what it looks like to embrace life in 2020, as we move towards Scotland after COVID-19, or living with COVID-19 as a reality in our lives, is that it's a question of developing an erotic force in the widest sense of the word. That is a way of saying love and life in all their fullness.

SB: But not confusing that with 'life in all its niceness', as churches are apt to do.

AM: No, that would be self-absorption. Whereas fullness means fullness – taking the strands of our lives, including all the lengths that we think we don't want, and allowing the creative power to weave something beautiful out of it. What matters is not the mess we're in, but what we do to draw out goodness from that mess. Then life becomes a work of joy.

Section Six – Art, Culture, Sport and Media

Sìth Sealach

Anne C Frater/Anna C Frater

Fhad 's a bha sin uile glaiste
bha na sìtheanan a' fàs
ri oir an rathaid:
neòinein agus buidheagain,
canach agus cailleachan-breaca,
agus sealastairean buidhe bòidheach
a' glacadh na grèine.
Chualas ceòl an teillein
agus clacharain a' gliogadaich;
uiseagan gu h-àrd agus smeòrach anns a' chraoibh.
Bha sinn a' coiseachd,
agus a' ruith,
agus a' cuachail
agus a' dabhdail,
bha sinn a' stad, 's a' còmhradh,
a' gabhail naidheachd
agus a' nochdadh coibhneis,
o nach robh cabhaig sam bith oirnn
rudeigin eile a dhèanamh.

Bha mi an dòchas gun robh sinn ag ionnsachadh.

Dh' fhuasgladh na bannan
agus ghearradh na sìtheanan,
chan eil sgeul air an t-seileastair
's tha an teillein ri caoidh
gun do thill sinn.

Nach do dh' ionnsaich sinn.

Fhathast.

CHAPTER 29

Transitory Peace

Anne C Frater/Anna C Frater

While we were all locked in
the flowers grew
by the roadside:
daisies and buttercups,
bog-cotton and spotted orchids,
and beautiful yellow irises
catching the sun.
We heard the bee singing
and stonechats clicking;
larks above and thrushes in the trees.
We walked,
and ran,
and wandered
and dawdled,
we stopped, and talked,
asked for news
and showed kindness,
because there was no hurry
and nothing else to do.

I hoped that we were learning.

The locks opened
and the flowers were cut,
the iris has gone.
The bee laments
our return,

and that we haven't learnt.

Yet.

CHAPTER 30

A Changing Landscape for Arts and the Media
Claire Sawers

WITH THE ARRIVAL of the coronavirus, the landscape for the media and arts in Scotland was shifted and jolted dramatically. What might emerge or change further in both spheres 'after' COVID-19, whatever that might mean? It is very hard to tell. But the recent terrain may render some clues as to what might be happening to reshape our cultural and media lives. First, however, comes the story – or, rather a series of snapshots in which this process can be observed.

Opening Night

On what would have been the opening night of the Edinburgh International Festival, huge dancing Batman beams of light were shot up from over 250 venues across Edinburgh into the night sky. From the right viewpoint, the spectacle was surreal; a dazzling reminder of all the venues sitting empty when they would normally be packed with crowds. People craned their necks out kitchen windows and car windscreens to watch. It's the first time in 73 years that there hasn't been a festival in Edinburgh. This summer there are no flyers being handed out on the High Street, no pop-up bars around town, no late-night venues packed with tourists and performers. While many mourn the temporary loss of August's annual juggernaut of international comedy, theatre, music, books and dance – and the surge of international visitors that it brings – others consider the hiatus as a much-needed time out for reflection and, maybe, radical change.

The impact on the incomes of many artists, technical staff, critics, bookers and arts administrators is devastating, just as it has been for all live events that have had to be cancelled. But in the arts world, as in so many other spheres, the COVID-19 curveball could hopefully be offering an opportunity for reinvention. 'Edinburgh lives matter' tweeted someone on the YouTube stream before the official light show from EIF began. #LetEdinburghHeal, someone else had joked earlier that day at a bus stop in Leith Walk, where billboards and lampposts would normally be covered in posters advertising shows.

Market Challenges

Concerns have been raised for several years now around the Airbnb rental economy that goes hand in hand with the Edinburgh Festivals. Many believe the growth in this kind of profit-making accommodation has become out of control in recent years, prioritising income over the welfare of its residents.

A survey led by Green MSP Andy Wightman in early 2020 confirmed that huge numbers of these short-term lets in Edinburgh were also operating unlawfully – making it the largest unregulated rental market in Scotland. With Edinburgh's cash cow out of action for the time being, it's a time to consider what the original artistic motives behind the Festival actually were, and whether the existing format, with its increasingly market-oriented approach, needs an urgent rethink.

With no audiences coming to visit this summer, many of the performers that would normally be on stage in Edinburgh went online instead. Scottish Ballet unveiled some exciting new digital commissions in August; *Indoors* by choreographer Sophie Laplane, created after the entire company of 36 dancers rehearsed together via Zoom and *Catalyst*, which was recorded on an empty stage and shared online. SHEDINBURGH, set up by theatre producers Francesca Moody and Harriet Bolwell and writer/performer Gary McNair, allowed Fringe acts to livestream from their own garden huts during August and September, as well as special sheds set up at the Traverse Theatre in Edinburgh and Soho in London.

Viewers were able to book in to watch via Zoom, and all monies raised went towards the Shed Load of Future fund for the preservation of the Fringe. Fringe of Colour Films launched in August 2020 as 'an online arts festival for Black & Brown/PoC creatives', making films available to stream for a week at a time. Since 2004, the Free Festival has provided a more affordable alternative for the masses of performers that can't afford the high costs of the official Fringe. They have grown to become the biggest comedy producer at the Fringe, providing a platform for a wider diversity of working-class, BAME and LGBTQI+ performers in the process. Like so many others, the Free

Fringe Festival chose to go online for 2020, with a daily schedule of cabaret, comedy, music and children's shows streamed on Twitch TV, and the usual invitation to donate what you could afford, this time through an online link, instead of the usual upside down hat by the exit.

A Calendar for Culture

The calendar for culture extends far beyond Edinburgh in August of course, and some of the organisations, venues and individuals creating Scotland's best art were also forced to adapt and innovate if they wanted to avoid becoming obsolete, destitute or both. For some, the potentially catastrophic circumstances also provided a shot at the artistic revolution they'd long been hoping for. Under the working title 'Not Going Back to Normal', Collective art gallery commissioned a radical manifesto by and for disabled artists in Scotland. Artists Harry Josephine Giles and Sasha Saben Callaghan used the intervention of the pandemic to gather ideas and art for 'Not Going Back To Normal' writing:

> Before COVID-19, disabled artists were already routinely excluded from visual arts and galleries… Now, at a time when all of our adjustments are suddenly reasonable, the world is experiencing just a fraction of our normal, and everyone else is suddenly interested in isolation, vulnerability and distance communication, we want to hand that provocation over to you. Because we're not going back to normal. The world is changing, so let's remake it with our ideas.

Noticing the lack of an official Pride celebration this year, and feeling the huge void where Glasgow's nightlife and after-party scene used to be, Glasgow queer club Shoot Your Shot presented a 12-hour livestream of performance artists and DJs on Twitch TV instead. The money that they raised through PayPal was then divided up between the otherwise out of work photographers, musicians, dancers and bookers, keeping a vital grassroots world alive.

Counterflows festival of underground, experimental and international music was due to take place in Glasgow in April 2020, but commissioned some of its performers in Scotland, Africa and Europe to make new videos and audio streams for the Counterflows website instead. Co-organiser Alasdair Fielding was also keen to use some of the repurposed budget on paying music writers to interview the artists, recognising the crucial role that they play in the music ecosystem.

A Culture of Cuts

The arts and media worlds are undeniably interlinked, and often suffering the same serious hardships, while also experiencing some of the same promising transformations. In a report released in July, the office of the National Union of Journalists in Scotland described how 'the COVID-19 crisis has hit an industry with underlying health conditions.' Years before the virus appeared, a lack of investment in journalism and a worrying trend towards commercialism rather than quality coverage has threatened the future of traditional media. The NUJ report confirmed that redundancies were planned across many Scottish titles, including the Reach publishing group, JPI Media and Newsquest, with pay cuts hitting many more union members hard at a time of lockdown.

While many publications failed to consult with recognised unions before making changes that would severely impact their workers, others were forced to reconsider their economic decisions – the NUJ supported action taken by members against the Reach group, who claimed pay cuts were essential while also sitting on a company cash reserve believed to be £20 million. As part of a UK-wide cuts programme, BBC Scotland also announced that it needs to save £6.2 million, of which £3.5–4 million would come from staffing, the equivalent of around 60 posts.

There were more encouraging examples of good practice, too. All staff at STV were placed on furlough, in rotation to avoid singling out individual members of staff, and the government furlough scheme payments were topped up to 100 per cent of normal pay. *The Big Issue* also responded to its steep drop in advertising revenue by opening up the pages that would normally have been filled with adverts and inviting charities, grassroots groups and companies to use them for free instead.

Many smaller, independent publications faced an enormous challenge. The community-based, employee-owned *West Highland Press* was forced to pause production of their print editions for several months, resuming in August 2020. The Edinburgh-based (but Scotland-wide arts and culture magazines), *The Skinny* and *The List* both stopped producing print issues, running a reduced amount of coverage on their websites and social media instead.

New Visions?

Now is a time of rapid change, where many already beleaguered arts venues and organisations are facing closure and the media continues in its usual phase of flux, albeit with more serious implications this time. New dreams and aspirations are emerging too, as communities re-examine their values, create new structures of power and imagine new realities. Mutual aid networks and community-led initiatives may thrive as larger institutions take less precedence. Community radio and newspapers may enjoy a healthy resurgence. Trickle down economies may be ditched in favour of something more egalitarian and effective. There is certainly the opportunity to think and act afresh.

The Edinburgh Festivals (some of which have adapted themselves online in the meantime) will officially return in 2021, as will many of the live festivals and arts events that were forced to cancel or postpone. Whether they will be wiser, stronger and more exciting in the post-pandemic world remains to be seen. There is nothing automatic or guaranteed about how established media and the creative arts will respond as we come to terms with a COVID-19-infected world. A huge amount will depend upon the wider economy, and who controls the resources required. But the opportunity for renewed vision is always there, and resides in those who continue to operate on a changed landscape.

CHAPTER 31

COVID-19:
Accelerating the (Un)Social Media Landscape
Jennifer Jones

'THEY SAY THAT to be popular on social media is like being rich from playing Monopoly.'

When I say 'they' – I mean, I saw it on a meme, a pixelated quote box, a screenshot of a tweet that had been tarted up and shared onto Instagram Stories.

'That's a good one, I'm keeping that,' I smirk. Right swipe replay. Double tap save. Scroll to refresh. Notification. WhatsApp.

'Are you ok? Did you see this?' Open Application. View Screenshot. Write message. Pause.

I've just been furloughed. It's my fifth hour flipping between Facebook, Instagram, TikTok and Twitter. Gormless, I examine contrasting, moving images at a quick pace. Saving and Liking with my thumb. Might post this later. Have a like, why not?

I flip back to my home screen. Select photo album. Examine the fruits of scroll. Something, possibly, I could post on my own feed. WhatsApp deposited screenshots from a group chat. View image. Hmm. Could be about me. Shouldn't be on this. Public, I was taking a break.

I deactivate my Twitter account, a precaution. Don't get dragged in. Can't be trusted. Holding down the wobbling square, commit delete. I pick up my book. Reading on for two minutes, my mind wanders. I need to write that down. Good line. Remember that. Pick up the phone. Swipe screen. My finger hovers. Fuck. I hate it.

Earlier, a refresh-scroll showed an ex-colleague posted he was giving up Twitter because of just how bad COVID-19 Twitter was.

We had met on Twitter over a decade ago, so I was a little bit sad at his departure. The good guys are leaving, leaving me here hanging onto this, whatever this is. Perhaps maybe more nostalgic for the good times, when you used to meet good people in that place. But mainly I am jealous that he got in there early with the digital detox. 'He'll be back,' tuts my inner monologue.

The explanation pinned to the top of his page states COVID-19 Twitter was too much, and he was only going to use his account for work, as a broadcast tool, a place to store up links to the content he was producing remotely during lockdown.

'So you haven't left then.'

Fourteen years of making tweets, I was already forming sentences that fit perfectly within a 280-character word limit and I knew I would drum up a few comments in return. It would give me a reason to open my phone. To check that I wasn't alone in my thinking. The lockdown had only magnified this craving. With what felt like only a screen for company – and no work to distract me – the caustic, *pithy* manner in which the website invites me in to have an opinion, to exchange in dialogue, was just too much of a temptation to resist.

Nothing more felt like a void than the first two weeks of lockdown. Something. Anything more than jokes about toilet paper.

When social distancing became an expression, social media became dominant. Overnight, my world shrunk. My job – local reporter at a print newspaper – was eventually mothballed after three weeks of pandemic publishing. We tried to push on as advertising dried up, the pages shrinking each week, but the words required to fill them growing, while being unable to wander far enough to know if something was true. News-gathering was reliant on refreshing Facebook to see if anybody was doing anything interesting that I could borrow.

With any form of storytelling, the quality of interactions with the subjects are important. Working from home should be easy when you are in the industry of producing words. Moving from the office to the kitchen table doesn't impact the bulk of the journalist's day job. However, in terms of news sourcing, repurposing popular things people said on social media was already creeping in as common journalistic practice before quarantine hit.

The sports pages went first, which makes up nearly a quarter of a newspaper. Shit. It was then followed by our community ones, the events people hold, the meetings in churches, community halls, councils, sports halls, pubs and event spaces. Only weeks before I had covered my first 100th birthday in a nursing home. Sweet and endearing, and very human to meet four generations of the one family, so keen to talk to a reporter to celebrate their elder's life. Gone as people stop meeting to protect themselves and their loved ones. The phone contributions that we rely on, the stories I got while having a beer in the local, or walking the dog in the morning, the chance meetings in the in between. They all disappeared as people stayed indoors and were asked to stay apart.

With newspapers on their knees, the paradox of encouraging people to buy a physical copy while reporting against unnecessary trips to the shop. Now, it felt like social media was now ready to shine up front and centre its vision to be the collective window into the world.

Screens became the replacement for everything. A work life, a social life, a fitness life, recovery and mental groups, a child minder, a home schooler. Screens.

The pandemic itself worked in the favour of technology companies who have been working for years towards forcing a digital transformation upon nearly everything. With eyeball time increased for so many – the complex and secretive algorithms, learning what tickles you, feeding you more of what you want to see, personalising, yet homogenising the online experience so you don't put your phone down.

I saw it in my eight-year-old nephew first. Fortnite, perhaps now a trigger word for some parents, a massively online shooting game (that openly boasts about using child psychologists to keep them engaged by the way), became the source of contention at the dinner table. Controlling screen time in favour of DIY home-schooling became a battle of wills between grown-ups and child, of deception and cutting off the Wi-Fi and the ask for 'just one more game' each time the game ended – refresh screen, scroll. But it was his social life, the only line out of my parent's house and into the realm of his friendship circle, while locking him into the dependency of a virtual world over the physical.

As the days blurred into weeks blurred into months, I was staring at my own phone in the same way. The lack of real interaction, the pregnant pauses in conversations, wondering what to do with your face when listening on a Zoom call and the softness of non-verbal cues was starting to mess with my head.

The only thing that appeared to have bonded people was how the broadcasting of our personal lives had now become content for others to validate and critique. The government locked us down, and then it was our job to provide the surveillance panopticon required to ensure people stuck to lock down. The smugness of sticking to the rules was as annoying as those who broke them. Each posting becomes flattened as they join the infinite timeline of unlimited information about what other people are doing in other homes. The frustration of not seeing our own loved ones became amplified as the behaviours of others were magnified. The self-ownership of not being able to resist the allure of the posting content, even if that content showcased one breaking the rules. The paranoia of tagging a location of your walk, as knowing others could triangulate your whereabouts and if you had crossed the five-mile threshold. Then, of course, Barnard Castle happened.

Social media was already robbing us of context and nuance before the pandemic happened. We were increasingly trying to make sense of the new digital world and our identity within it, combined with the noise of others doing similar.

Picking up and unlocking a smartphone screen is deliberately and purposefully designed so that you are sunk into an interface of your own making. The complexity of using a social media network, such as Twitter, Instagram, pick a platform where the user posts updates with the notion of multiple, fragmented audiences is wrapped up solely in the personality and identity of the user.

There is a relationship between the user and the content that they choose to create and deem worthy to share with their personal network. The virtual identity of the user becomes their public facing performance – authentic and relatable on the outside but mediated, nonetheless.

For the explicit social media professional, or *the influencer*, their curation of content and posting of popular content becomes part of their known identity – and takes the form of an affiliation, there are rewards for those who can attract and command attention.

It is a heady, alluring cocktail of self-obsession combined with easy reward, of assumed underdog and while expressing vulnerabilities in an intimate way – through the same phone screen as private thoughts and messages go – as the user performs and adapts to the telling stories and broadcasting thoughts that garner attention from others. They say things so others will like them, and will validate them, but those who criticise can be deemed haters and trolls.

For those who learn to harness the affordances of social media, the chance to be heard over others, becomes an attractive professional proposition. It becomes a career, a financial opportunity, a chance to feel visible. A status symbol of such. The building of a personal brand, individuals who have learned to navigate the 'many-to-many' properties of the social networking platform in order to promote and interact with an implied public audience. All from the comfort and the limited effort of using a phone.

This is not a new thing – although we still refer to it as 'new media' 15 years on from the early Web 2.0 interfaces. The draw of social media is that it makes one feel as if they have their own voice, a media democratisation that did not exist previously. It is clear that the social media brands look forward to empowering their users to act like the legacy media of the past, skipping past the 'gatekeepers' of big media such as newspapers, television and radio and direct their internal thoughts towards their own implied audiences. Ones that they can see in the form of numbers and interactions such as likes and retweets.

Is it such a wonder that much of the discussion on platforms such as Twitter is about media – or the gleeful gloating as Scottish journalism receives its own death knock. As the response to the pandemic, and the bottom falling out of advertising, newspaper companies began shedding jobs. Furloughed journalists became redundant ones. Despite rising clicks and record-breaking page views, none of the money reaches the people who create the words. Digital transformation is still touted as the solution, but giving away content for free is the horse that bolted. Some try to add a paywall, as technology companies that seem to specialise in mediated chaos finally admit that they might be publishers in their own right. Gesturing at Facebook, who are finally starting to remove sources of disinformation and labelling harmful content after years of being out of control.

Furthermore, every posting from traditional Scottish outlets such BBC Scotland and *The Herald* carries the hangover from 2014. A familiar response, multiple scotty dog avatars tweet gleefully that they look forward to the day the newspaper is dead and how they don't need it anymore. How many subscriptions has one person claimed to have cancelled over the years? Every posting from the Radio Scotland account and the BBC, hits out with bias and blame, it was the mainstream media (MSM) that did it. Absolving the social media that dominates and permeates everything that we do now from any responsibility. Is this because users feel that they are only minutes away from being part of the new media power grab? Well, it depends what team you support and how deeply down the rabbit hole you are.

Jia Tolentino, staff writer at the New Yorker defines this sensation in her book *Trick Mirror* which looks at how the internet has transformed society:

> The everyday madness perpetuated by the internet is the madness of this architecture, which positions personal identity as the center of the universe.
>
> It's as if we've been placed on a lookout that oversees the entire world and given a pair of binoculars that makes everything look like our own reflection. Through social media, many people have quickly come to view all new information as a sort of direct commentary on who they are. This system persists because it is profitable.

Taken together, the 'usefulness' of social media post-corona sits on a spectrum, where we need to be careful when accessing information as an individual node in a decentralised network of communities battling the economy of visibility. This includes the process of making media, who is allowed to make media and what can be considered a legitimate voice or influencer on these platforms. I'm a reporter, of course I am biased here – but if we lose the expertise, the specialisms, the quality and diversity of Scottish writing that comes from longer form publications, in favour of immediacy and resharing social clips, we also lose the ability to hold power, in both big P and little p politics, that comes with a robust Scottish media landscape. What is left but threads, rants and memes?

'They say that to be popular on social media is like being rich from playing Monopoly.'

References

Tolentio, J, 2018, *Trick Mirror: Reflections on Self Delusion*, New York, USA, Fourth Estate.

CHAPTER 32

'Abandon All Hope, Ye Who Enter Here': From Hell to Creative Scotland Form Filling A Short Journey

Flavia D'Avila

MY FIRST PROJECT of 2020 began by quoting the famous words said to be inscribed on the gates of hell. The project was a week of R&D for a new devised theatre piece based on the fifth canto of Dante's *Inferno*, the first part of the *Divina Commedia* trilogy. Little did my collaborators and I know how dramaturgically ironic these words would become a few weeks after the public sharing of our piece.

The thing is, unlike most of my peers, I did not find lockdown to be hell. Like many of them, I had work cancelled or postponed indefinitely. Like many of them, I was furloughed from one of my bill-paying jobs and had my freelancing income slashed. Like a lot of people I read about online, I had just moved in with my boyfriend, and even though we have been together for a couple of years, neither of us had ever co-habited with a partner before and now had to learn to be in each other's company 24/7.

However, unlike many of my peers and people whose lives I read about on the internet, my life had been radically interrupted before. I first moved to Scotland from Brazil in 2006 and after six years of a perfectly happy life in Edinburgh, en route to obtaining the much-coveted 'Leave to Remain', the then UK Border Agency brought about some drastic changes to immigration policies and I was forced to return to my country of birth in 2012, not knowing if or when I would come back. For the next three painful years, my personal life and my work existed in limbo which, according to Dante's *Inferno*, is the place that harbours those souls who have not really done anything wrong but simply are not eligible to enter Heaven. It is a points-based system, apparently.

That time in limbo delayed my life and still does. Everything I do, every decision I make, is driven by the Home Office rules. I managed to come back on a new Tier 4 Student visa to do a PhD, going back to university when most of my contemporaries just got on with their work and furthered their careers in theatre. For the past five years, I have had to work even harder to do my research while maintaining or establishing the connections required to achieve a minimum level of recognition in the theatre sector. As a self-funded international student, I have also needed to work in other jobs, usually zero-hour and minimum wage, to scrape a living, within the stipulated restriction of 20 weekly hours that my visa allows.

Being a non-European national also makes me ineligible for any type of government support, including Jobseeker's Allowance. Therefore, a long period of suspended activities and uncertainty followed by a period of financial instability, burnout and having to follow strict rules was not new to me.

Personally, the lockdown was actually exactly what I needed: it afforded me the time and space to finish writing my thesis and I found the focus that I had previously lacked due to being distracted by theatre projects and bill-paying work. Coming out of lockdown, on the other hand, and navigating this new era, has turned out to be infernal. I deliberately delayed writing my contribution to this volume to very close to the deadline because we are going through lightning fast changes these days. Time has gone completely wonky – it slowed down in many respects (I do not have anything resembling a routine anymore), but in terms of updates on how our world is changing, it has really sped up.

Keeping up with the news has become an endurance test. My boyfriend is English, so we are constantly discussing the different rules in England and Scotland with his family, and yet that is much less stressful than talking to his sister who lives in the US or to my family in Brazil, both of whom we had planned to visit at some point this year. We can see some friends in some specific contexts, but it is still weird not to hug them, and some of them still do not want to risk the outside world. And I preferred not being able to go to places because they were closed, not because I could not afford them.

Emerging from the peace and quiet of my focused thesis writing, post-submission I began to hear the screams. I took notice of the outpour of online content from theatre-makers everywhere, festivals delivering entire programmes online, whole lives moving to the web-space. I felt exhausted before even engaging with any of it, so I just looked away. Before the pandemic, the recurrence of film aesthetics in stage productions already bothered me. I believe we will never be able to compete with film and everything pertaining to this medium that we try to recreate onstage will be inevitably be subpar. The one thing that theatre can do that film absolutely cannot is offer the shared live experience.

I fully understand the anxiety caused by wishing to stay relevant and stay on people's minds, I fully understand that streaming makes theatre more accessible to many (except that digital poverty does not seem to have been taken much into account the past few months), but I did not get much from the handful of online pieces with which I engaged.

In addition to the race to upload content, any content, just put it out there right now, there has (also understandably) been a lot of very loud screaming from the people often left behind. People of colour, trans people, non-binary people, disabled people, migrants, work-ing-class people, grassroots artists, are all desperate not to have the few spaces they had managed to conquer within the performing arts taken away again.

New task forces and movements pop up every few minutes to co-ordinate efforts, whereas the establishment desperately tries not to crumble by keeping their high-paid executives in post with their full salary and making their ushers, cleaners and box office staff redun-dant. All the while, the actual makers are just trying to keep up with the news and adjust their emotions, plans and expectations every time they find out there is no support/there is some support/there is a grant or a commission but it is not for you. Two weeks after submitting my thesis, I muted the word 'theatre' from my Twitter feed.

The problem with the screams of all the tortured souls in hell is you cannot hear what they are saying, and their sins are irredeemable. In Purgatory, however, they can purge and eventually ascend after time allocated for contemplation and atonement. During a conversation with another researcher the other day, she pointed out she had not seen much from people working with live art during the pandemic.

My first thought was that the clue was in the name: *live art*. Though many people working in this medium have pioneered the use of var-ious digital technologies in live performance, they do absolutely rely on the direct connection with their audience for their art to work. I found myself thinking back to a show I saw at *Take Me Somewhere* last year, during which a woman flagellated herself with a dead octopus for ten minutes. If I were watching that online, I could simply close my browser window and walk away from any discomfort.

People did walk away in the Tramway, but that required walking through the performance and being seen/judged by performers and audience. Besides, all other senses were engaged directly as people could be hit with a bit of tentacle if they were sitting close enough and the octopus was slowly cooking under the theatre lights, filling the space with a terrible fishy smell, all of which fed into the dramaturgy of the piece. Live artists fully comprehend what they are and maybe this is why they have taken this as time out while they cannot perform live.

As a sector, I wish we could just go into Purgatory now and collectively atone. We have a spectacular chance to radically change theatre, but it will not happen without employing efforts to understand what went wrong and how to fix it. As a maker, I am much more interested in figuring out how we uphold the distinction between theatre and film clearly defined and find ways to maintain the shared live experience in a socially distant world. If we absolutely must work online, I wish established organisations would embrace the unknown and offer their low-risk platforms to artists who have not yet had a chance to work with them.

I wish artists would go beyond livestreaming through conference calls and making archival footage available and get creative with digital and online technology, pushing the boundaries of what dramaturgy can do. I wish there was enough monetary support fairly distributed for making no-strings-attached, high-quality work respecting creative freedom.

But sadly, this is not where I see us headed. At the time of writing, we are all still processing the news that 75 per cent of the latest government bailout money for the arts has been ring-fenced for regularly-funded organisations and is to be distributed by Creative Scotland. I have also observed that, in the eager attempt to save the arts, a trend towards advocating for socially engaged theatre has become prominent, which is not to say we should not do it, but I am concerned about it becoming the only way of being funded.

I have read excellent analyses of the new Open Fund by fellow theatre-makers pointing out that questions regarding equality and diversity, inclusion and outreach of projects seeking funding are repeated three times in the application form, thus indicating where the focus currently lies for the gatekeepers.

However, I do not agree that yet more tick-box exercises are the best way to respond to demands, when I have calculated that the salary paid to the Creative Scotland CEO would be enough for me to make three shows paying 25 freelancers in the process. This is why I am less scared of theatre dying out and needing to be rebuilt from scratch than I am of things just going back to normal. We have missed our chance to purge. After the virus, we will just keep screaming inside our burning coffins into eternity.

CHAPTER 33

Scottish Football in the Wake
of the Pandemic: Do or Die?

Paul Goodwin and Simon Barrow

'ONLY THREE THINGS matter in football – the players, the manager and the fans,' the legendary Bill Shankly once observed. 'Nothing else matters,' he added, with the categorical flourish of a man who knew his mind when it came to the game that had become his life. In terms of the immediacy of the sport he lived and breathed, that may be true. But in reality football in Scotland, as elsewhere, depends upon an infrastructure of support covering everything from governance and regulation through to finance, publicity, health and safety, and much more. The stark reality of COVID-19 is that it has reminded all of us associated with the Beautiful Game that much of this infrastructure is perilously fragile, unevenly spread and tremendously stretched.

So the virus has not just been an unprecedented event in terms of its own multiple impacts on society and on the sporting culture of the nation, it has also served as a further wake-up call regarding the future of our particular game, how it is run, and what it might need to prosper. This is a larger question than simply recovering from the shock of coronavirus. It is a question of facing the long-term and deeply damaging decline that has added to the vulnerability we are experiencing in these additionally perilous and economically enervating times.

Given the importance of sport as a whole in Scottish life (with rugby and golf chief among those endeavours ranking up alongside what many of us still regard as 'the national game'), the issues and challenges faced by football as a result of COVID-19 are by no means singular. But they are, in many respects, distinctive – and distinctly threatening.

A Different Scale of Challenge

As lockdown moved from weeks to months it became increasingly clear that its impact is going to be far worse than anyone could have predicted. The nearest thing we have to compare it to, many suggest, is the two world wars of the last century. Yet in a football context, that is an inappropriate analogy. During those wars, many fans joined the armed forces. Players (men) were also called up. The game was interrupted. Women's football rose to the limelight briefly, but then was supressed again – only more recently starting to gain the seeds of attention it richly deserves. However, after the break football resumed, buoyed by the post-war resurgence seen in many other areas of life, fans got something to cheer about again.

Indeed, football adapted and adjusted significantly during and after the war years. There was reduced pricing, alternative kick-off times and guest players – such as one Bill Shankly, then a star at Preston North End, playing for Partick Thistle here in Scotland. We even had wartime international matches, with huge crowds at packed stadiums. Football did its bit for morale during a period of national trauma. It lost players and fans to the conflict, and suffered from a reduction in revenue. But it mostly emerged from the crisis intact – though the Luftwaffe did manage to put one club – King's Park FC, the Stirling predecessor to Stirling Albion – out of business, when a stray bomb destroyed their Forthbank home.

It has not taken us long to realise that coronavirus is, proportionately, threatening to do much more lasting damage to the game's supporting structures and to some of its clubs – especially the smaller ones – unless a major rescue, recovery and renewal programme can be launched. As the weeks rolled by, with professional and junior clubs losing income and having little idea of when or whether they might be operational again, Scottish football managed to produce its own COVID-19 soap opera – with the end-of-season crisis morphing into a massive league reconstruction debacle. All we had to talk about was interminable football politics and threatened legal action, plus the latest 'classic match' reruns for those who supported higher profile teams.

A People-Shaped Economic Challenge

Economically, Scottish football is hugely lop-sided, and the danger is that this will only get worse. Half of those who support a team in Scotland opt for one or other of two Glasgow teams. The further gulf between a handful of other sides and the rest of the pack gets wider the further down the leagues you look. The billionaire English Premiership is another world, although one which feeds inflation across the whole game.

Meanwhile, while mostly existing on a relative pittance, some 60 per cent of total revenue in Scottish football is still derived from the paying customers, the fans. That is why it is essential to understand supporters, and why that knowledge is key for preserving the game and for any chance of building a sustainable football business.

We know that, for the vast majority of fans, their primary football concern is usually what happens at 3.00pm on a Saturday and in the ensuing couple of hours. What is important is the almost religious ritual of watching their current heroes trying to write another chapter of sporting history for their club. However, over recent years there has been a significant change to that dynamic.

A growing number of supporters are wanting and needing to understand how football works financially and practically. When it comes to the inner workings of their club and its place in the game, they appreciate that engaging with its commercial and political dimensions is now essential. It is a two-way process, in fact. Fans need to be understood (as enthusiasts, but also as customers and stakeholders), and they in turn need to understand how a football business works.

Fans to the Rescue?

In the context of COVID-19, this understanding translated into some remarkable gestures – such as the £25,000 voluntarily raised in a matter of weeks by fans of Dumbarton, located in an area of the central belt enduring some of the worst economic indicators in Scotland. As the chairman of the club acknowledged, this money has helped it to stay afloat.

The concern going forward for the game as whole is that, given the health crisis and accompanying financial meltdown, the impact this will have on football supporters attending games could be severe. We know that over 50 per cent of revenue is directly generated by gate and season ticket admissions in our lower leagues, and 43 per cent in the Premiership. Any downward pressure on those numbers could be critical to the financial viability of football. Expecting numbers to hold up is at best optimistic, and probably not realistic. The eventual return of spectators, under conditions of social distancing or otherwise, remains a great unknown at present. If the fall is significant, clubs could very well go out of business.

Given that there will be shrinkage, or at the very worst a collapse, in the sponsorship market, and that the Sky television deal will certainly need to be redrawn, Scottish football will need every fan it can find moving forward. Yet, as we know, football supporters are no ordinary customers. While their unique loyalty has often allowed clubs literally to 'bank' upon on their continued support, finding new customers and the next generation remains the biggest challenge all clubs face. Being a football fan takes years of inculturation to the ways of your club. That means finding new supporters to fill sudden or dramatic gaps in season ticket sales is virtually impossible.

Radical thinking might be the order of the day, but that is not something we have seen in the game. Even a small and possibly temporary reconstruction of the leagues was recently defeated by the votes of our professional clubs themselves, opting for a narrow view of their own immediate interests over a larger understanding of the ecology needed to ensure that the whole edifice of which they are part can survive and offer support to its constituent parts. A lack of faith (worse, real anger and frustration) at the governance failings of the football authorities is a major contributory factor to loss of nerve when it comes to facing change. In this context, and given the customary talking down of Scottish football in the media, converting Facebook and Twitter likes to visitors to a stadium will be an almighty challenge.

Much More Than Small Change is Needed

Is there light at the end of the tunnel? It is very hard to tell at this stage. On an uneven playing field, some clubs will have the adaptability and infrastructure to change, while others may well not. Two external donors have donated funds amounting to several million pounds in ameliorative funding, with an emphasis on community engagement as a key to survival. However, this is effectively for project spending affected by coronavirus, not for core costs. Yet it is core cost where the pinch is felt most for smaller clubs – and which could turn out to be a matter of life or death (a subject on which Bill Shankly also pontificated).

Above all, the pandemic highlights the desperate need for root and branch reform in Scottish football, starting at the top and prioritising the grassroots. Vastly improved governance, accountability and transparency, commercial acumen, positive PR, investment in youth and in the women's game, community ownership (and other collaborative forms of ownership), more adaptable structures, income generation, serious community partnerships, genuine engagement and representation of supporters as major stakeholders, a serious plan for the national team, a fans' parliament, the commitment of the Scottish Parliament to the future of the game – these are among the ground-breaking changes we need to negotiate. They are a key part of the agenda of the Scottish Football Supporters Association, the growing fans union that came into being in 2015 with the forthright affirmation, 'We Believe in Scottish Football'.

Survival first, then flourishing, is the usual order of things when you are planning to turn an industry around – including a cultural one, like a major national sport. In reality, Scottish football may not be able to do the former without the latter any more. It could be do or die. Are we up to the task? Is Scotland and Scottish sport more widely capable of making the huge transition required? The gauntlet has been thrown down by the circumstances of COVID-19 and it has revealed all about where the game is right now. Who will pick it up?

Section Seven – Ideas Scotland
The Power of the Past and the Future

CHAPTER 34

Zero Traces of Cringe 2.0
Christie Williamson

'I didn't want to hope. I didn't know how to stop.' – James Baldwin

sumeen's bön mövin da moontins aboot
caain ower molehills so da glib
onkerry o dir underbellies
trootle da time awa
laek da cracked mug slesters
aa da carefully brewed coffee
naewye hit's meant tae end up
doon fur ay tae da grund

aebdy staundin is marked an dey keen hit
furlongs sooth o plan F haein
twitched dir fill an mair o net coortins
eltit wi owerkill gel
roond da tickin furloughed clock

twinty twinty -
here wir bön fun oot
even whan wir aa stuck in

violence ony ivvir begat hitsel
ilka time hit screwed da bobbin
ower ticht ta slip da healin
remede o love fae haund tae haund
uncan an kith an kin as wan
severed fur ay fae da pasts teddir

CHAPTER 35

Scotland as Ark, Scotland as Lab

Pat Kane

I AM THE SON of a barrier nurse. We knew the tales; we understood the equipment. My mum was first trained to tend to tuberculosis patients, in the immediate post-war period and through the '50s. She told of relentless scrubbing of hands and boiling of objects; how important it was to make connection with the patient through all the protective layers.

In the early, plague-freaked days of HIV/AIDS in the 1980s, when no one knew exactly how the virus was transmitted, Mum threw herself into nursing the diagnosed. Like all good nurses, she both had a massive heart and was a geek for technique. Combining the two, caring through the danger, was her ethos. If she were alive and active at this moment, I've no doubt she would be up to her oxters, deploying protective measures.

So I am aware, maybe a little more than the norm, about what it's like to live close to an infectious, damaging and maybe fatal bug. But I'm mostly of the Scottish generation who came home from school grumbly and smarting, showing off to cooing parents the purple vaccination lumps on our upper arms.

Measles, mumps, rubella, tetanus, were dealt with by nurses with needles at the end of long queues to their offices. (Yet I seem to remember getting the first two of these infections, anyway.) In any case, despite the disgruntlement, there was a strong sense of us all dutifully having to submit to this. It was a collective mutual protection, which you'd have to be crazy not to go along with.

How much of that deeply assumed collective responsibility, facing ancient viral and microbial foes, is alive and operating today, under the threats of COVID-19 and coronavirus? Here, on these islands, it's hard to measure. My 1970s experience – a compliant population trusting the science and expertise of those in authority above them – seems to have been replicated in nations like Germany, Finland, New Zealand, Taiwan, Australia, South Korea, Iceland, Canada, Singapore. With the exception of the last, these are democratically advanced nations (half with women leaders). They also have strong bureaucracies and technocracies, and comprehensive welfare systems (Time, 2020).

Yet it's so early in the game of comparative research, and so difficult to draw conclusions. For example, you might imagine that high levels of trust in government would be a key indicator of anti-COVID-19 success – people's willingness to follow lockdowns, wear masks, clean hands, input reliably into monitoring apps. But the aforementioned nations are all over the place on (for example) the 2020 Edelman Trust Indicator – indeed, most are nearer the bottom of the scale (Edelman, 2020)

We also approach tricky waters around deep cultural comparisons – where the popular willingness for your personal data to be fully surveilled, and acted on, by a monitoring state is deemed to be rooted in a difference between 'Western' and 'Confucian/Buddhist' values. Less individualist, more subservient to a paternalistic state, the riff goes (*Asia Times*, 2020).

I'm not so sure about this. Towards the end of 2019, I reviewed a book by the US academic Shoshana Zuboff called *The Rise of Surveillance Capitalism* (Kane, 2019). In this, Zuboff accused American info-corps – not Asian ones – of being relentless 'instrumentarians'. Meaning that Google, Amazon and Facebook are hoovering up our interactions with our products and turning that data into ever more seductive and precisely targeted products. We supposedly sovereign Westerners submit to that meekly enough, speedily clicking through our EULA agreements on the way to the digital sweeties on our apps.

So no, I don't think the core challenge of COVID-19 is about diverse styles of governance, in the face of a biological threat. I have so little to say about the Brexitannic handling of this crisis – its arrogant exceptionalism, its cronyism, its systemic incompetence – that I won't bother.

I have little more to say about the Scottish response. The First Minister Nicola Sturgeon has certainly stepped forward and tried to inform and engage the Scottish public daily, taking the role of Explainer-in-Chief much more seriously than her Westminster counterpart. Yet as of the end of July, according to the Office for National

Statistics, 'excess deaths in Scotland were the third highest in Europe during the first half of 2020, with only England and Spain faring worse' (*The Herald*, 2020). Imagine that Scotland had voted for the essentially confederal, 'indy-lite' package in 2014's independence referendum. Under those circumstances, I don't believe we'd have been any less coordinated with Westminster's judgements and assessments that we were over the first eight months of the pandemic.

The challenge of COVID-19 in Scotland is much, much deeper than political point-scoring across the devolutionary divide. It seems that Sturgeon recognises this, amidst her calming daily narrations:

> I suppose the one thing I know beyond any doubt now is that I will not be the same coming out of this crisis as I was going into it... I don't mean fundamentally changed as a person, but my perspective and what I value in life. What is important and what's not important and the things that I get worked up about. I just think I will have a completely different perspective coming out of this. (*The Times*, 2020)

We'll await the FM's revelations. But I share her sense – if maybe not her conclusions – that COVID-19 compels a 'perspective shift' on what we value in contemporary Scotland, and on the wider modernity we are continuous with (and perhaps, still, want to be a nation-state within).

There are three elements to this shift for me.

First, COVID-19 makes climate breakdown intimate and real. It's here. I resist the idea that the coronavirus is somehow a separate, exceptional issue, compared to the urgencies of climate crisis. Just the latest instance of a perennial threat that humankind has had to deal with over thousands of millennia. The work of Rob Wallace and Mike Davis (particularly the latter's *The Monster Enters*) makes it hugely clear (Wallace, 2020; Davis, 2020). The relentless penetrations of capitalist agribusiness into virgin forest in Asia and Africa will generate even more virulent animal-to-human bugs in the future – that is, if the extractive and expansionist business model stays as it is. And if the bugs don't get us... then the likely outcome of a two degrees centigrade rise over pre-industrial levels by 2050 will be: hundreds of millions of people displaced by rising sea-levels from melted icecaps; severely damaged food supplies; and methane released from permafrost that will likely accelerate warming to three degrees. And at three degrees, says the eco-thinker Mark Lynas, 'we will stress our civilisation towards the point of collapse'. We will endure violently, uninhabitably hot summers, regular extreme weather, and no albedo-whiteness at our barren poles that could reflect sunlight back into space – accelerating change further (*New York Review of Books*, 2020). Scotland (and Scots) cannot disappear into a bubble of competently-managed, 'normalist' independence – where we pride ourselves on merely matching the average response to these biospheric disruptions (giving ourselves the excuse of early nation-building for mediocrity).

Second, we must massively reduce the 'material throughput' of our economies – which implies a full-system change. Some of the statistics on the inertia that impedes our response to a climate emergency are jaw-dropping. For example, we may believe we've raised enough of a fuss about the amount of discardable plastic passing through our lives but it is still on course to increase by three times as we get to the middle of the century (*The Guardian*, 2020). We seem deeply unwilling – as consumer/citizens, producers or governments – to even countenance something as design-able as a 'circular' or 'zero-waste economy', because it may challenge existing business models or our current habits of convenience. Bill McKibben makes this very strong point about COVID-19, and the near-total cessation of business-as-usual during the main lockdowns (*New York Review of Books*, 2020). We've just had an experience of the kind of thorough-going change in lifestyles and practices that a zero-carbon civilisation might demand. But there's a hard truth at its core: the bottom line was that (during the global lockdown) emissions fell, but not by as much as you might expect – by many calculations little more than 10 or 15 per cent. What that seems to indicate is that most of the momentum destroying our Earth is hardwired into the systems that run it. Only by attacking those systems – ripping out the fossil-fuelled guts and replacing them with renewable energy, even as we make them far more efficient – can we push emissions down to where we stand a chance. Not a chance at stopping global warming. A chance at surviving. We should be 'bouncing beyond' our current, self-terminating socio-economic norms – not merely 'bouncing back', to the same or merely better. The crucial, fundamental question is: what is the most effective and coherent polity that could affect these changes? And which could have the executive power, and the degree of collective commitment, required?

Many activists and thinkers believe this heralds the return of the city-state: the city being big enough to have effective infrastructures and budgets, and small enough to be able to mobilise and motivate civic and social behaviours (C40 Cities, 2020). I'm holding out (with faint desperation) for an independent Scotland state, as a potential model for an 'eco-nation' or 'eco-state'.

So third, Scottish independence can be an 'ark' to navigate these futures, and a 'lab' to experiment with new ways of thriving in them. It's been a truism of COVID-19 that it has revived our belief in the necessity of state action – to enforce lockdown, print money to sustain demand-free (and supply-free) economies, coordinate research and tracing within and across borders and communicate clear public health instructions to national audiences. Yet (as noted previously) not all states have properly executed their duties – and it's been a joy to see grassroots, community-level solidarity and mutual aid emerge, to quickly and effectively fill in the gaps (The Alternative UK, 2020). This COVID-19 mutualism can blend well with Scottish traditions and practices of community empowerment. Common Weal (on whose board I sit) has proposed a broad-ranging report on 'Resilience Economics', which is a deep rethink of socio-economic practice in the era of coronavirus (Common Weal, 2020). It focuses on making and repairing, the maximisation of territorial resources (land, wood, renewable energies), technology-enabled localism, radically shortened and circular supply chains. But the point is that scores, even hundreds, of strategic plans like Common Weal's should be encouraged in a Scottish eco-society (one of the first items on the innovation agenda being how purposeful projects can be initiated by virtual and remote means – an obvious ambition for a full national-public media infrastructure, beyond relying on Californian corporations to answer this challenge). This is 'Scotland as Lab', acting in a spirit of experimental pragmatism in the face of the dynamics of the climate crisis – what Roberto Unger might call a 'high-energy democracy' (Unger, 2020). But this would hardly be zero-carbon innovation just for the sake of it. Scotland possesses a unique combination of elements – a solid social consensus for a gently prospering country, and our scientific, humanistic and engineering excellence. Independence gives us the chance to be an exemplar: to show the way that modern societies must radically change their course, their speed and their style, as they face requirements to keep their material throughputs within planetary boundaries. This is 'Scotland as Ark'

– putting our resources, skills and social/cultural imagination at the service of living lightly on a damaged planet; confidently sailing in the right direction, urging others to follow.

COVID-19, and its inevitable sequel, and the climate disruptions that tower behind both, are a piercing challenge to us as individuals, communities, regions and nations. Yet Scots have been in the mood and mode to 'constitute' themselves differently for a century or more. To permanently imagine yourself in 'the early years of a better nation' was never more relevant or helpful a mindset than now.

References

The Alternative UK, 2020, 'We now have millions of "lockdown volunteers". How can they be resourced, supported and developed – for the next wave?', accessed at: www.thealternative.org.uk/dailyalternative/2020/7/24/lockdown-volunteers-support-develop

Asia Times, 2020, 'Confucius is winning the COVID-19 war', accessed at: www.asiatimes.com/2020/04/confucius-is-winning-the-covid-19-war/

C40 Cities, 2020, accessed at: www.c40.org

Common Weal, 2020, 'Resilience Economics', accessed at: www.commonweal.scot/policy-library/resilience-economics

Davis, M, 2020, *The Monster Enters*, O/R Books.

Edelman, 2020, 2020 Trust Barometer, accessed at: www.edelman.com/trustbarometer

The Guardian, 2020, 'Plastic waste entering oceans expected to triple in 20 years', accessed at: www.theguardian.com/environment/2020/jul/23/plastic-waste-entering-oceans-triple-20-years-research

The Herald, 2020, 'Coronavirus: Scotland has third highest rate of excess deaths in Europe after England and Spain', accessed at: www.heraldscotland.com/news/18618596.coronavirus-scotland-third-highest-rate-excess-deaths-europe-england-spain/

Kane, P, 2019, 'How surveillance capitalism is changing human nature forever', *New Scientist*, accessed at: www.newscientist.com/article/mg24132222-300-how-surveillance-capitalism-is-changing-human-nature-forever/

New York Review of Books, 2020, '130 Degrees', www.nybooks.com/articles/2020/08/20/climate-emergency-130-degrees/

The Times, 2020, 'Coronavirus in Scotland: Nicola Sturgeon looking to life after leadership', accessed at: www.thetimes.co.uk/article/coro-navirus-in-scotland-nicola-sturgeon-admits-pandemic-has-changed-her-outlook-on-life-x6f99wv0f

Time, 2020, 'The Best Global Responses to COVID-19 Pandemic', accessed at: www.time.com/5851633/best-global-responses-covid-19/

Unger, R, 2020, 'High-Energy Democracy', accessed at: youtu.be/UG0YXi4MpaA

Wallace, R et al., 2020, 'COVID-19 and Circuits of Capital', *Monthly Review*, accessed at: www.monthlyreview.org/2020/05/01/covid-19-and-circuits-of-capital/

CHAPTER 36

High Noon for an Imperfect Union:
The Search for a 'Settled Will'

Henry McLeish

THE EARLY YEARS of the new millennium have exposed the United Kingdom as consumed with a misplaced sense of history and a diminished sense of how to handle rapid political change and constitutional uncertainty. The financial crash in 2008, the independence referendum in 2014, the Brexit vote in 2016 and the arrival of populist authoritarianism in the form of President Donald Trump in the same year, have exposed a union which is unsettled, unstable and insecure. History suggests that some crises lead to long-term positive change. Could COVID-19 be Scotland's tipping point?

Impervious to the consequences of political turbulence, the union presently lacks a vision and any sense of collective ambition, aspiration or solidarity. Faced with this drift and the failure of the union to adapt to a changing world, Scotland, and Scots, could be forgiven for thinking that there must be a different way to build a new future.

The UK and Westminster are prisoners of the past. Prime Minister Johnson's handling of the COVID-19 pandemic, and his cavalier attitude and contemptuous outbursts towards Scotland, have only added to the growing sense of historic mistrust and alienation between London and Edinburgh.

The Challenge of a New Era

Devolution and the establishment of the Scottish Parliament opened a new era in UK politics. Scotland accepted the challenge, but Westminster did not. This has resulted in the pro-union parties failing to find any traction in Scotland in the post-devolution era. That has led to doubts about the commitment of Westminster to any further significant changes which would lead to a different model for the union – changes to our politics, governance, democracy and constitutional settlement. In other words, something that could provide a credible and popular alternative to independence.

Time is running out. The window of opportunity is fast closing. If Westminster and the major political parties are unable to change their mindset, the union will be furthered diminished, leading to independence within the decade, I believe. The Scottish Parliament elections in 2021 will be a further test of the union's resolve to urgently address 'the Scotland question' – but in the context of a much neglected and more immediate 'union question', which has been ignored following the Scotland Act of 1998.

A perfect storm of issues and events has engulfed the union. A new and possibly final phase of post-devolution politics is underway, which could provide a deeper, and more inclusive discussion of Scotland's future. But this can only happen if the Conservative and Labour Parties in London see the constitutional question through a new prism, and a painful transition to a new set of realities.

Self-Evident Truths Must Be Recognised

Scotland and Scots have grown in confidence in the post-devolution period. We are less deferential, more confident, less inclined to take matters of history for granted and unimpressed with the quality of governance on offer from Westminster.

The debate in Scotland is changing and evolving from narrow nationalism and spirited calls for freedom towards a greater recognition of better governance, learning from other countries and embracing a vision which is shaped by the challenges of the future and less concerned with our imperial past. Delusional assertions of everything having to be 'world beating' (the UK Government mantra) makes little sense: this is emblematic of Westminster's handling of the pandemic.

The consequences of Brexit will be deeply damaging to Scotland, but the lure of greatness (never defined) was the unspoken driver of this act of collective self-harm – a position that Scotland rejected.

The decline of the pro-union parties in Scotland, has been self-inflicted. They have rarely embraced the spirit of the constitutional settlement and its central importance both to political progress in Scotland and to the safeguarding of the union. Labour has been in denial, has lost political traction and finds adjusting to the new politics of Scotland unusually difficult. It has failed to answer the Scotland question, never mind understanding the incalculable damage being done to the union!

Obsessed with nationalism, opposing a second referendum on independence and remaining close to the Conservative Party's unionism: this is not a strategy. Labour has never accepted the practical politics of seeing Scotland as a new, exciting and distinct entity with needs and aspirations, requiring new thinking and a reimagined union.

After Devolution, What?

Post-devolution, a political vacuum existed in Scotland. After a period of adjustment, the SNP seized their opportunity, and from 2007 to the present day moved from the margins of politics and governance to the mainstream, and then to majority government. Independence is the only show in town.

There is no question about Scotland's ability to be independent. The real question is, should it be? Despite heroic overtures about saving the union and the dire consequences for Scotland if it left, nothing has changed at Westminster. Four nations politics remains a pipe dream.

This is a bizarre set of circumstances. The union is vulnerable, but there is no real interest at Westminster, only musings on the margins. There is no debate in Scotland, but instead a campaign for independence. There are no alternatives to independence, but merely negative anti-independence sentiment.

Undiluted centralism, status quo unionism or incremental concessions of powers are not an alternative, but a startling reminder that no serious defence of the union or plans for its future are being contemplated. Adding insult to injury, Prime Minister Johnson is in danger of strengthening the case for Scotland's exit. Reducing Scotland's future to a nationalism versus unionism trope is unhelpful. Westminster could embrace a commitment to reimagining a different union and evolving the idea of four nation politics, including England?

Unfortunately, there is a complex multi-layered blocking mechanism to be dismantled. Ideas of history, empire, sovereignty, exceptionalism, must be faced. Delusion, sentiment, nostalgia and the politics of invincibility add further layers of emotional band aid. English nationalism present through Brexit, and gaining strength in Boris Johnson's Government, is another obstacle. And now questions of political resilience, competence and authoritarian populism are emerging as issues.

A Prisoner of History

The union today is a prisoner of history and on a course that will wreck any prospect of change. England represents a disparate set of concerns, grievances and resentments that have no obvious solutions or immediate outlets of expression. England is unlikely to be an ally in the search for a new union, but it will be crucial in any restructuring.

Where does this dismal assessment of Westminster and the future of the union leave Scots who are interested in change, but see little prospect of change outwith the arguments for independence?

One of the notable features of present-day Scotland is the lack of imagination displayed by those making the union case. There is no alternative vision of what a reimagined union would look like or what it might be for. The trauma of Brexit could have inspired new thinking but did not. The pandemic provides another opportunity to rethink our future.

So there is no 'settled will' about the future of Scotland. Despite 150 years of intermittent constitutional debate since the 1870s, and 13 years from 2007 in which the SNP has dominated Scotland's politics and government, with an overwhelming focus on their signature policy of independence, a majority of Scots remain to be convinced of the idea of leaving the UK.

A handful of over 120 opinion polls since the 2014 independence referendum have shown a majority for independence. Scots remain divided. Recent polls, along with a changed mood and sentiment, are more supportive of the SNP's policy, but not overwhelmingly so, at least at this stage. Scotland remains a 50/50 country as far as its constitutional future is concerned. This suggests there is potential for a different debate.

When is a matter settled beyond reasonable doubt and what could be the 'settled will' of the Scottish people as described by the late John Smith at the Labour Party's Scottish Conference in 1994?

To be independent in the full constitutional, sovereign and political sense, requires a much greater degree of consensus and a better understanding of the likely consequences. A second referendum is inevitable, but its timing would make more sense if a greater proportion of Scots agreed about what is best for Scotland. This requires an inclusive campaign, possibly other questions on the ballot paper and not just another binary vote.

Traditionalists and fundamentalists, and those who argue for Scotland to be independent at any price, need no further persuasion. But the majority of Scots – passionate, proud, patriotic and pragmatic – remain unconvinced, though open to persuasion. Brexit has bitterly divided the UK and a simple majority to leave the EU has done nothing to settle the issue, or to promote any sense of national unity. Instead, a bitter legacy has befallen the defeated, and this is likely to be enduringly destructive.

Lessons must be learned.

An Alternative Approach to Scotland's Future

Politics is no longer the comfortable space of the past; shock developments are frequent, volatility is everywhere, and Brexit and the Johnson Conservative Party remain a serious threat to Scotland and the stability of the United Kingdom. Political certainties are being shredded and the mood of Scotland is being influenced by the pandemic too. The dynamic is changing. Dignity and Identity matter. A serious alternative to independence must be on offer.

The mindset gripping Westminster, the UK Government and the two main political parties must change. The ties that bind the union are weakening. A case must be made for its continued existence, reflecting the conditions and challenges of 2020, not 1707. Merely frustrating the legitimate concerns and ambitions of Scots in their quest for a new political settlement is not a strategy or a vision.

Power devolved can never be shared. Scotland has obtained three tranches of new powers, but after 20 years has no real 'power' or influence over Europe, international affairs and constitutional or political issues. Brexit was a humiliation for Scots, highlighting the shortcomings of devolution and exposing Britain's rotten political core.

A more explicitly flexible federal system is the only real alternative and would require a written constitution and some form of convention to discuss and shape a new structure for the future of the union. There is no fixed model of federalism. It is best defined as two levels of government, each of which has independent powers and neither of which has supreme authority over the other.

The idea of a Federal union has been around for a long time. Speaking in a House of Commons debate on 9 April 1889, Mr Hunter, the Honourable member for Aberdeen North said:

> I have come to the conclusion that the Federal form of Union is the one which gives the greatest hopes of obtaining the objects of representative institutions in the future... look forward to the day when England herself shall be merged in a higher unity, and when, although we may not live to see it, there will be established that which would be the greatest blessing to the world – namely, the United States of Europe. That is the direction of our ideas and inspiration.

A quarter of a century later, in a speech to his Dundee constituency on 9 October 1913, Winston Churchill spoke of the

> establishment of a federal system in the UK, in which Scotland, Ireland and Wales and, if necessary, parts of England could have separate legislative and parliamentary institutions.

These are inspiring ideas.

Devolution is not a form of federalism. Some form of federal structure for the UK would give England its place in the form of some administrative or legislative assembly or more specific powers for the regions, counties and cities: the pandemic has laid bare the shortcomings of England and the political tensions between the north and south.

A Federal Framework

A flexible federal framework would see the four nations in a more purposeful union. Other countries have a great deal to offer. Federalism makes sense of nation states that are large but require a way of governing that offers shared not devolved power, solidarity, social cohesion and a space where sovereignty of the people triumphs over outdated notions of absolute sovereignty and historical exceptionalism.

The European Union provides one idea of a model, where nations come together and share power, cede sovereignty and opt in and out, of policy. This would be a continuing process of self-determination for each of the nations and regions of the UK, developing at different times, and at different speeds, and dependent on different circumstances, diversity, challenges and social and economic conditions in every part of the United Kingdom. Westminster would downsize accordingly.

In Scotland there is a unique opportunity to build on the success and achievements of the Scottish Parliament, now come of age. There is more potential to be realised. A more assertive and ambitious Parliament could provide a progressive platform, the cornerstone of a new approach to move the Scotland debate forward and help resolve what the 'settled will' of Scots might be.

The Scottish Parliament would become a bigger player in shaping Scotland future. This would comprise a larger Parliament, more powers, less inhibition in developing, a more extensive international profile, remaining close to the EU, encouraging more cooperation and consensus, boosted by electoral reform by scrapping first past the post, pushing political boundaries and offering a more unified approach, by creating an inclusive cross-party platform.

We need to speak to London in a way that reflects the whole of Scotland and not one party or only 50 per cent of Scots: a more distinctive and consensual voice for Scotland, not a voice for independence. Traditional parties will be able to engage positively in shaping the future of Scotland, instead of sniping negatively from the bunkers of outdated thinking. Scotland's Parliament and Government should not be one and the same.

Will any of this happen? Probably not. This is a set of ideas designed to deepen the debate in Scotland and ignite some interest in the United Kingdom. The high noon for the union reflects a crisis of political neglect, amidst a world gripped by a pandemic, which screams out at us in terms of interdependence and internationalism, cooperation, consensus and the common good and a broader humanity.

Scots recognise the weaknesses of our democracy, governance and politics. Traditional loyalties and allegiances are breaking down and that sense of 'class' that so dominated my political generation is being refashioned as social, economic, technological and cultural change (and the politics of identity and dignity) seem to be outstripping the capacity of our institutions and politics to cope, manage and adapt. The Scottish Parliament elections in 2021 will provide little respite for the traditional parties.

Scotland Deserves a Choice

A form of Federalism deserves a serious airing. Scotland needs a consensus on a way forward. A new approach to the Scotland question could help avoid the bitter and divisive aftermath of Brexit. Federalism is all about 'effective power'. Rejection by the pro-union parties will lead to an independent Scotland. Supporters of independence could gain from a more critical examination of this idea too.

Scotland deserves a choice it is currently being denied. Churchill's speech asked,

> is federalism now inside the sphere of practical politics, or is it just about reflection and discussion rather than prompting action. Are we speaking of the immediate future or just dreaming of a new political order that can never be?

Over one hundred years on, is there more scope for optimism?

CHAPTER 37

Sure Foundations:
The Constitutional Basis of Scottish Statehood
W. Elliot Bulmer

THE CHALLENGE WE face today is helping Scotland recover – not only from COVID-19 and Brexit, but (many would argue) to recover its sense of self, its values and principles and its full potential after three centuries of absorption into the British Empire. All policy ideas about how to do this presume, however, that Scotland will have a functioning, stable and legitimate state: a state that is capable of winning and sustaining public loyalty, that keeps the peace and upholds justice, that can effectively tax and spend, that can manage public services and large infrastructural projects. We need a state that is able, as well as willing, to ensure the conditions for human flourishing. That is why the project of recovering Scotland has always been about recovering Scottish statehood: building a state that can serve the people well.

Here I examine the implications of treating independence as a state-building project, and in particular what that means for the constitutional question. Too often, the constitutional question is reduced to what Scotland's status should be in relation to England and the rest of the United Kingdom, independence or not. It is reduced to the sort of simple, binary choice that can be put on a referendum ballot paper.

However, mere independence – if that is to be – is only one part, and perhaps not even the most important part, of the question. Of greater significance, in terms of its effect on the future wellbeing of Scotland and its people, is not where power lies (Holyrood or Westminster), but the nature of power itself, its origins and its limits, its purposes and its procedures. These are the genuinely constitutional issues.

The Constitution is Fundamental

Before we can properly ask whether Scotland should be an independent country, we must therefore ask other questions. Should Scotland be a democratic country – one in which government is representative of and responsible to the people? Should Scotland be a free country, defending human rights, civil liberties, the rule of law and an open society? Should Scotland be a well-governed country, where the common good is nurtured and nourished, where the civil service and the judiciary are honest and competent, and where the ethical principles of good government are upheld? Should Scotland be a country that belongs to all its people, where we are *fellow citizens* and where everyone, regardless of their race, religion, gender, or identity, can enjoy equal opportunities, equal rights and equal respect?

If this is the kind of Scotland we want – democratic, free, well-governed, ethical, inclusive – then we need to make sure we get the constitution of the Scottish state right. The constitution, in this context, is a written *supreme and fundamental law*. It is supreme in the sense that it is the highest law, the law to which other laws must conform, and which can be changed only by a special process that sets it beyond the reach of ordinary working majorities in Parliament. Typically, a constitution might be amendable by a two-thirds majority vote in Parliament, although some provisions may require additional protection, for example by requiring a referendum to change them. The constitution is fundamental, in that it deals with the foundational values and principles on which the state is based, the basic rights of citizens and the institutional structures through which power is exercised. At the simplest level, the constitution prevents the government of the day, with a working majority, from unilaterally changing the basic rules of democracy as it goes along. It ensures that there are foundations in place that can only be altered by broader deliberation and consent.

The United Kingdom, of course, does not have a constitution in this sense of the word, relying instead on an unstable and ill-defined amalgam of ordinary statutes, judicial decisions, unwritten conventions and amorphous norms and practices. For a long time, it could be argued that in practice it worked well enough – after all, the flexibility of the UK's so-called 'unwritten constitution' enabled the state to develop from a Hanoverian limited monarchy in the 18th century to a parliamentary democracy in the 20th century without a revolutionary rupture. That pragmatic defence of the unwritten system can no longer be sustained. The unwritten constitution was based on a degree of moderation and self-restraint, an ability to enforce informally what was 'done' and 'not done', and an overriding notion of constitutional propriety, which our present rulers do not possess.

The rot has been setting in for some time, but has become painfully evident since the Brexit referendum. Since then, we have witnessed a double-edged dysfunction: on the one hand, it has failed to provide effective, coherent, capable government; on the other, it has failed to properly check, balance, constrain and limit the government. The government has been allowed to too little of what it should, and too much of what it should not.

This is evident in the mismanagement of Brexit itself and in the British Government's negligent and incompetent response to coronavirus. Thousands of people needlessly died – a death toll on a scale similar to that of the opening days of the Battle of the Somme – through government inaction, vacillation, bad leadership, corruption and carelessness. Preparations were hurried, botched and ill-thought-through. Vast sums of public money were funnelled off into companies associated with government advisers, whose owners profited while sub-standard equipment was supplied.

Corruption and veniality on this scale should have been stopped. It was not. Effective action in the public interest should have been pursued. It was not. Coronavirus was no one's wish, but the fact that it has hit in the midst of the biggest self-inflicted economic, diplomatic and political crisis in modern British history has exposed a deep-seated institutional, indeed constitutional, failure. From being the envy of the world (which, believe it or not, we once were, even well into the mid-20th century) the United Kingdom has become a laughing stock.

Not Simply a Political Crisis

The crisis is genuinely *constitutional*, and not merely *political*, in nature because it has exposed the inadequacy of the ground-rules regulating how power is exercised. Principles and conventions that were once thought to be settled have been challenged. On 15 January 2019, the Government was defeated on its flagship policy – the EU Withdrawal Agreement – and yet did not resign. It stumbled on in office, but not in power. Later, when the Labour MP Yvette Cooper sponsored a bill to prevent a no-deal Brexit, the Government toyed with the idea of advising the Queen to withhold royal assent, which would have overturned a three centuries old convention against the use of the royal veto. Most notoriously in Scotland, the Sewel convention, which is supposed to prevent the UK Parliament from legislating on devolved matters, was repeatedly pushed aside. This contemptuous treatment of Scotland, Wales and Northern Ireland shredded the trust and respect on which devolution depended, and so undermined the moderate pro-union case for the *status quo* as 'the best of both worlds'.

The picture that emerges is of a state where the ground-rules are increasingly unclear, unenforceable, illegitimate and under attack. The 2019 Conservative manifesto promised to establish a 'Constitution, Democracy and Rights Commission', whose function would be to review

> the relationship between the Government, Parliament and the courts; the functioning of the Royal Prerogative; the role of the House of Lords; and access to justice.

Promising though this might sound, the evident intent of the Johnson Government is to roll back the Blair-Brown reforms, not least the Human Rights Act and devolution, and to reassert the dominance of the central executive. It has already tried to marginalise Parliament, as shown most notably by the prorogation crisis, but also by over-use of press conferences in place of proper questioning on the floor of the House of Commons, by the deliberate delay to the formation of select committees and by trying to hand-pick the chair of the Intelligence and Security Committee. It has attempted to politicise the civil service, putting untold power into the hands of special advisers. It has packed the House of Lords with political favourites. It has revealed plans to undermine the judiciary, restricting access to judicial review in revenge for the Supreme Court's bold defiance against prorogation in the *Miller II* judgement. The lack of a proper constitution leaves all these elements of a normally functioning democracy – human rights, devolution, Parliament, the civil service, the courts – extremely vulnerable to attack.

More deeply, the frayed British system of government has ceased to provide broadly convincing answers to the fundamental constitutional questions that any state must be able to address. Who are we? What do we stand for? What will we not stand for? How should we govern ourselves? How do we discern the principles of the common good in our diverse society? What standards and principles should be reflected in our public life? How will these foundations be upheld? What guarantees do we have? How will any future changes to these fundamentals be renegotiated if required? Perhaps there was a time, not more than a few generations ago, when these things did not have to be written down or spelled out, because they were self-evidently understood by all who mattered. Perhaps, but it is not that way now.

A future Scottish constitution must be able to fill this gap, providing coherent, morally justifiable and politically persuasive answers to these questions. Some of the answers will be expressed in the symbolic parts of the constitution: in the preamble, in those sections of the constitution dealing with the foundational principles of the state, or defining the nature of the state itself. Some answers will be expressed in the constitution's substantive provisions: those dealing with rights, responsibilities, citizenship or religion-state relations. Some will be found in the structural parts of the constitution: those concerning the composition, selection and powers of the various institutions of the state – Parliament, Government, Head of State, the judiciary, local authorities, the Electoral Commission, civil service and so forth – and in those provisions regulating how these all relate to one another and to the public they serve. Examples of what this might look like in practice have been presented in my previous works, listed below.

The Task of Constitution-Building

It is a relatively easy technical task for a suitably trained legislative drafter to put these words on the page. There are many good examples (not least from Commonwealth countries that became independent from the United Kingdom during the second half of the 20th century) of how that might be done. Building on these examples, and on the previous work of the Scottish Constitutional Convention in the 1990s, which achieved important reforms such as proportional representation, there is no need to reinvent the wheel. A constitution of this type is tried and tested. We know it works and have many 'lessons learned' to draw upon.

Constitution-building is never, however, a purely legal-technical exercise. It is always intensely political. The words on the page derive their legitimacy and authority from being backed by a broad consensus of both parliamentary and public opinion. Reaching this consensus, through an organised constitution-building process that brings together political leaders of all parties, civil society and the general public, is as important as the text of the constitution itself. The process has the opportunity to be inclusive, to bring hitherto unheard voices into the discussion of the fundamentals by which we are to be governed. Nevertheless, political elites cannot be excluded from the process, otherwise they will inevitably wreck it.

A good constitution-building process brings elites, experts and everyone else to the table. For instance, a Scottish Constituent Assembly might consist primarily of politicians, who have the democratic legitimacy, as elected representatives, to negotiate and reach agreement. These would be supported by a competent secretariat and expert advisory committee. They would engage with the public and civil society through public consultation processes, public hearings, petitions and perhaps a final referendum. The details may vary, and are themselves subject to political negotiation, but if the process is to be successful there must be an attempt to achieve a sufficient consensus. It is good for the process to have a statutory basis, in the form of a 'Constitutional Transition Act', which would regulate – and fund – the process.

Beyond Defensiveness, Towards New Foundations

This need to reach consensus means that constitutions – those that work and endure – cannot reflect a divisive ideological position, nor the policy agenda of a particular party, but must seek to define the common ground. They should express and defend the fundamentals of a democratic political system and concentrate on those things that unite us as fellow citizens. The constitution cannot be a wish-list of progressive ideas designed as a shortcut to radical change, but can protect the essentials of democracy, human rights and good government that would otherwise be at risk. In this way, the constitution provides stability and reassurance. It might not in itself make things much better, but can help stop them from becoming worse.

This defensive or preventative function of a constitution must be taken seriously, even in an established democracy like Scotland. Many countries have gained independence only to fall into the hands of dictators and oligarchs. This is a risk to which oil and gas-rich states are especially prone – the stakes are higher, as is the threat of foreign interference. Nationalist or pro-union, it is in no one's interest for Scotland to go down that destructive path. If we are to become an independent country, we have to be prepared, do it right and make it work.

The development of a sufficiently robust constitution must therefore be central and integral to Scotland's restored statehood. The time for starting work on that is now. As in the 1990s, when work on what was to later become the Scotland Act began even when devolution seemed far off, those who believe in the possibility and desirability of a Scottish state should be laying foundation stones now, in building a constitutional consensus, even if a second vote on independence seems far off. Then, when the time comes, we can be ready. We can offer, in place of vague political promises, the clarity and reassurance an agreed draft constitution.

References

Bulmer, WE, 2011, *A Model Constitution for Scotland: Making Democracy Work in an Independent State*, Edinburgh, Luath Press.

Bulmer, WE, 2018, *Foundations of Freedom* (White Paper Series), Biggar, Common Weal.

Bulmer, WE, 2015, *Strengthening Scottish Democracy After the Independence Referendum* (2nd ed.), Edinburgh, Luath Press.

CHAPTER 38

The Changing Risks of Independence
Marco G Biagi

ECONOMISTS ARE TERRITORIAL. Rarely do they bestow their highest honour – the Nobel Memorial Prize – to someone outside the tribe. Daniel Kahneman, a psychologist by background, is an exception. The 2002 laureate, along with his frequent co-author, Amos Tversky, are known for challenging the economic orthodoxy that humans make decisions based on purely rational considerations of risk and reward. Instead, they found that people tend to be more motivated by the fear of loss than the prospect of gain. Their 'prospect theory' experiments have been repeated many times since initial publication in 1979 and the results have remarkably held across different countries and cultures.

These findings have revolutionised the scholarly discipline of economics but have made fewer ripples in academic work on politics. Their central insight is however a powerful tool to understand how the person-on-the-street will have weighed the arguments about Scottish independence. And this is as true for the mainly economic tussles of the 2014 debate as it is for the new post-Brexit, post-COVID-19 world.

The Independence Prospectus
Losses and Gains

To the typical voter in the early days of the independence referendum, the Yes campaign was offering much. A £600 per person per year bonus, based on official statistics of government revenue and expenditure, fronted one of the first Yes Scotland publications. In a *Scotland on Sunday* article in February 2013, billionaire Jim McColl described independence as a 'management buyout' that would lead to a better economy (McColl, 2013). Later, after the publication of the Scottish

Government's White Paper, massively expanded childcare became a core part of the independence prospectus too, invariably accompanied in promotional materials by images of smiling families.

All of these put the concept of independence in what prospect theory would call a 'domain of gain'. Take the chance, vote Yes and these will be your rewards. But it was not wholly so. And as time went on, independence began to be presented in other terms. In March 2013 the SNP's 'Kirsty' broadcast sought to put an independent Scotland side-by-side with a negatively portrayed UK (SNP, 2013). Scots were reminded that it was their government that would protect higher education from the tuition fees being imposed in Westminster. But was the imposition of tuition fees a realistic prospect when there was already devolution? Other spectres were tried too, but none of them stuck until late in the campaign.

The most significant evolution of the Yes message was the pivot to the NHS in 2014. Philippa Whitford, a breast cancer surgeon renowned in her field but relatively unknown in politics, released a YouTube video that made her a fixture on the panels in many pro-independence public meetings being held up and down the country. Suddenly an authoritative figure with no background in party politics was clearly and confidently arguing that one of the most cherished of 'British' public institutions was under threat from a No vote. Though it was unplanned and unexpected, the official Yes campaign saw the opportunity and started producing materials on the theme of 'Protect the NHS'.

It struck a nerve. In the August Holyrood debates even then-Labour MSP Malcolm Chisholm, usually noted for level-headedness, accused the Yes side variously of 'mendaciousness', 'disgraceful scares' and 'ill-informed, politically motivated scaremongering'. The 'Vow' front page of the *Daily Record* also headlined that additional powers promised to Scotland in the event of a No vote would allow the ongoing protection of the NHS. Difficult though it may be to be certain what was in voters' minds, the two competing campaigns clearly felt this was an issue that was resonating.

When asked what the two or three most important issues were influencing their choice after the referendum, 54 per cent of Yes voters chose the NHS, second only to disaffection with Westminster politics at 74 per cent and far ahead of jobs, named by only 18 per cent (*The Guardian*, 2014). No voters by contrast were more likely to mention the pound and pensions, which the Better Together campaign had made emblematic of the uncertainties of the vote. Both of these are very clearly in the 'domain of loss' – the argument was not vote No and you will gain, it was vote Yes and you will lose. As a campaign perceived to be for the status quo, this was the obvious strategy. And anyone who went door-to-door, as I did, could see that, for older people especially, no prospect of a better Scotland however well-presented was going to be enough to dislodge the perceived safety of the British pension payment. As the old saying goes, the bird in the hand was being seen as worth two in the bush.

2014 is now in the rear-view mirror and vanishing quickly. Curiously, many of the dire warnings of the Yes campaign have indeed come to pass. The United Kingdom has indeed left the European Union. The unpopular Boris Johnson is Prime Minister. There may not be a formal coalition between the Conservatives and one of Nigel Farage's parties but that is wholly down to the former adopting in its entirety the key objective of the latter.

After the vote on membership of the European Union, suddenly Scottish independence took on a greater element of being a protection against loss. For those who value their European identity highly, Scottish independence began to be the most obvious way to hold on to this connection. The problem however was that very few Scots actually felt European in their gut (Ipsos MORI, 2016). European referendums are traditionally decided on the basis of 'cues, community and calculation' but in Scotland the decision was mostly cues – all Scottish parties backed Remain – and very little sense of community (Hooghe and Marks, 2005). And, in late 2020, some four years after the referendum, the negative impacts of the decision to leave the EU are still not yet tangible. Analogised to a household wage, the UK's GDP did not take a pay cut, it merely took a pay rise smaller than originally predicted. Foregone gains are not as visceral in their political impact as an outright recession.

Enter COVID-19

Coronavirus has been very different. Everyone living in Scotland can relate to the consequences of the public health emergency. While many will not know anyone who has died, all have experienced lockdown. They have seen streets emptied and workplaces closed. Not since the Second World War have as many changes been brought to the lived day-to-day experience of citizens in a single year. 1974 brought a three-day-week; 2020 brought the *zero*-day-week for millions of people throughout the UK as furlough becomes the word of the year. The wearing of masks, physical distancing and the very long and slow path back to 'normality' serve as ongoing reminders. This year will be remembered and grandchildren will one day ask what it was like to live through 2020. They may learn in school about Zoom as we did about ration books.

Coronavirus has also given ordinary citizens a chance to evaluate their two governments. Side-by-side, Nicola Sturgeon is outscoring Boris Johnson in public affection. In July and August 2020 polling, even majorities of 2014 No voters and 2016 Leave voters were answering that she was doing a good job as First Minister. SNP support for the impending Holyrood election passed 50 per cent and independence began to take a lead over the continuation of the union. Though the UK Government has tried to claim credit for compensatory measures such as the job retention scheme, the scorecard suggests that this is less convincing than the visibly imperfect record of UK authorities in England in combating the virus.

But though a second referendum looks more likely than ever, no such vote will take place while the pandemic continues to exert its hold on the public sphere. Such a vote is only feasible once – hopefully – vaccines have been developed and distributed or – more darkly – science has been defeated and we have adapted our society to a permanent accommodation with COVID-19. What then will be the lessons? In a second referendum, what evidence will the unprecedented events of 2020 offer to the two campaigns?

Some of the themes of the first referendum could have been predicted in 2011. The 2008 financial crisis and rescue of the Scottish banks was also fresh in the public mind. The question of whether Scotland is a net contributor or recipient in the UK fiscal scheme has been debated for decades. The infamous Government Expenditure and Revenue Scotland (GERS) publication which attempts to estimate this every year was first published in 1992.

Similarly, the presence of weapons of mass destruction on Scottish soil has been a key theme of the independence movement since the 1970s. The question of currency was more surprising. In its early years the SNP supported membership of the Euro but by 2014 was advocating for the continued use of Sterling. Its emergence as a key battleground seems to have emerged from a mash of focus groups and the early media skirmishes in an almost Darwinian way. Many arguments were bandied about and, for whatever reason, the No campaign felt that this one resonated.

Just as the financial crisis still loomed large six years later, the political effects of the pandemic will persist. Independence will have to be framed in relation to what it has done to public expectations and campaigners on both sides will have to address the experiences.

To campaigners for the union, the strategy is obvious. They need simply swap the global financial crisis for the pandemic and repeat the arguments about the supposed 'broad shoulders' of the UK. Moreover, GERS has also been less superficially favourable to independence campaigners in subsequent years as the price of oil failed to meet expectations and dependence on oil now looks even less politically acceptable given changing attitudes to climate change. They can again present themselves as 'steady as she goes' in their messages – the option that offers certainty and protection while independence puts households at risk. A status quo campaign finds it hard to offer gain – the obvious question is always if it can be offered why is it not being offered already – but its natural territory is the fear of change and risk of loss.

The opposite numbers on the nationalist side do not necessarily have it as easy as they think. The pain caused by the pandemic will be in the past tense by the time of any second referendum. A suggestion that staying in the Union presents an active risk to the safety of the people of Scotland would depend on people thinking that the biggest public health crisis since 1918 stood a reasonable chance of being repeated in the near future. That seems unlikely. A second Yes campaign may therefore also have to fight on much the same territory as the first – a prospectus for a different Scotland combined with a stark portrayal of the contemporary UK.

Whether the result is any different will therefore hinge on two competing factors. For the union, the upheavals of Brexit and COVID-19 might heighten *all* sensitivity to risk. People who have never felt more at the mercy of great events may well respond by being even more risk averse than before. Whatever the rational calculus of traditional economics may suggest, the post-Kahneman orthodoxy prevails in this scenario, with the feeling of insecurity being accentuated and winning out over any willingness to strike out for better.

But the same can hold for nationalists. The *credibility* of the pro-union claims may have been significantly damaged. How does a Better Together 2 campaigner argue convincingly that Britain protected Scotland if people feel that the UK suffered more in the pandemic than our European neighbours? The financial crisis damaged the case for Scottish independence so much because the SNP had built up neighbouring nations such as Ireland as an 'arc of prosperity' only for them to be seen as hit far worse than the UK. But during coronavirus it is the Irelands, Denmarks and New Zealands of the world that have suffered least. If the status quo is Boris Johnson and Dominic Cummings, that status quo could well become the greater risk – the 'domain of loss' while the credibility of the better Scotland is enhanced.

To Independence?

Risk will never be seen in entirely rational terms. Rightly or wrongly, a good story beats a good statistic in any political debate. Coronavirus has been an epoch-defining experience on at least a par with any in our lifetimes. We have seen society changed more in a relatively short space of time than any of us have ever before had to face. The great upheaval has given both sides in the constitutional debate new stories to tell and has reinforced emotional connections with institutions such as the NHS that were tapped the first time around.

If it occurs, an independent Scotland may well be described as one of the outcomes of the pandemic by the next century's historians. But the future is not set. Other factors, such as the growth of English nationalism post-Brexit, cannot be discounted. And there are plausible permutations that would lead to a second rejection of independence after the campaigns have made their new (and old) cases. But great changes have already occurred. The immediacy of events to people's lives goes far beyond even the tangibility of the doctor's appointment or the pension payments debated in 2014 and they are social, not individual. For months our entire way-of-life was altered and may never be quite the same again. We may well stand now at a fulcrum of history.

References

The Guardian, 19 September 2014, 'Scottish independence: poll reveals who voted, how and why', accessed at: www.theguardian.com/politics/2014/sep/20/scottish-independence-lord-ashcroft-poll

Hooghe, L and Marks, G, 2005, 'Calculation, community and

cues: Public opinion on European integration', *European Union Politics*, vol.6, issue 4, 419–443.

Ipsos MORI, 9 June 2016, 'The "Tinman" referendum: the EU debate in Scotland is lacking heart', access at: www.ipsos.com/ipsos-mori/en-uk/tinman-referendum-eu-debate-scotland-lacking-heart

McColl, J, 3 February 2013, 'Business billionaire Jim McColl backs independence', *Scotland on Sunday*, accessed at: www.scotsman.com/news/scottish-independence-will-be-management-buy-out-1-2773456

SNP, 22 March 2013, 'Two Futures', Greenroom Films, YouTube, accessed at: www.youtube.com/watch?v=qetvDbl4Xfs

CHAPTER 39

Scotland, Brexit and Europe: Challenges Ahead

Kirsty Hughes

Scotland did not vote for Brexit. But at the start of 2020 – on 31 January – the UK formally left the European Union. This major change in the UK's relationship with the EU and its 27 member states represents a sea-change compared to the last almost 50 years. But this huge shift was partially obscured as the UK spent the rest of 2020 in a transition period, staying inside the EU's single market and customs union. That, together with the dominance of the COVID-19 crisis, meant that, despite the big political and legal change of leaving the EU, the full economic, political and social impacts of Brexit will only really hit home on 1 January 2021 when transition ends.

From March 2020, there were tortuous negotiations between the UK and Brussels on the nature of their future relationship. But it is clear that deal or no deal, the UK – and Scotland – will face a very different future relationship with the EU.

The EU and the COVID-19 Crisis

This substantive change in the UK-EU relationship was already apparent as the COVID-19 crisis unfolded – with the UK following its own separate path. The European Union stumbled at the start of the crisis as member states responded in very different ways. Attempts by the European Commission to encourage and lead a coordinated response foundered initially due to the rapid onset of the virus, the fact that powers over health reside mainly with member states not Brussels and the lack of response from member states when EU requests were made early on to help Italy (hit hardest at the start in early March).

But EU solidarity started to become more obvious as the epidemic continued into summer. And, at a major four-day summit in July, the

EU's leaders agreed a €750 billion package to provide grants and loans to EU countries hardest hit by the virus. This package was notable too as it allowed the European Commission, for the first time, to raise funds on financial markets and distribute around half the funds as grants to member states. This didn't just show solidarity; it represented a rather major step forward in European integration – a step initially resisted by four member states at the July summit (Austria, Denmark, the Netherlands and Sweden) but who finally gave in and the package was agreed.

At the same time, the European Commission had undertaken other steps including launching joint procurement programmes to buy personal protective equipment, and agreeing a deal with the French company Sanofi to secure supplies of a potential COVID-19 vaccine – one that would then be available to all 27 member states.

The UK, outside the European Union, had no role to play in these developments – with no seat, vote or voice any longer at the summit table. It could have joined in the EU's joint procurement programmes but chose not to (with a spat in early summer over whether the EU had properly informed the UK of this possibility or not). If the UK had still been a member state, it would certainly have had a big voice in the debates over how the EU could and should respond to COVID-19. But outside the EU, the UK was left looking rather isolated as it forged its own path and its death toll rose to be one of the highest in the world.

Since health is devolved in the UK, Scotland could respond somewhat differently to the rest of the UK to the epidemic – something that the Scottish Government did more around lockdown-easing, rather than at the start of the crisis. But, given that Brexit had happened, the Scottish Government was not in a position to join in EU programmes that the UK had refused to participate in (which the UK could have, as it was still in the single market and customs union). And since the UK was not in EU meetings, there was no route for Scotland to influence by pushing its views via the UK Government (should the latter have listened to them).

Questions for Scotland After Brexit and After COVID-19

The impact of Brexit and the impact of COVID-19, in different ways, will be with us for a long time to come. The COVID-19 crisis is first and foremost a health crisis but rapidly became an economic, social and cultural crisis too – raising many questions for our globalised world already in a sustained and existential climate crisis. Meanwhile, Brexit had already had negative economic impacts on the UK even before leaving the EU or its single market (due to lower investment, amidst considerable uncertainty about the future and lower growth as a result). But the damaging economic effects of Brexit will get worse in 2021 once the full reality of leaving the EU and its single market and customs union becomes clear. And Brexit, like COVID-19, is also a political, social and cultural process, changing the opportunities and ways the UK and Scotland can and will relate to other European countries in future.

The Future EU-UK Relationship

How the UK's future relationship with the European Union will evolve is, to some extent, an open question. The Withdrawal Agreement, agreed between the UK and EU in autumn 2019, came into force once Brexit happened at the end of January 2020 and sets some basic parameters, with three central aspects to the agreement. Firstly, the two sides agreed on the UK's outstanding financial obligations – the divorce bill some called it. Secondly, EU citizens living in the UK, and UK citizens living in the EU 27 member states, were given rights to stay in those countries – 'settled status' – under certain conditions. Thirdly, there was a separate and striking deal for Northern Ireland.

To ensure the border between Northern Ireland and the Republic of Ireland stayed open, without border infrastructure, UK Prime Minister Boris Johnson agreed that Northern Ireland would stay, effectively, in the EU's single market for goods (but not services) and in its customs union. This was an extraordinary thing to agree – to put a customs and regulatory border within the UK, between Britain and Northern Ireland, and something that Theresa May when Prime Minister had long resisted. It means that there are now substantial checks on goods going from Great Britain to Northern Ireland, and more bureaucracy and form filling for exports of goods and agricultural products – with knock-on damaging economic effects but with the great plus of helping to preserve the peace process as set out in the Good Friday Agreement.

Even with a basic free trade deal, future trade between the UK and EU will be more problematic than before Brexit. There may be tariffs, there will be other customs rules and checks to manage, and there will be regulatory checks at Dover and all other ports. These will add to costs of trading with the EU, will get in the way of 'just-in-time' supply chains and discourage foreign direct investment – and access for a range of service sectors to the EU market will be severely limited. A range of studies, including ones by the UK and Scottish Governments, have shown that these barriers to trade will significantly reduce economic growth compared to what it would have been otherwise.

And there will be a whole range of other effects – from longer queues for UK citizens travelling to EU destinations, new rules on health insurance or pet passports and less freedom to live and work in any of the EU 27 countries.

Nor will the UK-EU relationship be fully clear by January 2021. As geographical neighbours who will still trade and interact with each other a lot, there will be much to discuss, whether on foreign policy in an increasingly unstable global environment or on cooperation on climate change, on the COVID-19 pandemic as it unfolds, on future agreements on transport, on whether the UK will participate in EU research and educational programmes and so on.

Scotland's European Choices

Where does all this leave Scotland as the UK heads off on a new trajectory outside the EU? Overall, it leaves Scotland in a position that is far from where the majority of its voters and government wanted it to be. Scotland is no longer in the European Union, despite a 62 per cent 'remain' vote in 2016. The option of the UK staying in a very close relationship with the EU, perhaps like Norway in the European Economic Area, never looked likely and has not happened.

So the hard Brexit option of leaving the EU's single market and its customs union is what Scotland, alongside the rest of the UK now faces. And while the Scottish Government, as early as December 2016, proposed a deal not so dissimilar to the one Northern Ireland has – suggesting Scotland could stay in the EU's single market even if the rest of the UK did not – that didn't happen either (true it was never that likely but even less ambitious proposals such as giving the Scottish Government and Parliament more control over migration were rejected by the UK Government too).

The Scottish Government had precious little advance information from the UK Government about the UK-EU talks in 2020, let alone any chances to influence the negotiations in a substantive or strategic way. And, as has become increasingly clear, Brexit has substantial implications for the devolution settlement too. In the EU, the UK and Scotland were part of the EU's single market – with Scotland having devolved powers to implement EU laws in environment and agriculture. But the UK has moved to create a UK internal market having left the EU one, resulting in a major dispute between the UK Government and devolved governments in Scotland and Wales about this re-centralisation of powers – or power grab to put it more bluntly. Scottish Government plans to stay as close as possible to EU environmental laws may well fall foul of these UK internal market plans.

There will be areas where different governmental, business and civil society relationships between Scotland and the EU can still be partially protected and developed without UK Government interference. The Scottish Government has offices – 'hubs' – in Berlin, Brussels, Dublin and Paris and can invest in relationship-building from those. Businesses will still trade with the EU, charities and cultural bodies will still interact and work with their partners in Europe. But overall, to build relationships and even have some voice and influence on EU policies and strategies post-Brexit, will require much more effort for much smaller impact – that is the new reality of Scotland's position within the more restricted, more distant UK-EU relationship.

Independence in the EU?

Scotland's constitutional debate remains centre stage. The Scottish Government, and the SNP, have a strategic policy stance of seeking independence in the EU. But post-Brexit is this realistic and is it a good idea? And will the EU be open to an independent Scotland in the future as it integrates further in the face of the COVID-19 crisis and deals with many other challenges?

If at some future point, there was a legally and constitutionally sound process whereby Scotland chose independence, then certainly it could, as a European state, apply to join the European Union. Unlike in 2014, post-Brexit, independence would mean Scotland being an EU member state with a seat at the table while the rest of the UK would remain outside with whatever set of deals and agreements it had made with the EU by that point in time.

This raises a number of questions but it clearly means that the EU's external border, with Scotland as an EU member state, would run between Scotland and the rest of the UK (or more specifically England and Wales given Northern Ireland's special deal). From 2021, the UK and Scotland will face a harder border with the EU. But an independent Scotland in the EU would no longer have a hard border with its fellow EU member states – there would be no customs barriers. But instead Scotland would have a new hard border with the rest of the UK. Just as with Brexit, this border with the rest of the UK would have some negative economic effects. The debate over how big these effects might be and how they might be offset by being independent in the EU will surely be a sustained one.

But there are other questions post-Brexit and post-COVID-19. For now, there is no reason to argue that the big economic and political challenges posed by the pandemic have made the EU less open to new member states joining. There is an accession process for several western Balkans states – one that is moving slowly but is nonetheless progressing. For the EU to absorb a small, advanced country like Scotland – and one that had already been in the EU for 47 years – would not per se be disruptive. Scotland would still have to meet all the EU's criteria including debt and deficit rules (see Hughes, 2020). These economic criteria might become less rigid following the COVID-19 crisis as EU member states debt levels have mounted sharply but it is certainly not to be relied on.

Scotland would also need to debate whether the EU's path to more integration on economic and fiscal policy, its approach to tackling the climate crisis, its challenges over migration, and more, were ones it wanted to be part of. There is an alternative: to be like Norway, in the EU's single market but not part of its wider political institutions. But this would mean newly independent Scotland would need to follow EU rules but with no vote or voice. And on the tricky border challenges, it would leave Scotland with a customs border to the EU (Norway is not in the customs union) and a regulatory border to the rest of the UK – quite likely the worst of all worlds. Moreover, at a time of substantial global instability, it would also mean not being part of the EU as a political and diplomatic block.

Where Next?

For now, as part of the UK, Scotland is on a trajectory away from the European Union. Scotland's European relationships will be strongly influenced by how the future UK-EU relationship evolves; but in the current UK political situation it will have little say over that.

The UK has chosen to reduce its influence in Europe just as global crises, most of all climate change, COVID-19, and geopolitical instability, have made the EU a more vital alliance than ever. In this insecure world, Scotland – with its constitutional debate – still faces a choice between two unions.

References

Hughes, K (ed.), 2020, *An Independent Scotland in the EU: Issues for Accession*, Scottish Centre on European Relations.

CHAPTER 40

From Downton Abbey to the Blitz Spirit: Living with the Ghosting of Britain

Gerry Hassan and Patrick Wright

GH: Your book – On Living in an Old Country – *was hugely influential in developing an understanding of Britain and what it is, and how the past is a living set of collective memories being remade (Wright, 1985). England and the idea of Britain are sometimes presented as synonymous and overlapping, but are increasingly a major fault-line in British politics and the British state.*

Why did you write the book, and how have its ideas endured since its first publication in 1985? Thirty-five years on – after Thatcher, Blair and New Labour, ten years of Conservatives and austerity, Brexit and now COVID-19 *– where is the notion of 'living in an old country' and whose, and which, country are we talking about?*

PW: I began writing the book in 1979, after five years in Canada. There, I had started thinking about how the British state clothed itself in synthetic ideas of national and imperial tradition. I was partly spurred into reflection by the glaring disconnect between Anglo-Canadian ideas of 'the old country' and the disintegrating Britain I had known in the early '70s; not least the three years spent at the University of Kent which felt, in those years of turmoil and crisis, less like the building site it was and more like the ruin of a promised future collapsing around us.

Back in England, I formed this sense of separation that became central to the book, planning it as a doctoral thesis. But without funding, I wrote the book while making a living doing other things. For these reasons, it was a series of connected essays many focused on suggestive, conventionally overlooked manifestations; the whole thing threaded together with theoretical perspectives and various strategies of assertion and accusation.

I yawn when I hear *On Living in an Old Country* counted among the books that launched the critique of 'the heritage industry', and contributing to then yet-to-be invented 'museum studies'. The question for me was to understand how a selective idea of national tradition had become the willing attendant to a disruptive political project (Thatcherism) that was fundamentally destroying tradition. How did this idea serve to legitimise the deindustrialising 'modernisation' being pursued then? What made 'the past' so compelling in peoples' understanding, and what were the consequences of invoking a unified and 'organic' conception of national heritage?

I looked for other writings about this sort of 'nationalism' but found little. Hobsbawm et al. helpfully gave us 'the invention of tradition' but much academic research seemed content with the idea that 'nationalism' was really only significant as a third world development project. I went elsewhere for views on how ideas of tradition become attached to aspects of everyday life – a key point that seemed vital to understand to get beyond thinking that it might be enough to show up the falsification, the 'inventedness', in popular conceptions of history.

I had read Tom Nairn on the case for a new articulation of England in *The Break Up of Britain* and his essay on the English literary intelligentsia, and it was obvious that it was not ideal to tackle this subject from English experience alone (1977). I wanted to expose some of the murkier aspects of inherited ideas of English identity but felt some tension between the direction Nairn was indicating (the break-up scenario) and other requirements of the time – to defend educational and welfarist elements of the British state faced with aggressive ideological attack, privatisation etc. In the end, *On Living in an Old Country* was really an incomplete act of 'reconnaissance' of a terrain I have continued to investigate.

GH: *The power of the past seems everywhere in Britain – not just the Blitz spirit that Angus Calder was trying to demythologise nearly 30 years ago, and the Battle of Britain and Dunkirk, but military triumphs like Trafalgar and Waterloo are regularly commemorated (Calder, 1991). This continued love of heritage and reproduction, and repacking of Britain's past and its upper classes –* Downton Abbey *and more – also sells overseas. What does this rise and grip of a very selective past – something you foretold in* On Living in an Old Country *–*

mean? How can it be understood, what does it say about the present, and can we escape from it?

PW: Overseas images of Britain can indeed have a kind of potency – whether *Downton Abbey*, or older propaganda films like *Mrs. Miniver* (1942) made to project an image of England to encourage American efforts in the Second World War – or Afro-Caribbean immigrants raised with schoolroom ideas of Britain who then found themselves in a very different country when they got beyond the passenger terminal. Much expatriate memory of Britain is absurdly disconnected from reality. It is a form of timeslip memory and the fact that it misses out many decades of recent history makes it convenient to those who think the country has spent those decades going to the dogs.

Recent events have indeed confirmed that we must understand 'the past' as a present construct that may, especially under pressure or crisis, owe precious little to the actual truth. We have seen successive remobilisations of the memory of the Second World War, and Remembrance Day has definitely not become irrelevant as some feared it might as the war faded from living memory. We may start by recognising that the British Empire's participation was a virtuous moment as a struggle against fascism – that also commanded considerable solidarity across the British nations. This should make us more inclined to call out some of the things done with its memory over subsequent years. For two or three decades after 1945, the memory of the war found testimony in institutions of the post-war settlement – the welfare state, public education, industrial policy – and, for the veterans who favoured it as an alternative to war in the early 1970s, membership of the European Economic Community.

I tracked this gathering tide of allegedly 'creative' destruction in *A Journey Through Ruins* (Wright, 1991). One of the first moves in bringing national history into play was to repossess the memory of the Second World War, concentrating it around the Battle of Britain and the 'Blitz spirit' and then to assert that it had actually been betrayed by the peace built in its name. In this version of the war, the post-war settlement with nationalisations and the welfare state, was restaged not as the reforming expression of popular desires for social justice, but as the betrayal that gave birth to a state that was bungling, incompetent and barely distinct from the Soviet equivalent.

Some veterans of the Second World War were influential outliers.

SCOTLAND AFTER THE VIRUS

For example Antony Fisher, the former Battle of Britain pilot and en-
trepreneur who founded the Institute of Economic Affairs, or the an-
ti-fluoridationist, Patrick Clavell Blount, who spent the war cooking
for RAF bomber crews and felt that the state that later presumed to
impose 'mass medication' was not worthy of their sacrifice.

By the late '80s this cranky current had taken centre stage even
though its champions still liked to position themselves as valiant patri-
ots who had resisted while many submitted to corruptions of the post-
war decades. By the time I started mapping this story, the memory of
the war was being redeclared against all sorts of modern encroach-
ments – the state, trade unions, immigration, permissiveness, youth
etc. Over and again, and in many different fields of public life, the
same version of post-war history appeared. First there was this great
and noble victory achieved at considerable sacrifice; then the supposedly degenerate peace that betrayed that sacrifice in diverse fields of
post-war development. The third part was always the promised and,
thanks to the heroic endurance of its champions, no longer impossible
moment of recovery in which the nation returned to its true path.

I called this narrative 'the revivalist fable' in *A Journey Through
Ruins*. Preliminary versions may have seemed fairly trivial – for example, when right-wing cynic Auberon Waugh described Shirley
Williams, Labour Minister for Education, as 'worse than Hitler' for
promoting comprehensive schools. In 1989, the same 'theory' of national history informed the poster that Saatchi and Saatchi produced
for the Victoria and Albert Museum's exhibition of Prince Charles' ar-
chitectural 'Vision of Britain'. 'In 1945,' it said 'the Luftwaffe stopped
bombing London. Two years later the Blitz began.' In that case, the
answer was to revive traditional forms of architecture, and the classi-
cal revivalist Quinlan Terry became the architect with the 'answer' to
problems of failing council housing estates. And in 1999, the *Sunday
Times* accused Michael Nauman, then Germany's Minister of Culture
(who claimed with good evidence to have been falsely presented) of
daring to suggest that Britain was 'obsessed with the memory of the
Second World War' and was alone in Europe in having it embedded
at the core of its national identity. Predictably enough, the tabloids
reacted in a way that only served to prove Nauman's point.

All this happened in another century, but more recent events confirm the potency of simplifying and politically motivated narratives
that appeal to British patriotism in public life. The Revivalist Fable has

endured as a rallying cry not just in the battle against the now largely dismantled welfare state, but also in the rhetoric of Euroscepticism. We might argue about how much the case made for Brexit amounted to more than a fantasy dressed in lies and appeals to an allegedly lost purity. There can, though, be little doubt that it relied on the same sort of appeal to an allegedly interrupted national past, or that it was advocated by the same politicians who led the attack on post-war social democracy in the last century. There is a direct continuity between these two onslaughts. The perceived enemy may oscillate back and forth – between Europe, the welfare state and migrants – but from the '80s onwards we've been locked in the same battle.

GH: The left's failure in all this is profound. Why has this happened, and why has the right successfully captured mainstream stories of England and Britain, telling accounts about the past which validate reactionaryism in the here and now? Was there ever a time, 1945 apart, when the left successfully told a counter-story about Britain that dislodged the right? And if 1945 is the exception, what does that say about Labour – which has been a deeply conservative institution – and the broader constituency of the left?

PW: Looking at the situation now, some of the recent anger and desertion among voters may still stem from the catastrophe unleashed on the Middle East in 2003, and how the Labour people responsible – Blair, Mandelson, Campbell and others – thought it fine to lecture us on the moral void in which they brought their government to a close. It's also time to recognise the absolute dereliction of Trojan Horse tactics pursued by Seamus Milne and others who should understand dangers associated with the British Labour movement's long-standing habit of fighting challenges of the present with attitudes and instruments of the past. It is not just in Scotland that the Labour Party has seemed lost in internal feuding, timorous calculation and incompetence.

It is the consequence of Labour's failure to grasp the situation, to produce an alternative sense of possibility within a transformed present reality, which allowed a defensive and backward-looking version of English patriotism to win. The 'England' that has prevailed is less a modern society in search of a future than a tribe along the lines of GK Chesterton's 'secret people' – slow, rooted and instinctive, but also outwitted and betrayed from above; a 'silent majority' reduced to finding consolation in diverse conspiracy theories tossed down to them by members of the Brexit elite. It is a tough call, but we must surely wish Keir Starmer well as he tries to widen rather than narrow our sense of possibilities, to establish a more truthful understanding of the discontents caused by so many years of austerity and to produce a principled set of policies that are not just Tory-lite, or defensive, or in denial about the new liquidity in people's political allegiances.

GH: You talked in On Living in an Old Country *about the left's unease about invoking and representing the nation(s) in the UK. I recently wrote a book about Labour, its ideas of Britain and Britishness –* The People's Flag and the Union Jack *– partly because such a study had never been done (Hassan and Shaw, 2019). All histories and studies of Labour, even of a left-wing kind such as Ralph Miliband, assume its Britishness and never critically investigate what this might mean and the political consequences that flow from it. What have been the consequences historically, and in the here and now, of this unease, evasiveness and avoidance by Labour, and most of the left, about Britain, Britishness and talking about the nation – allowing for the UK not being a nation but a nation-state?*

One counter-tendency on the left has been continual citing of the political agency of 'the people' to be put in opposition to 'the nation' – and lots of left-wing thinkers have at times posed this binary division. This seems a disastrous political logic, leaving the emotional and popular terrain of national imagination at a British level to be articulated by the right, which has its own myopic reading of what Britain is and what the past is. Why have Labour and the left been so consistent to an almost dogmatic degree – wanting to avoid the terrain of talking about Britain, Britishness and nation(s)? What are the consequences and is there any prospect of change?

PW: It is a fundamental question that reminds me of how easy it remains in England to underestimate the extent and consistency of Labour's rout in Scotland as well as in the so-called 'red wall' constituencies to the south. I agree that the Labour Party has conventionally assumed that its 'people' existed within a generalised British identity – a conservatism that can be traced back to the days when George Lansbury could take a train from London to Edinburgh and insist that nothing really changed when you crossed between the two countries. In recent years, the party has had to wake up to an increasingly obvious reality, but its attitude to thinking about Britishness and any further constitutional realignment remains dawdling, reluctant and defensive – trying to hold the line rather than thinking creatively about a transforming set of relations in the British state.

Those who have tried to address the question within the Westminster party have quickly found themselves facing powerful figures who continue to believe that these issues are either marginal to the political project or so tainted by secessionists and racists that they are best left alone. This has to change, and the Labour Party (which would certainly have served us all better had it really considered the likely impact of Brexit within the British state) should now be leading the necessary exploration of what a transformed future might look like.

As for Labour's assumptions about 'the people' – these may have been slightly adjusted by the many analysts who have tried to apply Gramsci's idea of the 'national popular' to the British situation and to understand the actual and diverse composition of the working-class today, but the supposedly natural link with 'the people' is definitely broken and the Party won't be remade without coming out its mental bunker and pursuing a different kind of engagement with present realities. The disconcerting fact is that many of 'the people' have marched out of the frame in which the Labour Party has long liked to contain them – in Scotland to the SNP, and in England to the appeal of a right-wing Brexit.

Long ago Tony Benn urged us to remember the Chartists and create a new legend of Robin Hood. I doubt the wisdom of trying to provide already aroused Englishness with more congenial anti-racist contents even though those may exist to be dug from the historical record. Much better to work for a fuller understanding of the present causes behind this efflorescence, and who is actually responsible for the economic, social and technological changes that, in the absence of other alternatives, have granted so much allure to right-wing populists. Jurgen Habermas once wrote that the task of critics and intellectuals was to clarify 'murky realities'. COVID-19 may certainly have been revealing as well as alarming, but it is Brexit and the extremely murky atmosphere in which it triumphed and now proceeds, that brings my attention back to the question of Englishness.

References

Calder, A, 1991, *The Myth of the Blitz*, London, Jonathan Cape.

Hassan, G and Shaw, E, 2019, *The People's Flag and the Union Jack: An Alternative History of Britain and the Labour Party*, London, Biteback Publishing.

Nairn, T, 1977, *The Break-Up of Britain: Crisis and Neo-nationalism*, London, New Left Books.

Wright, P, 1991, *A Journey through Ruins: The Last Days of London*, London, Radius Books.

Wright, P, 1985, *On Living in an Old Country: The National Past in Contemporary Britain*, London, Verso Books.

What Could It Mean to Flourish 'After the Virus'?

Simon Barrow and Gerry Hassan

THIS IS THE third book we have edited together in the space of three years. The first, *A Nation Changed?*, looked at the SNP and their impact on politics and society ten years after they became the governing party (2017). The second, *Scotland the Brave?*, addressed wider society and its development in the 20 years following the establishment of Scotland's Parliament in 1999 (2019). We have covered a decade of party politics and two decades of Scotland under devolution, and now, with this book, address how our society is being impacted by a pandemic neither of us would have envisaged a year ago. In so doing, we open up questions about what its aftermath could look like – something which will likely be with us for at least a decade to come.

All three of these books have been collaborative efforts in mapping modern Scotland, engaging a wide range of voices – ones which embody a considerable amount of experience and expertise – in considering the significant degrees of change we have all been living through. However, the approach of *Scotland After the Virus* turned out to be quite different. As we began to conceive this volume, it became apparent that a set of essays on public policy issues, pertinent though those might be, was simply not adequate to the task of truly considering the many dimensions of the human condition in Scotland – and beyond – in the light of the pandemic. Yet this, we realised, was precisely what was needed. For that reason, fiction and poetry were essential. And the story behind our cover shows the importance of the visual, the artistic, the cultural and the emotional in coming together to revive the human spirit in an ongoing moment of trauma and uncertainty.

The Unanswered Question

The other issue we needed to negotiate was the title. Should the phrase 'Scotland After the Virus' have a question-mark after it? Or would that in itself simply create even greater anxiety? Should we avoid explicit mention of the virus in the title altogether, as one contributor persuasively suggested to us, positing 'Recovering Scotland' as another vibrant possibility. In the end, we decided that the coronavirus had to be acknowledged and named. That is, after all, why we are all here, in our different spaces, mindsets and psychologies. We are dealing with a reality which for most of us came out of the blue but cannot be sidestepped or shied away from.

But that question-mark still looms for us, tantalisingly and agonisingly. As it does for you, in all probability. Questioning and probing is both essential and unavoidable at a time like this. But as TS Eliot reminds us, in a phrase which is at once humane and caustic: 'Humankind cannot bear very much reality' (1936). So we also need to find reassurance and relief – of the kind that the imaginary, the artistic and the poetic can truthfully but pointedly offer. The issue here is not escapism (though we all need that from time to time, too). It is engagement with those dimensions of human experience which cannot avoid a degree of existential dread, but which also longs for a better world and better way of being together in the midst of both challenge and unfinished business – and which need to find that in the midst (as Eliot avers), not simply in some ideal future forever postponed. Politics and public policy, such as we consider in the second half of the book are essential to that future, whatever it may be, of course. But they are also palpably insufficient on their own. As we cling to friends and loved ones, or find that because of social distancing we cannot, that becomes very obvious in ways that the regular worlds of public affairs and multiform media are so good at avoiding.

Is There an 'After the Virus'?

In the old days 'the $64,000 question' meant the question that has to be asked at a certain crucial point but which was feared because there is so much at stake. In Scotland's and the world's case right now, the *technical* question is 'Is there an "after the virus"', or is COVID-19 and a world of future pandemics simply something we will have to live with for an indefinite period of time? In all honesty, no one knows the answer to that, which is why it is so terrifying. The possibility exists, distinctly or not, that things we have simply taken for granted in the modern era – like large gatherings, sporting events and concerts – may not ever happen again in the ways that we have been used to.

What we are working for, of course, is a solution – which most people think of as a vaccine. Humankind, staring that reality straight in the face, needs to acknowledge right now that so far in our history we have never found a vaccine for a coronavirus. This one, we are all assuming, with some supporting evidence from epidemiologists and research scientists, is the one we *will* crack in the near future. Forecasts are being made, as we write, that a vaccine could be made available as soon as a few months' time, or perhaps a year, or maybe 18 months. Some are claiming that the essential breakthrough has already been made. It is now mainly a question of testing and trialling. But in reality we do not know.

This in itself raises the most profound questions imaginable about our relationship to the earth, and to its ecology and life-chains – ones which are only hinted at in this book. Equally, the reality of globalisation in the broadest sense (the existence of the world as a single, if complex and monopolised, economic fact) is about to be tested to the possible destruction of some of us if and when that vaccine arrives. The Pope is among those world leaders who have homed in on the moral imperative to ensure that everyone has access to the COVID-19 'cure', with special attention to the poorest and most vulnerable – those who corporate globalism, economic nationalisms and nativist populisms often leave out of the equation in the rush to power.

These profound challenges – along with the other looming catastrophe of human-assisted global warning, and the daily crises of war, abuse of rights, human suffering and dislocation – are also the very ones that point to COVID-19 as posing the $64,000 *ethical* question. Are we really one humanity? Are our rights (let alone our responsibilities) truly universal? How can we find ways of being and flourishing in particular places (like Scotland, and the British and Irish Isles) which benefit both our global neighbours and ourselves? Is a path beyond survivalism and towards mutuality really possible?

That is why this book, in addition to its poetry and prose, also has chapters on psychology and spirituality – the former not presuming a 'one size fits all' model of framing the human psyche, and the latter not assuming that the realm of the spiritual is necessarily either religious or non-religious, scientific or extra-scientific. What our different contributors have done, in a variety of compelling ways, is to open doors of perception. In this afterword, we will now look at a few of those windows of opportunity – lessons and patterns which might help us into a sustainable, usable and flourishable future.

Interconnected Realities and Challenges

But just before we open those doors, it is worth noting that all the questions we are negotiating, or will have to negotiate, in contemplating Scotland and the world 'after the virus' will need to be faced in the light of the many other things we have learned afresh over the last year or so. That includes the toxic nature of white supremacy, the divisions brought about by identity politics and the extent of abuse and corruption within institutions which have presumed upon being advanced and civilised.

What COVID-19 is teaching us, perhaps, is that in spite of the technological, intellectual, cultural and organisational advances we have made across the modern and post-modern eras, we are not 'in control of the world' in the way that doctrines of progress and modernity (not to mention capitalism, communism and religions of different stripes) have mostly assumed. The *Vorsprung Durch Rethink* we need (a phrase from sociologist Goran Therborn, reworking the old Audi advert) may therefore be more fundamental – in the non-fundamentalist sense of that term – than any of us has the capacity to envisage right now. We just have to go on seeing if it is possible to see – most likely – through a glass, darkly.

How Can we Learn Differently From Here?

Through the many voices of this book some emerging patterns may be detected. We will identify just a few here. We hope that there might be ways of engaging fruitfully about such learnings through and beyond this particular set of texts.

Firstly, there is the sheer adaptability, resourcefulness and resilience of human beings in adversity. Faced with a pandemic which less than a year ago virtually no one was predicting, people have made enormous changes to their lives. The capacity to cope is quite extraordinary. This is not simply an evolutionary instinct to adaptation, in the reflexive nature of human consciousness, it is a moral one too, and a matter of engaging active imagination with the practicalities of daily life. Of course, we should not forget those who have not coped or are not coping. But there is something we can do about that

– individually, communally and in larger collectivities and systems of organisation. How those are, and what they are, should be at the forefront of our political and neighbourly considerations right now, and on into the future.

Secondly, the pressures which people have faced have not been borne equally. The rich and privileged have managed to have more control and, if very wealthy, to buy their way into a degree of security in the pandemic. Those who are low paid or vulnerable have suffered the most – sometimes tragically with their lives. The world is deeply divided in terms of wealth and power, in terms of access to health, technical capabilities and much more. The effects of the pandemic are structured along class lines, deeply gendered and marked by historic patterns of racism, colonisation and injustice. These also constitute another ecological and planetary threat, felt first by the poorest.

Thirdly, some of the reflections in this book are confirmations of what we already knew or should have known. Indisputable facts, such as the fact that poverty and inequality kills; that Scotland is not that equal a society (which we have previously charted); and that some of our poorest communities have some of the bleakest life circumstances despite living in one of the richest countries in the world. Concomitantly, democracy reduced to the rituals of majoritarianism, or with the de-liberative engagement of the people disconnected from representative institutions, puts us in a weak place to negotiate collaborative means of survival in a time of crisis which could be chronic as well as acute. So we have to work better and harder at the processes of learning, partic-ipating, choosing and deciding (see Ainsley, 2018; Geoghegan, 2020).

Fourthly, some things which have been revealed over the course of this pandemic and in this book are matters we did not know pre-COVID-19, or knew inadequately. These include the degree to which Scotland as a community has shown an overwhelming desire to have a unity of purpose in the face of this crisis – and whatever other differ-ences we undoubtedly have – to listen to authoritative knowledge and expertise, and to act in the interests of a common good which we all, at some level, recognise.

The Scottish Dimension of an Emerging 'New'

A related point here is the journey we have been going on as a nation, as a society and as a particular historically-conditioned set of communities and cultures in our wider home of northern Europe. At the outset of this pandemic, when UK Chancellor Rishi Sunak announced his furlough scheme, some in Scotland thought this was conclusive proof of the benevolence and power of the British state and hence making the case for its continuation.

Yet, as the scale of the crisis became more self-evident and the incontrovertible fact that small affluent states such as Denmark, Norway and New Zealand ran similar schemes and were also more competent, the argument about the power of the UK Government and Treasury has not been persuasive. Rather, this crisis has yet again shown the fleet-of-foot nature and adaptability of a host of small-sized states which have chosen to prioritise social cohesiveness and national unity, and the disastrous choices of a range of larger sized states – from the UK to the US, to Brazil and Mexico to name the most obvious.

Maybe what this presages, under the pressing conditions of a pandemic, is that our particularities can indeed find a degree of common ground and aspiration, both within and outwith constitutional questions. While the toxicity of certain parts of social media rumbles on (and probably always will), the remaking of the public sphere offers us opportunities to explore better ways of having conversations, connections and even disagreements. There will be, in the future, new and better languages of public exchange which are more rooted in what binds us together, rather than what divides us, but the challenge is how do we aid that future into being in the here and now? How can we make a route map from the present impasse to a better terrain – and one which in so doing takes on and defeats the populists, ultra-tribalists, conspiracy theorists and hatemongers?

Equally, can we reframe those points of difference in ways which acknowledge both the viewpoint of the other (so closely called to our attention as we have listened to each other's COVID-19 experiences and stories), and also the vulnerability of what we think of as our own non-negotiables? For instance, can the concept of a union acknowledge the need for a real, not cosmetic, ceding of Westminster sovereignty in the search for workable patterns of democracy, polity and economy? And can the debate on independence be mature enough to adapt to the new pro-independence majority which emerged in the summer of 2020? For example, pro-union arguments should recognise the democratic impulse that is behind most independence arguments; while the independence case has to recognise that in the inevitability, even necessity, of interdependence, some form of union and unions will continue to define Scotland's future (Jackson, 2020). The debate has to move on to what kind of union, co-operation and democratic institutions, this might involve.

As we search for new ways forward, better ways of differing, fresh grounds for unifying and improved hopes for the future, perhaps one mediating concept that could bring together the best elements both of a union state and of independent nationhood would be *confederalism*. This, distinct from federalism, assumes different nations and more empowered regions in control of their own destiny (including an independent Scotland), but which then looks for voluntary agreement and where appropriate contract, to work together across borders, markets, legal systems, polities and democratic structures in order to achieve a genuine 'family of nations'?

For if the COVID-19 pandemic has taught us anything in this regard, it is surely both that we need the very particular resources that each of us can bring, and which have to be developed through particular disciplines or communities (scientific ones, for instance); but also that we need to bring these resources and spaces together in ways which appreciate difference and complementarity while maximising cooperation. Rather like having fiction, non-fiction, poetry and art all under one cover, but distinct and independent in their own contributions, for example.

Contemplating the Critical Questions

All of this surely raises large questions about our near and longer-term future, both as Scotland and as part of an interconnected world. At this juncture it is perhaps best to pose these boldly, rather than seek to answer them editorially – though we hope the preceding pages contain more than enough ideas and clues to begin to do that.

- How do we nurture our connectedness, shared humanity, and jointly cultivated values across our differences? How can we recognise and act upon the fact that whatever we think about politics, the constitutional question or values for society, what unites us is more than what divides us if the key issue is survival (and with it, flourishing)?

- In this, how do we aid better, more honest, deeper debate – where we can disagree openly with each other and agree to disagree, without the need to insult or devalue the humanity of the people we disagree with? This is surely one of the critical questions of our age both in Scotland and globally?

- How do we deal with the rise of populism and hate-mongers in this an age where the answers to most of the big issues involve complexity, plurality and ambiguity, and are not amenable to simple soundbites and slogans?

- How do we address those issues which can be divisive and all-consuming in the present such as what are called 'culture wars', controversies over 'cancel culture' and the rival claims in the debate on trans rights, to name some of the most obvious, respecting their importance, while placing them in proper context of issues of power, voice and inequality?

- How can we achieve the most appropriate balance between focusing on issues which are of immediate concern and controversy while also having an awareness and focus on the long-term?

Part of this debate has rightly already begun. The Royal Society of Edinburgh (RSE) set up a Post-COVID-19 Futures Commission to address the landscape that will emerge, although criticisms were made that this involved a narrow selection of the great and good, with a minimal degree of participation and engagement (RSE, 2020). More ambitious and far-reaching were proposals from Common Wealth, a centre-left think tank, for a post-COVID-19 programme of government which challenged many of the orthodoxies around economic growth, the economy and society, and set out a detailed policy prospectus (Macfarlane and Brett, 2020). The truth is that we need a range of ideas and initiatives, from established and traditional bodies to new voices and radicals, with the richer and more pluralist the mix the better.

'Viviculture' Revisited

This returns us to the idea of 'viviculture', which was in *Scotland the Brave?* drawing on the thoughts of Fintan O'Toole and others.

In the reception of that book, including a number of events which flowed from it, we noted how receptive people were to this notion. Viviculture, in summary, means *love of life, and love of those cultures which express and nurture life*. How do we bring this simple but profound idea – one capable of limitless elaboration – centre stage, to nourish and nurture it? In what ways would a Scotland aiming at the practices of viviculture look different to the present one? What do we need to do to develop the kind of human character that makes live-giving a priority, and develops the virtues and habits associated with viviculture?

That, clearly, is a question about how we deploy our humanity to one another in health and social care, in our politics and corporate life, in the psychological services, in the development of civil society, in the religious and non-religious 'communities of character', in our food cultures, in education (both schooling and lifelong learning) and in the practices of both environmental justice and deep ecology. There is so much to explore here, both in a global sense – but ultimately in a very local one – related to Scotland's natural environment, cultural and linguistic inheritances, institutions, businesses, neighbourhood gatherings, sporting occasions and civic organisations. One particular issue here is as to whether a Universal Basic Income (UBI), currently being explored in Scotland and many other parts of the world, would ultimately enable the kind of independent action – free of the fear of destitution – which would enable people across society to invest in viviculture? It is worth thinking about in these terms, as well as in relation to redoing our economics and guaranteeing social security and liveable habitation for all.

Fundamentally, what the notion of viviculture embodies is respect, empathy and regard for our fellow human beings and putting that centre stage in everything we do in public policy while doing so in a way which has an environmental consciousness and groundedness (McIntosh, 2020). There have been numerous stress points over the course of the COVID-19 pandemic in Scotland and the UK and examples across the board where the Scottish and UK authorities have been found to have fallen significantly short.

However one particular area is worth particular comment and that is the attitude of the UK Government towards asylum seekers and refugees. The UK as we write has literally no humanitarian legal route by which migrants can enter the UK which has been a major contributory factor in the dangerous and illegal crossings of the English Channel by thousands of migrants in July and August 2020. At the same time the UK Government's official policy – with the actual title 'No Recourse to Public Funds' affects hundreds of thousands of citizens and most damagingly and inhumanely falls on refugees and migrants who have no official safety net.

The direct consequence of this UK policy is the tragic death of Mercy Baguma, a refugee from Uganda, who died in Glasgow on 22 August 2020, destitute, deprived of the right to work or claim benefits, and who was found with her young baby, alive but suffering from malnutrition, by her side. This morally scandalous case brought the usual platitudes and evasions from the UK Home Office who are responsible for the policies that brought this about, leading to Robina Qureshi, head of Positive Action on Housing, declaring that the asylum system 'seems designed to break spirits' (Positive Action in Housing, 2020). Any discussion of all the progressive, humane values we want to see embodied in the Scotland of the future, and indeed, the UK, has to starkly recognise the brutal consequences of UK Government policies.

Reimagining Power Through the Power of Imagination

This brings us, lastly, to something quietly running through this book – occasionally explicitly stated, often implicitly implied: the issue of power. Namely, who has it in Scotland? How did they get it? How do they exercise it? In whose interests do they exercise it? And who are they accountable to, in its use and necessary limits? These questions have inevitably been foregrounded as we have needed to rely on the public authorities in relation to handling the COVID-19 pandemic, as they have needed to seek consensus from both expert communities and the public, and as the question of power and its exercise for and in Scotland has rubbed noses with power at Westminster, economic power and so on.

At one level, the people of Scotland have collective power – and there is the oft-used language of 'the sovereign right of the Scottish people'. But to fully understand power we have to move beyond such abstracts and generalities – and to talk about insider groups. One narrow interpretation of power in Scotland sees a select group of elites and privileged players have access and influence with those who make critical decisions: political, economic and civic.

It is a telling state of affairs in Scotland that coming up to the 2021 elections – after 22 years of the Parliament and 14 years of a SNP Government – there remains a lack of genuinely independent and well-resourced research agencies feeding our public life, and interacting with the development of strengthened forms of civic engagement and deliberation (forums interacting with elected bodies, and the like). Instead, we have a policy environment which, while not as regressive as the corporate capture of Whitehall, is not as ethical and transparent as many would think it to be. An example is the role of the corporate lobbyists at the heart of policy-making and government. This matters even more so given the lack of countervailing forces – from think tanks to trade unions and NGOs.

The issue here is developing an ecology of recognised power which involves both countervailance and a willingness to break the dominance of special interests – specifically, those massive concentrations of corporate, economic muscle which so readily and regularly overcome our political, environmental, democratic, educational and cultural institutions. James Burnham, author of *The Managerial Revolution* (1941), wrote in *The Machiavellians: Defenders of Freedom: A defense of political truth against wishful thinking*:

> No theory, no promises, no morality, no amount of goodwill, no religion will restrain power. Neither priests nor soldiers, neither labor leaders or businessman, neither bureaucrats nor feudal lords will differ from each other in the basic use which they will seek to make of power... Only power restrains power (1943).

The point of this is not that we are left with an unassailable 'will to power' which must inevitably corrupt all attempts at public virtue, sharing, equality and reasoning, but rather that we need to tackle and face power relations openly and honestly; to pin down the leviathans that would rule us with a thousand Gulliver-like pegs, perhaps.

One way of finding out how to do that is to give far greater prominence (and, yes, power) to the poets and storytellers in our midst, as we have tried to do in this book. These people are the developers of the moral vision (the ethics and practice of viviculture) that we need in order to be able to renegotiate our uses/misuses of both power and language. They are the painters, prophets and practitioners of a future that is really worth having: a Scotland, and a world, which is not driven by fear, loathing, panic and pandemic, but by a sense of community which is built out of the fabric of daily life, rather than left to idle on the shelf of imagination afforded to us by our dreamers of a better tomorrow. The future of Scotland after the virus has already begun, so we had better start imagining, creating and building – to prevent a return to the values that existed pre-COVID-19.

References

Ainsley, C, 2018, *The New Working Class: How to Win Hearts, Minds and Votes*, Bristol, Policy Press.

Burnham, J, 1941, *The Managerial Revolution: What is Happening in the World*, New York, USA, John Day Co.

Burnham, J, 1943, *The Machiavellians: Defenders of Freedom: A defense of political truth against wishful thinking*, New York, USA, John Day Co.

Eliot, TS, 1936, *Burnt Norton*, San Diego, California, USA, Harcourt.

Geoghegan, P, 2020, *Democracy for Sale: Dark Money and Dirty Politics*, London, House of Zeus.

Hassan, G and Barrow, S (eds), 2017, *A Nation Changed? The SNP and Scotland Ten Years On*, Edinburgh, Luath Press.

Hassan, G and Barrow, S (eds), 2019, *Scotland the Brave? Twenty Years of Change and the Future of the Nation*, Edinburgh, Luath Press.

Jackson, B, 2020, *The Case for Scottish Independence: A History of Nationalist Political Thought in Modern Scotland*, Cambridge, Cambridge University Press.

Macfarlane, L and Brett, M, 2020, *Charting a Just and Sustainable Recovery for Scotland: A Plan for Scotland's Programme for Government*, Common Wealth, accessed at: www.common-wealth.co.uk/reports/charting-a-just-and-sustainable-recovery-for-scotland

McIntosh, A, 2020, *Riders on the Storm: The Climate Crisis and the Survival of Being*, Edinburgh, Birlinn.

Positive Action in Housing, 2020, 'Mercy Baguma', 25 August, accessed at: www.paih.org/death-of-mercy-baguma-glasgow-statement/

Royal Society of Edinburgh (RSE), 2020, 'Post-COVID-19 Futures Commission', accessed at: www.rse.org.uk/inquiries/ rse-post-covid-19-futures-commission/

CONTRIBUTORS

JANETTE AYACHI is a Scottish-Algerian poet based in Edinburgh. Her debut poetry collection *Hand Over Mouth Music* (Pavilion Press, 2019) won the 2019 Saltire Poetry Book of the Year Literary Award. She has been published widely in various anthologies, collaborates with artists, and has appeared on BBC television in the arts series *Loop* and *The Edinburgh Show*. She is working on her book *Lonerlust,* a nonfiction narrative about travelling alone searching connections between landscapes, culture and human connection.

SIMON BARROW is Director of Ekklesia, the beliefs and ethics think-tank. He has written and contributed to numerous books, including co-editing *Scotland the Brave?* (Luath Press, 2019) and *A Nation Changed?* (Luath Press, 2017), both with Gerry Hassan. His latest volume, on composer Michael Tippett, will be published in 2021. He is also a co-founder of the Scottish Football Supporters Association. He was previously assistant general secretary of Churches Together in Britain and Ireland, the official ecumenical body. He lives in Leith, having moved to Scotland ten years ago.

JULIE BERTAGNA is an award-winning author for children and young adults, published around the world. Five novels have been nominated for the Carnegie Prize and other major shortlists. A graphic novel on Scots-born environmentalist John Muir won a Gold Standard in the US. Julie is writing an adult novel, adapting her acclaimed climate change *Exodus* trilogy for the screen and is a writing mentor for Scottish Book Trust.

MARCO G BIAGI was elected as SNP MSP for Edinburgh Central in 2011 after a decade of involvement with the party. He stepped down in 2016 to begin a PhD in Political Science while continuing to provide commentary and analysis on Scottish politics. He holds degrees from St Andrews, Glasgow and Yale Universities.

ALAN BISSETT is an award-winning playwright, novelist and performer from Falkirk, who now lives in Renfrewshire. He is most well-known for the novels *Death of a Ladies' Man* (Hachette Livre, 2009) and *Boyracers*

(Birlinn, 2001), and his 'one-woman show' *The Moira Monologues.*

W. ELLIOT BULMER is a Lecturer in Politics at the University of Dundee and formerly Senior Programme Officer (Constitution Building) at the International Institute for Democracy and Electoral Assistance. He specialises in the comparative study of constitutions and the politics of constitutional change. His latest book is *Westminster and the World* (Policy Press, 2020).

THOMAS CLARK is a writer and translator who works mainly in the Scots language. He writes a regular column for *The National*, and was formerly Scots language editor at *Bella Caledonia*. His books include the poetry collection *Intae the Snaw* (Gatehouse Press, 2015) and the award-winning children's novel *Diary o a Wimpy Wean* (Black and White Publishing, 2018).

TOMMY J CURRY joined the Philosophy Department at the University of Edinburgh in 2019. He is the author of *The Man-Not* (Temple University Press, 2017), which won the 2018 American Book Award and *Another White Man's Burden* (SUNY Press, 2018). He is also the editor of the first book series dedicated to the study of Black males entitled *Black Male Studies* (Temple University Press). His research has been recognised by Diverse as placing him among the Top 15 Emerging Scholars in the United States in 2018 and has been past president of Philosophy Born of Struggle, one of the oldest Black philosophy organisations in the United States.

FLAVIA D'AVILA is a Brazilian-born theatre director based in Edinburgh. She is the Artistic Director of Fronteiras Theatre Lab, working with new writing, devised, multilingual and transcultural theatre. Flavia is the Events and Membership Coordinator of Theatre Directors Scotland, part of the core group leading the Migrants in Theatre movement, and has recently completed her PhD thesis on syncretic theatre and devising at the Royal Conservatoire of Scotland/University of St Andrews. You can follow her constant rants on Twitter: @fronteirastl

OLIVER ESCOBAR is Senior Lecturer in Public Policy at the University of Edinburgh and Academic Lead on Democratic Innovation at the Edinburgh Futures Institute. He combines research and practice to advance democratic reform and social change. His academic work is shared in 50 publications, including the new *Handbook of Democratic Innovation and Governance* (Edward Elgar Publishing, 2019). Before academia, Oliver worked in literature, radio, retail, fishing and construction.

CHERYL FOLLON is a poet living in Glasgow. Her latest collection is *Santiago* (Bloodaxe Books, 2017).

ANNE C FRATER/ANNA C FRATER was brought up in the village of Upper Bayble in the Isle of Lewis, in a home and a community where Gaelic was the main language. Her work has been published in various anthologies, as well as her collections, *Fon t-Slige* (Gairm, 1995) and *Cridhe Creige* (Acair, 2017).

SALLY GALES is an ex-architect turned writer. Originally from Florida, she moved to Scotland to pursue her Doctorate in Fine Arts (DFA) in Creative Writing at the University of Glasgow. When she isn't working on her novel or essays, she can be found hiking in the hills, climbing a crag or exploring Scotland's forgotten ruins.

BRONAGH GALLAGHER is a member of Enough!, a Scottish degrowth collective and a collaborator with The Outside, working on systems change with equity at the centre. Building on over 15 years' experience in the voluntary sector, her work blends enabling people to take action together with the integration of complex living systems perspectives. She believes that both of these are needed if we are to radically transform our political, institutional and economic systems for a fairer, climate-stable future.

DANI GARAVELLI is a freelance journalist and columnist with bylines in *Scotland on Sunday*, *The Times*, *The Guardian*, *The Big Issue*, *Prospect* magazine and *Tortoise*. She recently co-wrote and presented the BBC Radio 4 documentary 'Scotland's Uncivil War'.

MARJORIE LOTFI GILL's writing has won competitions, been published widely in the UK and abroad and performed on BBC Radio 4. *Refuge*, poems about her childhood in revolutionary Iran, is published by Tapsalteerie Press. She has written for the St Magnus Festival, the University of Edinburgh, the Talbot Rice Gallery, the Fruitmarket Gallery and CAMPLE LINE. She is an Ignite Fellow with the Scottish Book Trust, and a Co-Founder and Director of Open Book.

PAUL GOODWIN is a marketer to trade and a passionate football fan. He created the campaign to convert Stirling Albion into Community

Ownership and worked to help a range of clubs on the Community Ownership pathway and has a forthcoming book titled: *How to Buy and Run a Football Club* (Luath Press). He is a Partick Thistle fan and long-time Tartan Army member and is a co-founder of the Scottish Football Supporters Association.

HANNAH GRAHAM is a criminologist who works as a Senior Lecturer in the Scottish Centre for Crime and Justice Research at the University of Stirling. Outwith the university, she is a member of the Scottish Sentencing Council, an independent advisory body.

MICHAEL GRAY is a trainee solicitor and writer from Glasgow. After campaigning in the 2014 independence referendum, he worked in journalism as a reporter and columnist. He co-founded Skotia Media, a platform for campaigning journalism. He is now working in private practice having recently graduated in law. He tweets @GrayInGlasgow

GERRY HASSAN is Research Fellow in contemporary history at Dundee University and has written and edited over two dozen books on Scottish and British politics including *The Strange Death of Labour Scotland* (with Eric Shaw, Edinburgh University Press, 2012), *Caledonian Dreaming* (Luath Press, 2014), *Independence of the Scottish Mind* (Palgrave Macmillan, 2014), and *The People's Flag and Union Jack* (with Eric Shaw, Biteback Publishing, 2019). He edited with Simon Barrow two previous collections: *Scotland the Brave?* (Luath Press, 2019) and *A Nation Changed?* (Luath Press, 2017). He has written and commented widely in the Scottish, UK and international media and his writing and commentary can be found at: www.gerryhassan.com

KIRSTY HUGHES is a writer and commentator on Scottish, UK and European politics. She was the founder and director of the Scottish Centre on European Relations from 2017–2020. She has researched and published extensively on European issues including the EU's several enlargements and prospects for an independent Scotland to join the EU.

KIRSTIN INNES lives in the West of Scotland. She is the author of the novels *Fishnet* (Freight Books, 2015) and *Scabby Queen* (Fourth Estate, 2020).

JENNIFER JONES is a reporter at the *Stranraer and Wigtownshire Free Press* and a (recovering) academic. Amongst the writing about issues important to the south-west of Scotland, she also occasionally writes about journalism, digital culture and social media. She founded Hack/Hackers Scotland, running workshops and seminars about the Scottish media landscape, misinformation and trust in the digital age. Twitter: @jennifermjones Email: hello@jennifermjones.net

PAT KANE is a musician, writer, consultant, curator, futurist, father. He is the author of *Tinsel Show* (Polygon, 1992) and *The Play Ethic* (Macmillan, 2004). Pat consults globally on play, creativity and innovation (see www.patkane.global). He was on the board of Yes Scotland during the first Scottish independence referendum, and writes for *The National* newspaper. Pat is also the co-initiator of the democracy lab The Alternative UK. He is still one half of Hue and Cry.

KAPKA KASSABOVA is a writer of narrative non-fiction. Her latest books, *Border* (Granta, 2017) and *To The Lake* (Granta, 2020), explore the trans-boundary human geography of the southern Balkans. *Border* was shortlisted for many non-fiction prizes in the UK and won the British Academy's Al-Rodhan Prize, The Saltire Book of the Year, The Stanford-Dolman Book of the Year and the Highland Book Prize. Kapka grew up in Bulgaria, was university-educated in New Zealand, and since 2005 has lived in Scotland.

ALASTAIR MCINTOSH is the author of books including *Soil and Soul* (Aurum Press, 2004) on land reform and community, *Poacher's Pilgrimage* (Birlinn, 2016) on the spiritual journey, and most recently, *Riders on the Storm* (Birlinn, 2020). He is an Honorary Senior Research Fellow at the University of Glasgow, a fellow of the Centre for Human Ecology and a founding trustee of the GalGael Trust in Govan.

HENRY MCLEISH has been in public service for 50 years, 30 years elected. He is a former professional football player, began his political life in Fife in the early 1970s, worked in local government, was first elected to the UK Parliament in 1987 and became a member of the Labour Government in 1997 as Minister for Home Affairs and Devolution. Elected to the Scottish Parliament in 1999 he became First Minister of Scotland in 2000. Life, after elected politics, has included more public service, including, lecturing, writing, chairing, broadcasting, advising and agonising over his first love, the future of Scottish football.

HUGH MCMILLAN taught History for many years in south-west Scotland. He is an award-winning poet and writer. His last collections *Heliopolis* and *The Conversation of Sheep* were published by Luath in 2017 and 2018 respectively. In 2020 he was chosen as a 'Champion' by the Scottish Poetry Library to commission new work for the library.

JAMES MITCHELL holds the chair in Public Policy at Edinburgh University. He is the author of numerous books on Scotland, the UK and territorial politics including *The Scottish Question* (Oxford University Press, 2014) and *Hamilton 1967* (Luath Press, 2017). He is also editor (with Gerry Hassan) of *Scottish National Party Leaders* (Biteback Publishing, 2016).

ANGELA O'HAGAN is a Reader in Equalities and Public Policy and Glasgow Caledonian University where she is also Deputy Director of the WISE Centre for Economic Justice. Angela has been an advocate and researcher on gender and human rights budgeting, and gender and public policy for many years and has been a member of a number of government and other advisory boards on social security, taxation and budget processes in recent years.

ALISON PHIPPS is UNESCO Chair in Refugee Integration through Languages and the Arts at the University of Glasgow and Professor of Languages and Intercultural Studies. She is Co-Convener of Glasgow Refugee, Asylum and Migration Network (GRAMNET). She was Distinguished Visiting Professor at the Waikato University, Aotearoa New Zealand 2013–2016, Thinker in Residence at the EU Hawke Centre, University of South Australia in 2016, Visiting Professor at Auckland University of Technology, and Principal Investigator for AHRC Large Grant 'Researching Multilingually at the Borders of Language, the body, law and the state' She is currently Co-Director of the Global Challenge Research Fund South-South Migration Hub. She is an academic, activist and published poet.

CLAIRE SAWERS is a freelance journalist specialising in music, the arts, travel and food. She is a regular contributor to *Wire* magazine, *The Quietus* and *The Times*, and was deputy editor at *The List* for five years. She loves to show support for Scotland's exciting underground scene, which includes DIY performance art, LGBTQI+ events, experimental dance and grassroots, community activism. @claire_sawers

CATHERINE SHEA is a psychotherapist and accredited Cognitive Analytic Therapist with specialist training in trauma work. She has been a clinician, supervisor and trainer for more than 40 years. She moved to Scotland in 2004 and feels more at home here politically and socially than anywhere she has lived previously. She believes passionately that Scotland's health would be hugely improved by self-determination. Her comments here reflect a community of clinical experience and owe much to what colleagues have shared.

CATHERINE SIMPSON is a novelist and memoir writer based in Edinburgh. Her novel *Truestory* (Sandstone Press, 2015) was inspired by raising her autistic daughter, Nina. *When I Had a Little Sister* (Fourth Estate, 2018) is a family memoir about being raised on a Lancashire farm and the suicide of her sister, Tricia.

MIKE SMALL is a writer and activist. He is the editor of *Bella Caledonia* and part of the Enough! Collective. He is currently writing a biography of Patrick Geddes.

ANNA STEWART is a writer whose stories have been published in *Riptide Journal, Gutter Magazine, New Writing Dundee, The Weekend Read, Scots Hoose* and *A Short Affair*. She was awarded a Scottish Book Trust New Writers Award, and shortlisted for the Royal Academy and Pin Drop Short Story Award, and Bloody Scotland's Short Story Competition. She was one of Cove Park's Scottish Emerging Writers (2019). She can be contacted via: www.annastewartwrites.com

WILLIE SULLIVAN is a campaigner. He is particularly interested in ways that power can be better shared through political and democratic innovations. He was a founder member of Compass and Common Weal and works for the Electoral Reform Society heading up campaigns across the UK.

KATHERINE TREBECK is Advocacy and Influencing Lead at the Wellbeing Economy Alliance and co-founder of WEAll Scotland. She sits on a range of advisory boards, holds several academic affiliations and is a Distinguished Fellow of the Schumacher Institute. Her book *The Economics of Arrival* (with Jeremy Williams, Policy Press) was published in 2019.

STEPHEN WATT is the author of four poetry collections. Since being appointed Dumbarton Football Club's Poet in Residence, Stephen became the first crime poet to appear at Bloody Scotland Crime Writing Festival, was appointed Makar for the Federation of Writers (Scotland) in 2019, and edited two poetry collections on behalf of Joe Strummer (The Clash) and Pete Shelley (Buzzcocks).

LISA WILLIAMS founded the Edinburgh Caribbean Association in 2016. She runs educational programmes and walking tours of Edinburgh and Scotland's Black History and curates a range of cultural events across Scotland. She has a Master's in Arts, Festival and Cultural Management and is an Honorary Fellow in the School of History, Classics and Archaeology at the University of Edinburgh.

CHRISTIE WILLIAMSON is a poet and essayist who lives in Glasgow. His poems have appeared in magazines and anthologies since 2003 and he has read his work at major festivals including Aye Write, StAnza and the Festivale Internazionale de Poesia Granada, Nicaragua. His latest collection is *Doors tae Naewye* (Luath Press, 2020).

PATRICK WRIGHT is Emeritus Professor of Literature Culture and Politics at King's College London. He spent many years as a freelancer in the last century, working variously as a feature writer for *The Guardian* and a presenter of Radio 3's Night Waves. His documentary series for Radio 4, 'The English Fix' (2016–17) is available on BBC Sounds. His books include *On Living in an Old Country* (Oxford University Press, 1985), *A Journey Through Ruins: The Last Days of London* (Oxford University Press, 1991), and *The Village that Died for England* (Faber and Faber, 1995). *The Sea View Has Me Again* is forthcoming with Repeater.

SUZANNE ZEEDYK is a developmental psychologist, based for 20 years at the University of Dundee. In 2011, she set out to boost public awareness of the science of connection, becoming one of a leading voice within the Scottish ACEs Movement in the process. Her key message is that the decisions we take about caring for our children are integrally connected to our vision for the kind of society we wish to build. Details of her work can be found at her website: www.suzannezeedyk.com

Luath Press Limited

committed to publishing well written books worth reading

LUATH PRESS takes its name from Robert Burns, whose little collie Luath (*Gael.*, swift or nimble) tripped up Jean Armour at a wedding and gave him the chance to speak to the woman who was to be his wife and the abiding love of his life. Burns called one of the 'Twa Dogs' Luath after Cuchullin's hunting dog in Ossian's *Fingal*. Luath Press was established in 1981 in the heart of Burns country, and is now based a few steps up the road from Burns' first lodgings on Edinburgh's Royal Mile. Luath offers you distinctive writing with a hint of unexpected pleasures.

Most bookshops in the UK, the US, Canada, Australia, New Zealand and parts of Europe, either carry our books in stock or can order them for you. To order direct from us, please send a £sterling cheque, postal order, international money order or your credit card details (number, address of cardholder and expiry date) to us at the address below. Please add post and packing as follows: UK – £1.00 per delivery address; overseas surface mail – £2.50 per delivery address; overseas airmail – £3.50 for the first book to each delivery address, plus £1.00 for each additional book by airmail to the same address. If your order is a gift, we will happily enclose your card or message at no extra charge.

Luath Press Limited
543/2 Castlehill
The Royal Mile
Edinburgh EH1 2ND
Scotland
Telephone: +44 (0)131 225 4326 (24 hours)
Email: sales@luath. co.uk
Website: www.luath.co.uk